Slave Badges and
the Slave-Hire System in
Charleston, South Carolina,
1783–1865

# Slave Badges and the Slave-Hire System in Charleston, South Carolina, 1783–1865

HARLAN GREENE *and*
HARRY S. HUTCHINS, JR.
*with* BRIAN E. HUTCHINS

McFarland & Company, Inc., Publishers
*Jefferson, North Carolina, and London*

*The present work is a reprint of the illustrated case bound edition of* Slave Badges and the Slave-Hire System in Charleston, South Carolina, 1783–1865, *first published in 2004 by McFarland.*

This book was written by Harlan Greene
based on the research of Harry S. Hutchins, Jr.,
and supplementary research by Harlan Greene;
numerical estimates are by Brian E. Hutchins.

LIBRARY OF CONGRESS CATALOGUING-IN-PUBLICATION DATA

Greene, Harlan.
Slave badges and the slave-hire system in Charleston, South Carolina, 1783–1865 / Harlan Greene and Harry S. Hutchins, Jr., with Brian E. Hutchins.
p. cm.
Includes bibliographical references and index.

**ISBN 978-0-7864-4090-0**
softcover : 50# alkaline paper ∞

1. Slavery—South Carolina—Charleston—History. 2. Slavery—Law and legislation—South Carolina—Charleston—History. 3. Slaves—Employment—South Carolina—Charleston—History. 4. Slaves—Legal status, laws, etc.—South Carolina—Charleston—History. 5. Badges—South Carolina—Charleston—History. 6. Charleston (S.C.)—Race relations. 7. Charleston (S.C.)—History. 8. Charleston (S.C.)—Economic conditions. I. Hutchins, Harry S., 1945- II. Hutchins, Brian E. III. Title.
F279.C49N425 2008
326'.09757915—dc22

2003025050

British Library cataloguing data are available



Manufactured in the United States of America

*McFarland & Company, Inc., Publishers*
*Box 611, Jefferson, North Carolina 28640*
*www.mcfarlandpub.com*

# Contents

# Acknowledgments

This book would not have been possible without the earlier works of others, most notably that of Theresa Singleton, whose early monograph was for years the only reliable source on the topic. The other published (and manuscript) sources from which we benefited are cited in the text and notes. These we have tried to follow as closely as possible as to spelling and capitalization; very few, it must be noted, capitalized the word "Negro."

We were fortunate to have encountered people whose generosity and cooperation enriched us immeasurably. Nic Butler, a fine scholar documenting Charleston's early musical history, passed on information he gleaned from early newspapers, making this work much fuller and allowing us to interpret many things we had found puzzling. Mary Edna Sullivan told us of the Jane Waring estate book, and Judith Shanks shared records from the estate of Henry Aaron Alexander. Our entire task was made much easier by the professionalism of Charleston's librarians and archivists and the helpfulness of Steve Tuttle of the South Carolina Department of Archives and History in Columbia, S.C. We thank our families for putting up with this obsession and also note our gratitude to Jonathan Ray for his editorial and computer help.

Special tribute must be paid those who shared their badges with us, and, most notably, to Sharon C. Pope, who introduced us. Without her, there would simply have been no book. Thank you, all.

*Harlan Greene*
*Harry S. Hutchins, Jr.*
*Brian E. Hutchins*

# Introduction

In August 1863, Federal troops began their assault on Charleston, South Carolina. To take the city, they hurled shells from adjacent swamps and islands into downtown streets, splintering glass and brick, tearing up flagstone, slate and tree. Over the next few weeks those who did not flee town retreated instead to the safer, out-of-range areas north of Calhoun Street. Church bells, already melted for Confederate cannons, no longer sounded. The shriek of incoming shells was the sound of the city during the two-year siege.

When 18 February 1865 dawned, however, the Confederate defenders were gone and an eerie silence greeted those left in Charleston. At 8:00 A.M. an explosion, like that of death throes, shook the northeast part of town as the railway depot, filled with explosives, blew up. Two hours later, a batch of Federal troops arrived by water and set foot on Broad Street. With every forward step, they brought freedom to where it had never been; in taking control, the soldiers, for the first time since European occupancy, abolished bondage between the Cooper and Ashley rivers that defined the peninsular city.

Slavery had been part of the civilization of the area since its founding in 1670. In disembarking, the original colonists had brought with them the seed that would sow their descendants' destruction 195 years later in an 1865 whirlwind. Indeed, it is believed a slave was one of the first inhabitants to live on the tongue of land that became Charleston.[1]

Of these original European colonists and their descendants, much is known. Their faces stare from portraits; their names are cut in tombstones and stitched into the fabric of history. Faded grants proclaim their ownership of land; church registers record their marriages and baptisms. Their names live on in streets, such as Tradd, Bull and Coming; schoolchildren recite their deeds. The same, however, cannot be said of the unwilling Africans who came with them. Little is known of these slaves other than a name, a reference, or an estimated value. Despite this, they nevertheless constitute a presence; one can see their handiwork, and intuit their existence, in the bricks they made, in the iron they wrought, and in the houses and families they raised. As black holes in space do, these lost people pull on the imagination and intrigue with their mystery. Researchers work to fill in the blanks of slaves' lives, trace their genealogies and document their stories. More and more books on slaves and slavery are being published with each passing year, and each era claims its "seminal" work on the subject. Like abolitionists and fire-eaters, scholars and apologists continue to proclaim their view of things. Each side claims it has the truth and urges the other to enlist in its view of slavery, as benevolent guardianship or unmitigated tragedy.

In February 1865, with the war winding down, some sensed this might be the case in coming years. So, accompanying those Union soldiers taking Charleston and abolishing slavery were journalists and photographers. With glass plates and a chemical mix, photographer Charles Barnard fixed forever the images of the deserted, burnt city, and James Redpath of *The New York Daily Tribune* used words to record his view. He wrote of stumbling across a jumble of slave traders' letters in a slave mart on Chalmers Street: "We carried off, among us all, the entire correspondence of these establishments, the bell, the auctioneer's block, the locks and one sign."[2] *The Boston Daily Journal* writer Charles Coffin followed, and wandered into the large holding pen and three-story jail immediately behind Ryan's Mart. He pried loose the wooden steps traversed by the slaves and found the jail's key. He carried these relics back to the victorious North, where curious mobs turned out to view the war booty. "Let these infernal hieroglyphics and symbols of the worship for the Anti-Christ be carefully preserved," the poet John Greenleaf Whittier wrote. "Lay them side by side with the racks of the Inquisition and the keys of the Bastille. Let them tell the generations to come of the most hideous form of human depravity."[3]

Those next generations have continued to be fascinated and horrified with slavery, its artifacts and aftermath. It is manifested in the words we use, the music we listen to, in what we eat. It is present in economic inequalities and spun out in the double helix of owners' and slaves' chromosomes and genes. It looms large in abstract notions and sociological manifestations and is present, too, in tangible things, items that are literally stepped over in the street. Archaeologists sift and dig, and men and women in empty lots wave metal detectors back and forth like scythes; suddenly, with a magnetic click, the past reappears.

This, in fact, is how this study had its beginnings. One cold February morning in 1995, a collector, pursuing his weekend hobby of metal detecting, heard a sound in the soil beneath his feet. He leaned over, kneeled and freed from the dust a metal octagon. The metal slave badge he found was heavy with dirt, corrosion and history. Holding it in his hand, the digger could trace indentations, almost like fingerprints, where the last man to touch it, a slave no doubt, had tried to close, or perhaps force closure, on the object, by bending it in half, and then tossing it aside. Brushing it off, the man puzzled over the words on it—"No. 14," "Fisher" and "1800." Trying to find out what those words meant, the collector turned to the authors for help in figuring out and decoding (in Whittier's words) the slave badge's "hieroglyphics."

But it was not easy; all the scholarly books consulted only mentioned the badges in passing. Professionals had dismissive attitudes and organizations offered to accept it as a gift but could not help unravel its mysteries. We discovered that a few others before us had also tried to decipher the meaning of badges. The first documented interest we discovered of someone trying to decode these metal pieces came from ca. 1901 when Charleston was home to the South Carolina Interstate and West Indian Exposition, a type of regional world's fair and business proposition. The Exposition brought many people to the South and to the city. This was a generation after the end of the Civil War, and a year or two after the National Reunion of United Confederate Veterans was held in Charleston's Thompson Auditorium, later the Charleston Museum. Slavery, by then, was already a dim, mysterious thing to the visitors. Many coming to Charleston were intrigued with all things Southern; some were excited to find trinkets displayed in local shops. These, the tourists were told, were attached to every slave in the city, who were numbered and sometimes named, always marked as property. Horrified, the tourists snatched up the items, eager to take the objects back home and tell what they had learned.

One day in this era, local writer and amateur historian John Bennett got wind of this. He entered a shop on King Street and found "an old-fashioned platter ... filled to overflowing with pieces of copper, brass, zinc, rusted tin and badly oxidized thin iron in various shapes: oval, square, circular, oblong, octagonal, hexagonal, and round.... On each was stamped a name and a number: each was perforated at the upper edge and hung by a little ring: over the whole bunch was the label, 'Slave tags.'"[4] Of the dozens Bennett saw and described, only one was really authentic: "Charleston," it read, "Porter, 1376, 1842." Others said RR and SCRR and had numbers, really just being claim tags for railroad lockers and other similar objects. But the storekeepers, perhaps not knowing better (or perhaps eager for a sale), made up tales, and the tourists believed them. "Porter" must have been the slave owner's name, the merchant told Bennett; all slaves were tagged, he decreed. Although originally from Ohio and new to the city, Bennett knew this could not be true. He went to check the statutes in his father-in-law's library. Bennett found out that only slaves who were hired out had worn tags. Appalled at the misinformation, he wrote an article in the local paper to refute the claim and explicate the true history of the objects.

Yet still, misinformation grew. Ten years after this first article on slave tags appeared, the trade in fakes was still brisk. Daniel Elliot Huger Smith, an aristocrat who had been born before slavery's end and who remembered slave tags and the slave-hiring system, went on record about the process. "Many negroes, especially the mechanics," he wrote, "were allowed to 'work out' or to 'hire their own time.' For these the city authorities issued a license, as was and still is done in many occupations. These were of brass [really copper]," he wrote inaccurately, "as ... the dray-licenses and cart-licenses are to-day, and were numbered in sequence, I believe. A most ridiculous trade is ... carried on in the curiosity shops, which sell the very ordinary bits of brass as 'slave badges' at high prices, the number being supposed, I believe, to represent the slave's number on his master's plantation or in his household, just as a convict is known by his number in a penitentiary. Doubtless many have been dispersed over the North as curiosities of slavery."

Smith went on in his memoirs. "A man who 'hired his own time' paid a fixed sum to his master by the month," he believed, "and kept his surplus earnings for himself."[5] This was highly illegal, however, and reveals either the faultiness of Smith's memory or the extent to which the laws were flouted. Even a runaway slave in Charleston who had published his memoirs in England in 1862 passed on erroneous information about the badges. Fleeing his owner's plantation and trying to get on a ship to take him North, he went to work on the docks as a porter.

> I joined a gang of negroes working on the wharfs, and received a dollar-and-a-quarter per day, without arousing any suspicion.... One morning, ... one of them asked me if I had my badge? Every negro is expected to have a badge with his master's name and address inscribed on it. Every negro unable to produce such a badge when asked for, is liable to be put in jail."[6]

Truly, slaves without badges could be jailed, but the badges themselves carried no information about the owners' addresses or names.

As time went on, memories continued to dim and misapprehensions grew. I. Jenkins Mikell, who was a boy during the Civil War, also passed on wrong information in his 1923 autobiography. "No slave was allowed out after a certain hour at night without a slave badge," he wrote, "a copper badge with his number on it, to be returned to his master the next morning."[7] Worse still, a pamphlet put out by the Old Slave Mart Museum (occupying the Ryan's Mart building the journalists had stripped of slave materials after Charleston's fall) supplied incorrect information in its attempt to set the record straight. "Slaves," it noted, " were required to wear tags. These were made of light weight copper cut about two inches square with a hole punched in one corner so that with a string they could either be worn around the neck or attached to the clothing. Serial numbers that were registered in the owner's name were stamped upon the tags, together with the year and occupation, i.e., carpenter, porter, drayman, or spinster, etc." Much of that was not true, but worse still, it explained that, "A spinster was a spinning woman." "These tags also represented a head tax which varied according to the vocation followed by the Negro. The tax averaged from fifty cents to ten dollars according to the yearly assessments."[8]

With no accurate information on badges available, it is not surprising that novelists employing them in their fiction would also make mistakes. In 1970, playwright and novelist Patricia Robinson and Nancy Stephenson, later Lieutenant Governor of South Carolina, included a character in *A Clearing in the Fog* horrifying and shocking the city of Charleston by wearing a bracelet of slave badges from plantations dipped in gold leaf.[9] (Only slaves hired from the city had to wear them, not slaves on plantations.) In 2000, novelist Pam Durban showed a character in the Charleston market searching for a runaway. "The slaves," she saw, "wore copper badges that named their occupations—Baker, Seamstress, Cooper."[10] No badges ever sported these categories.

Over the years, many excellent books such as Richard Wade's *Slavery in the Cities* and Michael Johnson's and James Roark's twin works, *No Chariot Let Down* and *Black Masters,* appeared, but they examined the issue of slave hire and the badges the system produced tangentially, albeit quite brilliantly. No one could state with authority who made them, how many were made and what they meant to the economics of Charleston or slavery. Indeed, Wade stated that "municipal income from this source never proved very great," and as for hiring out, "there is no way of knowing how many slaves actually acquired this privilege."[11] The first systematic study of badges and the system that produced them was published in 1984. Working at the Charleston Museum, Theresa Singleton looked at the objects and published a scholarly article on the subject, calling for more study to clear up many of the unknowns and ambiguities related to the artifacts.[12] Although it was a time of much scholarly interest in slavery, Singleton got little praise for her efforts. Other scholars, ignorant of the field, dismissed her work as unimportant. Singleton was told to turn her attention to other things.[13]

If the knowledge of slave badges languished, interest in them did not. South Carolina's tricentennial in 1970, the country's bicentennial in 1976, and the explosion of interest in slavery attending the publication of Alex Haley's *Roots* caused many people to comb through not just books and documents, but old houses, empty lots and privies. This frenzy has continued; as the city of Charleston is developed more and more, as archeologists continue to investigate, and nearly every plot of soil on the peninsula is turned, more and more tags are being unearthed. Many more, unfortunately, are being fabricated and sold as authentic items to the unwary. Encouraging this is the growing collector's market for racist and slave memorabilia. Badges once tossed away as trash are now the subjects of articles in treasure magazines. They are being bought and sold by collectors, museums, and the curious, in auctions, on the Internet, and more and more frequently in counterfeit. (Some institutions hold counterfeit badges and display them as true relics.) Often sold for $2 in Bennett's day, badges have leapt in value, often selling for over $10,000. One badge at auction sold for more than $25,000 in late 2002. The time to demystify them certainly is here.

If anything is to come of the attempt, it must be from Charleston sources; for it is the *only* place in the country that seems to have actually issued tags, though other cities legislated hiring out procedures. But for many years, the city's historical records were uncatalogued, scattered and in disarray. It was not until the 1970s that a records management program was established and a municipal archives created. City archivists Margaretta Childs and then Marie Hollings combed through all the centuries of materials, but no books documenting the sale and creation of slave tags appeared. So scholars were stumped; Theresa Singleton had only the statutes and the few tags amassed over the years by the Charleston Museum to guide her. Until now, no one has been able to locate sources that could serve as a Rosetta stone to translate the tags and their meaning. (Many more records that could clear up other mysteries are still missing.) The sources were in plain view, much like many of the tags themselves, lying on the surface on the past. One just had to look.

And look and look. What compelled us to keep searching were the objects themselves. (Once one has seen one of these badges, the fascination becomes understandable.) For although what they represent is appalling, badges make abstractions real; they objectify slavery like shackles, auction blocks, or bills of sale do. But, most of all, the fascination is that the badges tell a story peculiar to Charleston, and tell a tale, too, of slavery and not-slavery. Those who wore the tokens, "tickets or badges," as they were called, often had a symbolic ticket to another way of life. Although these tags could not literally transport their wearers to geographic freedom, they could nevertheless unleash the power of metaphor and simile. Those wearing them could act *AS IF* they were free. For if a slave put on a tag, he or she could often act as his or her own master, act *as if* he or she had control of his or her own destiny. What did it feel like to wear a badge? John Bennett asked a former slave in 1903. Were they badges of shame?

"Shame' fo' wear badge?" the ex-slave answered in Gullah, the language of the low country African Americans that Bennett was also studying. "No," she laughed, "ain't shame' fo' mek money—ain't 'shame' fo' wuk—why dey bin 'shame' fo' wear badge fo'?"

Other evidence Bennett turned up verified that; he asked an elderly white resident his memory of the system. "Lazy negroes did not like to be hired out," the man answered, "but industrious ones did like it, as they brought only a stipulated amount to their owners and could make much more for themselves. Bricklayers, carpenters, blacksmiths, mechanics, in short, were constantly hired out—[only] a few private families having work to employ them all the time. Persons going away for a length of time would sometimes hire out their house servants. I knew well in the old-time, one [slave who] was a tailor, who made in two months thirty dollars for himself over and above his wage, while the other, a bricklayer, made twenty-five dollars for himself in the course of the winter.... [T]he men were always proud of their badges," Bennett's informant continued, "as they attested that the wearers were trusted."[14]

Indeed, in 1822, a slave with one of these badges accused of being an accomplice in the Denmark Vesey slave rebellion declared that his badge could vouch for his innocence. Because he was hired out, and thus had a badge, he said, he was "master of his own time, as good as free, as happy as the day is long." (Why then, he argued, would he have participated in a plot to free himself?) Further inquiry on the part of the inquisitors, however, proved the obverse. For another slave who did participate in the plot also had a badge, and thus was free of daily tasks; with no particular chores to pursue, he could give all his time and energy to the conspiracy. His cohorts were asked to chip in and give him money, which he then turned over to his master, ostensibly the cash he earned for being hired out.[15]

Some poor whites did not like this and grew irritated. "[S]laves are permitted to go at large, exercise all privileges of free persons, make contracts, do work, and in every way live and conduct themselves as if they were free," white mechanics, in competition with hired-out slaves, complained indignantly in the late 1850s.[16] "Whenever a slave is made a mechanic," echoed South Carolinian James Henry Hammond, "he is more than half freed."[17]

But as powerful as they were, badges could not save a slave entirely. (In 1822, for instance, the white inquisitors of the slave did not believe his story that the badge made him content; the slave William Garner was tracked down and hanged.) Even with a badge, there were certain things a slave had to do. He or she had to wear the badge visibly. In time, one category of slave, "servant," would not have to wear the badge, but just carry it on their person; while one badge in a private collection still has vestiges of thread used to attach the badge to the slave's clothing. It appears that some slaves altered their badges so they could sew them on their garments. Any white person, seeing a hired-out slave on the street, could demand to see the badge, and, if not produced, the slave could be taken to the workhouse and held. And if a slave counterfeited one, as many would no doubt be tempted to do, he or she could be whipped publicly.

So the badges are not just emblematic of the lives of those who wore them; in fact, they sum up a whole peculiar variation on the theme of slavery, namely slavery in an urban center, and in the city of Charleston particularly. For although other southern cities such as Savannah, New Orleans, Richmond, Wilmington, North Carolina, and Mobile passed ordinances similar to Charleston's slave badge laws, only Charleston seems to have manufactured them, or at least only badges from this city have been found, and perversely, this is fitting. As Edward Ball has noted in his personal recounting of slaves owned by his ancestors, *Slaves in the Family*, Charleston was "the Jerusalem of slavery, its capital and center of faith."[18] More slaves were imported through Charleston than any other single American city. Charleston, quick to claim its uniqueness, now has another unique story to tell—its variation on the theme of human slavery.

To do this, one must decipher and follow many different threads and themes. First there is the body of slave tag law to discuss, which is a bit of a misnomer, for they were never called that in the nineteenth century. "Slave tags?" queried the ex-slave Bennett interviewed in 1903. "I ain't never year 'em called that. Badges, that what dey is."[19] The following chapters will describe the system that called the badges into being and estimate the numbers of badges that were made by what men in each year between 1800 and 1865, and link the information to larger issues. Just as the poet William Blake attempted to see the world in a grain of sand, so one can intuit and summon up a whole world of slavery, slave-hire and slave life by decoding these items.

The story of how the system came about is nearly as fascinating as the badges themselves and reveals how Charlestonians, in an odd collision of time, place, greed, human weakness and economic necessity, came to devise a contradictory and Kafka-esque system. They created a bureaucracy out of human paradox and necessity. Slavery was not a simple black and white issue, but a complex creation of many colors and hues. Just as relations between blacks and whites produced people of mixed ancestry and status, so slavery itself produced odd and contradictory statuses, not just black and white, slave and free, but an amalgam of each. For those who wore badges were free and not free simultaneously. Perhaps like no other object that has survived from the time, the badges objectify all the oddness, gothic horror, and even the human side of slavery.

Charleston, of course, did not invent slavery or its laws. Both had been part of human history for millennia before the city's founding. The codes Americans used were based on Roman slave laws that had evolved over the centuries. Many original Carolinians, slave and free, came from the Caribbean, where slave codes were on the books before 1670. Once they appeared here, Carolina slave laws were codified as early as the 1690s. The early slaves, with their different languages, religions and customs, were so vastly dissimilar from the white Europeans that the masters could almost believe slaves were another species. With time, however, the two races began to interact; the Africans, despite what many Europeans did not want to believe, were humans with the same desires and innate natures and possibilities. Slaves raised children and were taught to read, but were also taught skills. (Many scholars believe that slaves from Africa actually brought the skills of rice planting that made wealth for their masters possible and their own slavery a corollary.) In this frontier settlement, it took all to pull together; it took a while to create elites. Slaves worked alongside whites, often becoming the greatest contributors to a family's prosperity. So one can easily see how the change allowing slaves to be hired out developed. A slave might have a skill a master did not need, and if the slave was not sold, the owner had someone on his or her hands who could provide services that others desired. It only seemed natural, then, that the owner should employ the slave in doing the work he or she did best, and which could bring the master income. The master could put a slave in his or her shop, could use him or her to carry on a trade, such as fishing, carting, designing and fashioning furniture and wrought iron, dressing hair, and dress making. Slaves increased; owners could sell them and certainly did; but they could be hired out, or leased to someone else, and turned over to some other use, directed by someone else who would pay the slaver owner a fee; and one could even allow a slave to go out and earn money and turn the profit back in. So Charlestonians and colonists elsewhere did all of these. Suddenly these Africans were not under lock and key, but were often out on their own, providing services, supervised or not, for others.

Another way slaves won a measure of freedom was with their master's death and being inherited by other members of the family. The spouse, children, and other heirs may not have known how to carry on the trade that the slave owner had followed, but the slaves who had assisted in the shop, smithing, making barrels, or selling behind the counter, did. Many orphans and widows thus turned to their slaves to support them, and they turned the business or the farm over to slaves to run. This brought slaves into competition with others who did similar tasks or ran similar businesses. Because slaves required no salaries and were given only the barest of necessities, they undercut the competition; many whites, with no slaves of their own, and only their white skins to separate them from their competitors, began to feel the economic pinch, possibly in the same way domestic workers would come to feel the competition with lower-paid laborers in third-world countries. Jealousy and anger at the slaves arose as they produced crafts, dug ditches, watched children, did laundry and other tasks cheaper than whites, who had to pay rent and taxes and tried to save money. These lower strata whites, now squeezed, complained bitterly. They were, after all, free; how could a slave, thought to be inferior, be allowed to prevent a free man from making a living? This slave should act like a slave, be on the mudsill, not competing. (It was South Carolinian James

Henry Hammond who would come up with the rhetoric of the mudsill, the slave base on which the economy and white society should rest, and reach its peak, like a pyramid.) As time passed, the poorer whites grew angry and vocal. Those who wrote the laws were called on to intervene. The lawmakers, having already written laws to enslave human beings, had no problem legislating around the practice of hiring out slaves or allowing them into trades. As life got more and more complex, slavery and its regulations did, too. This, therefore, was the beginning of the system that eventually resulted in the slave badge creation.

What follows are chapters on the laws that describe the legal side of the slave hiring-out practice. Then come chapters on the actuality of the practice, how the workings of the system and the badges themselves evolved and developed over the years. Much of the primary evidence is presented verbatim so that others will not have to repeat the same searching through microfilm and other sources we did. By presenting the contemporary data, we hope to let the materials speak for themselves and to document as fully as possible the basis for our conclusions which, in fact, we hold to a minimum. Theresa Singleton, as noted, in her first landmark article on the subject, was told that the subject was not worthy of her study. The slave-hiring practice upset the easy theories of those wishing to neatly categorize human behavior and human slavery. Students of human history and behavior know, however, that these issues do not fit neatly into categories. It is our hope that with presenting all our data, the field will attract more scholars who may be able to refine our findings.

We also hope that this book can do something to heal the ill feelings and bridge the gap between those dismissed as looters, or treasure hunters, and the scholars and museum curators and archaeologists who feel that they alone are entitled to interpret and dissect history. Certainly looting is not just illegal but reprehensible; looters should be prosecuted. But many "treasure hunters" obey the laws exactly, gaining permission from property owners, sharing their findings, literally bringing to light items and ideas that but for their work would have remained buried. Slave badges were meant to be discarded. One had to get a new one each year. So they were tossed away randomly, perhaps like old credit cards are today, or old rabies tags for dogs (the city would also make dogs wear badges in the antebellum years). Will archaeologists of the future be angry with "treasure hunters" who pull debris from the vast trash piles we are now making? Badges were meant to be disposed of, and were. Many cannot be found where they were originally thrown, for dirt and debris have been hauled off the peninsula to areas of landfill, and there badges are often discovered. Much earth was moved around Charleston in the antebellum era, as well. City Council minutes in the 1850s constantly mention filling in low-lying areas of the city and moving earth around to grade streets. If not for treasure hunters, this book would not have appeared, and many of the

**1806 Porter, No. 36. (Charles Prince). When finished with this badge, the slave might have been the one to break it in half. Furthermore, it seems he or she "signed" the badge with an "X," just visible to the right of the numerals 36.**

badges now present in museum collections would never have been discovered. Scholars, archaeologists and museum curators, we hope, will not be so quick in their judgments, but will work with amateurs in the field discovering objects which, without their work, would remain entombed under new construction in asphalt and concrete. Technically, the nineteenth century journalists who took away much of the slave material from Charleston at the end of the Civil War were looters; but nevertheless, they managed to save much that might have been later tossed away. Perhaps, then, if there is openness on both sides, a registry of found items can be devised, and images made and items catalogued and even purchased by museums, before they are dispersed privately. The authors are partisans of no particular group, but merely want to promote cooperation and sharing of knowledge for the benefit of all interested in this field.

# Part One

## The Badge Laws: A Summary, 1670–1866

"Many negroes discover great capacities, and an amazing aptness for learning trades, where dangerous tools are used, and many owners from motives of profit and advantage, breed them to be coopers, carpenters, bricklayers, smiths, and other trades."

—Alexander Hewatt, *An Historical Account of the Rise and Progress of the Colonies of South Carolina and Georgia*, 1779.

# Chapter 1

# 1670–1822: Laws of the Colony and the Early Republic

To date, the earliest Charleston slave badges found bear the year 1800. Although laws called for them earlier, and contemporary evidence from newspapers proves that they were both made and sold in the 1780s (if not earlier), no such badges have surfaced. Because of this, the period of 1800 to 1865 is this book's main focus. But just as the metal artifacts did not just magically appear, but were smelted out of ore, so the body of badge laws did not come from thin air in 1800, but in turn came out of the yore of earlier practice and laws. Laws demanding that hired slaves wear badges had been evolving for over a century.

In 1690, just twenty years after the first ships sailed into Charleston harbor, there was already a law on the books to regulate movement of slaves on their own. All going "out of their plantations" needed a *ticket*—a written slip stating the slave's name, the slave's place of origin and destination.[1] This early law, attaching a "ticket" or information to a slave, was reiterated in the slave laws of 1712, which also included this new provision:

> *Whereas* several owners of slaves used to suffer their said slaves to do what and go whither they will, and work where they please, upon condition that their said slaves do bring their aforesaid masters so much money as … is agreed upon … which practice hath been observed to occasion such slaves to spend their time … in looking for opportunities to steal, in order to raise money to pay their masters, as well as to maintain themselves, and other slaves … in drunkenness and other evil

> courses.... *Be it enacted* that no owner or master or mistress of any family, after the ratification of this Act, shall suffer or permit any slave to do what, go wither, or where, they please, upon condition aforesaid, under the penalty of the forfeiture of five shillings for every day he, she, or they shall suffer any slave to do aforesaid; *Provided nevertheless*, that nothing in this Act shall be construed or intended to hinder any person from letting their negroes or slaves to hire, by the year, or for any lesser time, or by the day, so as such negro or slave is under the care and direction of his master, or some other person by his order instructed with the slave, and that the master is to receive the whole of what the slave shall earn.[2]

Inferred in the legal language are a number of interesting issues: by 1712, slaves were already acting as if they were not slaves, i.e., they were working where and when they wanted to. Being hired out sometimes freed the bondsman from having to work all the time. Once he or she made the amount the master demanded, he or she could rest and pursue luxuries and ease. It made some whites angry to witness such privilege. So a law was passed stating that those slaves hired out had to be under control of someone responsible, and slaves had to turn over all money made to the master; those owners who did not see to this were to be fined. This was not meant to stop the hiring-out practice. Indeed the law went to great pains to demonstrate that this was not at all its intent. By 1712 hiring out was already a boon to slave owners and would not be abolished. The law only made sure that *slaves* were not to benefit from their hired-out status.

Despite the law, it appears the practice continued, for with a new code of laws coming out in 1722, the 1712 statute was repeated and finessed. The newer version of the law stated that the five-shilling per day fine would be paid to the informer, a ploy that would encourage all whites to pay more attention to hired-out blacks and be not just vigilant, but vigilantes. It also built on the 1690 idea of a ticket, for now the law demanded "that the person employing such a slave have a certificate, note or memorandum, thereof, in writing, from the owner, attorney, or overseer of such slave."[3] The evolution of slave badges was well underway.

The laws on the books were not enforced, it seems, for in March 1733-34, seeing "that it is a common practice by several Persons in *Charles Town*, to suffer their Negroes to work out by the Week, and oblige them to bring in a certain Hire, which is not only contrary to a Law now subsisting, but a great Inlet to Idleness, Drunkenness and other Enormities," the Grand Jury resolved to do something about it (*Gazette*, 30 March 1733–4). Its action was to reprint the 1722 law in the newspaper, in a format nearly verbatim as the version given above. It appeared, for instance, in the *South-Carolina Gazette* issue of 27 April 1734. And to make sure that it was obeyed, a note was printed beneath it:

> N.B. *The foregoing Extract of the Negro-Law is here published, that no one may for the future plead ignorance. The several Constables in and about Charles-Town will have Warrants given to them, empowering them to take up all Negroes, which shall be found without proper Tickets: And all Masters, Mistresses, or others, offending in any part of the foregoing particulars, will be prosecuted as the Law directs.*

People still flouted the law. Masters, and slaves themselves, refused to obey; some masters apparently had to take out advertisements warning against hiring out their slaves without their notice. In 1744, "Elizabeth Grove gave notice that anyone who hires her Negro wench Jenny without her knowledge or ticket from Mr. James Paris, will be prosecuted."[4] A generation later in 1772, David Rhine took out an advertisement to forewarn

> all Persons in general, but in particular Cabinet-Makers, House-Carpenters, and Joiners, not to employ, at any Time, without his Knowledge, and Consent first obtained, his NEGRO-MAN, named York: Otherwise, they may be assured of being prosecuted as far as Laws and Justice will support him.[5]

As time went on, further unanticipated effects of the hiring-out practice grew. In 1742, white artisans presented a grievance about "the want of a law to prevent hiring out of Negro tradesmen to the great discouragement of white working men coming into the province."[6] Slave hiring out, even legally done, they complained, cut down on white immigration. But the slave owners and vested powers in the province made money hiring out their slaves and wanted to continue.

Laborers lower down on the economic rung, those whites with no special skills who eked out a living fishing, pulling carts, acting as haulers and drayers, etc., began to feel the competition of the hired-out slaves. It was apparently in response to them that in 1751 the government in Charleston declared that,

> NOTICE IS HEREBY GIVEN, that no Slave belonging to any Person living without the Limits of *Charles-Town* except the Slaves belonging to Orphans, whose Parents were Residents in *Charles-Town* at the time of their Decease, and even in that Case, not above two belonging to any one Estate, and those such as have heretofore been employed in Town, shall be permitted to work for Hire in Town as *Porters, Laborers, Fisherman*, or *otherwise.* And that no Inhabitant of *Charles-Town* shall be permitted to keep more than *two* Male Slaves to work out for Hire, as Porters, Laborers, Fisherman, or Handicraftsmen in Town, on Pain of forfeiting *Five Pounds* for every Day such Slave shall be kept on Hire. And that no Slave work for Hire as a Porter or

> Labourer in *Charles-Town*, until the Owner or Person having Charge of such Slave, shall have obtained a License from the Commissioners of the Streets for so doing: And if any Person hire or employ any Negro, not having a Badge or Ticket, he or she so offending, forfeits the Sum of TEN SHILLINGS *Proclamation Money* for every Offence. *By Order of the Commissioners,* JOHN REMINGTON.[7]

So, in other words, only those living in Charles Town, or those slave-owning orphans of parents who had lived there at their death, could hire out slaves for these tasks, and then only two *males*. (Those slaves had to have already been hired out, as well.) Abusers of the law were to be fined, and for the first time, it was necessary for these two slaves to be licensed (instead of just the earlier certificate required). Licenses were to come from the Commissioners of Streets, and would result in a "ticket or badge." Those using unlicensed slaves were punished with fees.

The law was finessed (with the gender male not being solely specified, allowing female slaves to be hired out, too) when in 1764, the colonial government stated, "That no person whatever shall be permitted or suffered to keep more than two slaves to work out for hire" in Charles Towne; five pounds current money continued to be the daily penalty for owners to pay for having more than two hired out. At the same time, it was "further enacted by the authority aforesaid, That it shall not be lawful for any slave to work for hire as a labourer or porter in Charlestown, until the owner or person having charge of such a slave shall have obtained a license from the said commissioner [of Streets] for so doing; and every slave for whom such license shall be obtained shall wear a public badge or ticket." Licensing had been required before; now what was new was that a ticket (which sounds like paper) or badge (which does not) had to be *worn*. That certainly sounded definite, but obviously the legislators had not thought everything through. The ticket, they stated, would be worn "in such a manner as the said commissioners, or a majority of them, shall direct or appoint" something they obviously had not done by 10 August 1764 at the passage of the law.[8] Nevertheless, the wearing of a badge or something similar was legislated by 1764. The same earlier penalty for those hiring out a slave without such a ticket was repeated. This penalty would be enforced "except in cases of necessity, of which the said commissioners, or a majority of them, shall direct and appoint."

In this same act, the commissioners were also authorized "to ascertain the rates of porterage and labour of such slaves and also, to appoint the places where such slaves shall ply in the same town." This they did just a bit later; "the Commissioners for regulating and taking care of the Streets ... at a general meeting of the board, held at the State-House, August 23, 1764," set the rates for various items, distances, and rates of Negro porters as well. If hired-out slaves labored at the wharves, their pay would be ten shillings a day; if they drilled wells, or pursued any task that required them to stand in water, also ten shillings. For rolling rice, or other common porterage, they could expect seven shillings and six pence a day. Common labor would bring just two shillings and six pence for two hours, and three shillings and nine pence for two to four hours; they would get five shillings for a half a day.

Nothing was left to the Negro workers to decide for themselves. All those licensed "shall ply at the Curtain-line, between the Watch-House and the Gap opposite to Col. Beale's house, and not elsewhere," the law decreed. The Board also decided that the commissioners would meet on the upcoming Wednesday, 29th of August, from nine until 12 in the "forenoon" and three to six in the afternoon, "in order to grant licenses for negro porters, to be hired out in the said town."[9]

Those slaves refusing to work at the ascertained rate could be reported to any commissioner who could then order the slave "to be publicly whipt, not exceeding twenty stripes, by the scavenger or scavengers to be appointed."[10] (The term "scavenger" applied to the person appointed to clean up detritus around town; whipping slaves was to be another one of his duties.) The new law did not mention if the badges were to be annual, lifetime or what, again showing that the law was not well thought out. It did stipulate that the money accruing from those fees would be appropriated towards keeping the streets in Charlestown clean and in good repair. All contemporary accounts report the city's streets as fouled and often impassible, perhaps another circumstantial bit of evidence suggesting the lax adherence to the law. And indeed, there is contemporary evidence to support this.

In August of 1772, an Englishman who signed himself "The Stranger" began a series of letters to the editor of the *South Carolina Gazette*. In them, he took the government to task for its inability to enforce its own laws. Many subjects caught his attention, but on the issue of slaves and Negroes, he was most indignant. He referred to secret slave and Negro dances and parties going on outside the city; he described the difference between country and city Negroes, and how Negro women wore fine attire, eclipsing white women of the same economic class. But the hiring out of slaves really fueled his ire. He quoted the law and then wrote that

> What regard is paid to this regulation may almost every day be observed in and near the lower Market, where ... constantly resort a great number of loose, idle, disorderly negro women, who are seated from morn 'til night, and buy and sell on their own accounts, what they please, in order to pay their wages, and get as much more for themselves as they can; for their owners care little, how their slaves get the money, so [long as] they [the masters] are paid.

These women bought food and fruit brought in from the country and then resold it at sometimes a 150 percent mark up. "I have known those black women," the scandalized Stranger continued, "to be so insolent, as to even *wrest* things out of the hands of white people, pretending they had been bought before, for their masters or mistresses, yet expose *the same* for sale again within an hour, for their own benefit."[11] The editor teased his readers with promises of more letters from the Stranger; meanwhile the locals took to heart what he wrote, for soon after, on 10 October 1772, the following advertisement appeared in the same paper:

> WE the Subscribers, living on *Charles-Town* Neck, having been much injured by the great Number of NEGROES who are continually passing and repassing, selling Vegetables, &c. without Tickets, so that we cannot distinguish the Run-Aways or others that rob us, DO give this public Notice, That we have determined forthwith to put a stop to this pilfering Trade by Seizing whatever we shall find in the Possession of any Slaves, not having Tickets, specifying the particular Articles they are entrusted with, and by executing the other Powers wherewith we are invested by the Negro Act.

It appeared over the names of John Crew Robinson , John Donavan, Charles Strother, John Douglas and Melchior Werly. These angry gentlemen leave no doubt that the laws against Negroes were not being enforced on the neck, the area north of present day Calhoun Street. Their advertisement also suggests that it was impossible to distinguish valid sellers from illegal runaways, suggesting that tickets as required by law were not being worn, or somehow not being displayed.

This same 1764 Negro Act that required hired-out slaves to wear tickets or badges also addressed other related issues. One section of the law was aimed specifically at keeping slaves from competing with the "mechanics" or artisans and skilled laborers in town, a risingly vocal group who would eventually band together and help overthrow the British autocracy. The lawmakers had decreed,

> That it shall not be lawful for the master or owner of any negro or other slave whatever, hereafter to permit or suffer such negro or other slave to carry on any mechanick or handicraft trade of themselves, in any shop ... in Charlestown, under pain of forfeiting the sum of five pounds, current money, for every day that any such slave shall carry on such trade....

Furthermore, the law forbade "a negro or other slave apprentice or otherwise, to learn any mechanick or handicraft trade of another slave in the said town, upon pain of forfeiting the sum of one hundred pounds, current money." This significant fine hopefully would stop the propagation of more slaves learning more trades to interfere with the white artisans. Such a strict code could hurt those already making profits from slaves who were working as artisans. To placate this category, the canny legislators affixed the following clause to the act:

> Provided, always, nevertheless, that nothing herein contained shall extend, or be construed to extend, to hinder any mechanick or handicraft tradesman in the said town, from teaching their own negroes or other slaves the trades which they respectively exercise, so that they have and constantly employ one white apprentice or journeyman for every two negroes or other slaves they shall so teach and thenceforth employ....[12]

So a slave-owning craftsman could use and teach mechanic slaves in his shop if they carried out the same trade he did, and there was the correct ratio of white to black.

Other slaves did not have this rationing restriction applied to them, and many wealthy owners grew wealthier hiring them out. Henry Laurens, a merchant and slave trader who would take a diplomatic role in the War for Independence, wrote a letter to his brother, James, in 1775, in which he told his brother, now in London, how he had devised his (James') slaves:

> Auba ... hired to Mr. Thompson Schoolmaster for £90 per An[num] from 12 June 1775. Statira—[hired] the 28 June to the Reverand Mr. Tennant for easy Service in the House at £60 per An[num]. Ishmael—brought in 30/. Said he had earned as a porter. I gave him the money [a flagrant violation of the law] together with a reprimand which he thought a good couplet—he is to go to service 3d July, with Robt. Pringle Esq. at £7 per Month. George—the 29 June hired to Mr. Lody £7 per Month. Cato—to go to Mr. Phipse the 3d July £6 per month. Chloe—to work out at a ... stated Washerwoman's [wage] & bring in her wages weekly 30/ per week and maintain Stepny.... I shall hire Frost I mean prentice him to a Tayler, or send him to Mepkin—her wages to commence 3d July.[13]

Carolinians, both high and low, ignored the laws passed in the 1760s, which lasted through the break with England and the Revolutionary War. Early on, Charleston saw a victory over the British at a palmetto log fort on Sullivan's Island in 1776. After that, the area saw little military activity until Charleston fell to the British and was occupied in 1781-82.

When the war ended, a new country emerged. South Carolina became a state, and Charleston was incorporated as a city in August of 1783. There was still a great black majority in the low country area around Charleston, and slave control remained a paramount issue, so much so, in fact, that the twelfth law passed in the just-created city dealt with slavery.

In November of 1783, this new law declared that

> after one month from the publication of this Ordinance, no owner or other persons having the care and government of negroes or other slaves, shall permit any such slave, to be employed on hire, out of their respective houses or families without a ticket or badge first had and obtained from the Corporation of this City, under the penalty of three pounds for every such offense.

Those employing the unticketed would be fined 20 shillings each day. Furthermore,

> for each ticket or badge ... the several sums shall be respectively paid (viz)—For a butcher, 40 shillings; for a carpenter, bricklayer, fisherman, blacksmith, wheelwright, pump or block-maker, cabinet-maker, painter or glazier, and gold or silversmith, 20 shillings; for a tailor, tinman, tanner or currer, 15 shillings; for a mariner, cooper, shoemaker, barber, hatter, ropemaker, turner, or any other handicraft tradesman, 10 shillings; and for all others the sum of 5 shillings; which said ticket or badge shall continue for one year and no longer, but may be renewed at the end of every year on payment of the fees aforesaid.[14]

So, in 1783, just after Charleston's incorporation, for the first time, a staggered fee structure was named in the statutes. The annual fee and "renewable" nature of the badges was specified for the first time, too.

Many more particulars were spelled out. No Negroes or slaves (licensed or not, excepting licensed fishermen) could "presume on their own account" to sell any goods or wares, etc. Too, no Negro or slave could sell any item at all for a white person "without a written License or Ticket" specifying the amount and quantity, etc. "And whereas the practice which has hitherto prevailed among negroes and others, employed in selling fruit and other articles, of taking seats and stations at the corners and in other parts of the streets" which "does greatly impede and obstruct the free passage of industrious citizens"; therefore, the law ordained that all such materials had to be sold in "open market, and under such regulations as are or shall be established by the Commissioners of the Market."

The same regulation proclaimed,

> That no owner, or other person having the charge and government of negroes or other slaves, shall permit any such slave to carry on any mechanic or handicraft trade of themselves in any shop or otherwise in this city, on pain of forfeiting Twenty Shillings for every day that

> any such slave shall carry on any such trade; nor shall any person whatever hereafter put a negro or other slave apprentice, or otherwise to learn any mechanic or handicraft trade of another slave within this City, under the penalty of Fifteen Pounds for every such offence: PROVIDED nevertheless, that nothing herein contained shall extend, or be construed to extend to hinder any mechanic or handicraftman from teaching their own negroes or other slaves the trades which they repeatedly exercise, upon condition that they have and constantly employ one white apprentice or journeyman for every two negroes or other slaves they shall so teach and thenceforth employ.

Whites must have been worried not just over slaves, but also over those few blacks who were free. The law also specified that

> every free negro, mulatto, or [mestizo], living or residing within this City, shall be obliged ... to register him, her, or themselves, in the office of the City Clerk, with the number of their respective families and places of residence; and upon the removal from the City, or changing of the place of abode ... every such person shall be obliged previously to give notice thereof at the said office.

Now free Negroes had to wear badges, too, for, the law continued,

> every free negro, mulatto, or mestizo, above the age of fifteen years, shall be obliged to obtain a badge from the Corporation of the City, for which badge every such person shall pay into the City Treasury the sum of Five Shillings, and shall wear it suspended by a string or ribband, and exposed to view on his breast.

For not wearing the badge, registering or noting change of address, the Negro would be fined three pounds; if not paid within ten days, he or she could be taken to the workhouse and committed to hard labor for up to 30 days.[15]

There is no doubt that these free badges were made and worn, for some have been found. Different sources claim some are of brass, some of copper; there is even a silver one known, as shown in the referenced image. All bear numbers (all lower than the 600 or so free people of color in Charleston around 1790), with numerals sometimes engraved and sometimes stamped. Although they had to be worn, some do not have holes in them to allow for suspension. Most do. All are oval, with a design of a liberty cap on a staff, similar to a design motif of the seal of the city. "City of Charleston" surrounds the image. Although at least four are known, no slave badges from this era have been identified. It may be worthwhile then to examine the language of the laws for possible reasons why. For free people of color, the statute states that *badges* are to be obtained from the city and attached to clothing; for slaves, the wording is ticket or badge. The same law links the word "ticket" to license, possibly a written piece of paper. There is no stipulation in the law that these hired-out tickets or badges be worn, as is stated with the free people of color who are to wear it on their "breast." This disparity might suggest a difference in the type of item needed by free people of color and hired-out slaves. It may seem that although the city produced badges for people of color in this era, it might not have produced similar *wearable* slave badges. The great amount of information given, noting what each type of badge or ticket would cost for each profession tends to suggest, however, that badges or licenses of some sort *were* made; and the following leaves no doubt. It appeared in the *South Carolina Gazette and General Advertiser* issue of 20 December to 23 December 1783, exactly a month after the statute calling the badges into being was passed. That statute said it would go into effect within a month. And, so a month later, the following appeared: "BADGES ARE now ready to be delivered to Persons as have Negroes to Hire, at the CITY CLERK's OFFICE."

Now it can be definitely stated that slave-hire badges (in some unknown configuration) were created and sold in Charleston in the 1780s. Later notations in the newspapers also state that "negro badges" (with no distinction noted between those for free people of color and those for slaves) were both made and sold. They did exist, but what did they look like? This question will probably not be settled until a definite artifact turns up.

Another thing of great interest regarding the badges is their assumed impermanence. The section of the law dealing with *slave* badges or tickets states that they can be renewed at the end of every year as long as the fee was paid. But there is no mention of renewing *free people of color* badges. It seems that once purchased, they could be worn in perpetuity, and the fact that the surviving badges bear no date further suggests that the free person of color object might be of a more durable nature. On the other hand, the renewable nature of the slave-hire badges is confirmed in the following advertisement in the *South Carolina State Gazette and Daily Advertiser*:

> WHEREAS many persons in this City have neglected to renew their BADGES FOR NEGROS, which they hire out—This is to acquaint them, and others who, contrary to the Ordinance of the City Council, hire out Negroes, without Badges, that unless they call and take out new ones, on or before the 1st day of March next, the law will be strictly put in force against them by P. Bounetheau, *City Clerk*, 23 Feb. 1785.

Although many people did not follow the law, badges were available and renewable, meaning, apparently, that new ones were to be taken out each [calendar or fiscal] year.

Continuing on with its attempt to regulate blacks, the 1783 statute declared that any free Negro, mulatto or mestizo counterfeiting

> any of the badges hereafter given as above recited by the Corporation, or shall wear one without having first registered his or her name with the City Clerk, and paid for the same, shall forfeit the sum of Five Pounds for every such offence, and on nonpayment thereof, shall suffer such corporal punishment, not extending to life or limb, as the Court of Wardens shall in their discretion award: And any negro, or other slave, who shall presume to wear any badge in the similtude or likeness of those to be issued as above to free negroes, shall be publicly whipped at the discretion of the Court of Wardens, not exceeding thirty-nine lashes, and be put into the stocks, there to remain at least one hour.[16]

Obviously, whites realized how powerful the badge could be and how it could allow slaves to do certain things. To encourage people to ferret out offenders, fines paid were to be split between those informing on the offenses and the city.

This was the law, but the public obviously disobeyed it, as remarked in the 1785 notice quoted above. The flouting is further confirmed by the fact that on 26 July 1786, a new provision to the law was deemed necessary since, "many persons have neglected to take out the annual Badge, or permission to hire out their Negroes to work." This is what the City Council took note of as it announced in the *Charleston Evening Gazette* of 28 July 1786:

> *Be it therefore Ordained* by the Honourable Intendant and Wardens … That from and immediately after the passing of this Ordinance, every Negro working out on hire, shall wear the Badge received from the City Clerk, on some visible part of their dress; and the constable or any other person or persons are hereby required and authorized to command any negro applying for hire or working out, to produce his or her badge, and upon refusal or not being able to produce one legally obtained for the year in which the demand shall be made, immediately to convey such negro to the Warden of the Workhouse, who is hereby commanded to receive and secure such negro. And the constable apprehending such negro … shall within three hours after delivering him or her to the … Workhouse, give notice thereof to the Clerk of the City Council, who shall thereupon immediately issue a notice to the owner or person having charge of such negro.

That person or owner would be billed the accruing expenses, including the three-pound fine imposed in the 1783 ordinance, a ten-shilling reward for the constable or other person apprehending the Negro, and all other fees. The warden was forbidden to release the Negro, who instead had to be kept at "hard labour for the space of one year and one day." After this draconian measure, the Negro was to be advertised for sale for six weeks, the name of the owner listed and the cause of the sale. Once sold, the amount realized would be turned over to the city treasurer, after the warden deducted all his costs of keeping and advertising the slave. The treasurer would then deduct all his expenses, turning over what was left to the owner.

This addition to the law books shows that drastic measures were being taken to make sure the slave badge laws were respected and enforced; at the same time, it seems to confirm the different status given to the slave-hire badges or tickets, for no lack of adherence to the free person of color law is mentioned. The new law is no longer ambiguous; it no longer uses the phrase "badge or ticket," but the term "badge" exclusively. Now it states that the badge has to be worn and produced; the similarity of the language in the 1783 law which resulted in the creation of metal free person of color badges suggest that similar objects for hired-out slaves were now in use.

The Act further ordained "That no person whatever shall be permitted ... to keep more than two slaves to work out for hire in the city, except any mechanic or handy-craft trade, under a penalty not exceeding one pound for every day such slave shall be kept for hire as aforesaid." Should the owner refuse, the slave could be sold by the warden of the workhouse.

The ordinance then in a very extraordinary fashion tried to limit the number of slaves in town; no more than four slaves could be allowed for the head of a household "and one to each white person in the family, exclusive of children ten years of age, under penalty of being doubly taxed for each and every slave above the numbers limited aforesaid." The statute continued,

> *And be it further Ordained*, That every owner or person having charge of any slave, shall make a return on oath to the City Clerk, between the first day of August and the first day of September in every year, of the number of white persons in his or her family, and of all and every slave he or she shall retain in the city, whether for domestic purposes, or for hiring out, and specifying the same in such return under the penalty of Ten pounds, to be recovered in the Court of Wardens; one half to the City Treasury, and the other half to the person suing for the same. And the Clerk of the City, is hereby ordered and directed to keep a fair register of all such returns, which register may be examined by any person during the office hours of the said Clerk.

To summarize, this 1786 law was exceedingly strict, demanding that those working without a badge be immediately taken to jail, the clerk notified within *three hours* of the fact, the slave kept at hard labor for a year, and then sold. Furthermore, the number of slaves in town was limited and they were registered, and people were allowed only so many slaves per household. Those holding more would pay double amount the taxes for their excess slaves.

To make sure that this law regarding badges was enforced, the city government had the following advertisement placed in the local paper (*The City Gazette and Daily Advertiser*, 7 January 1788):

> Badges, Cart and Dray Licenses. NOTICE is hereby given, That badges for the year 1788, are ready to be delivered to the owners of slaves who go out to work on hire; Also, licenses for all carts and drays in this city. *By Order of his Honor the* INTENDANT. JOHN M'CALL, City-Treasurer. City-Treasurer's Office *Jan.* 1, 1788.

Financial reports found from these years cast some light on the use of badges, but also cast doubts and raises questions as well. (These records do not exist in the City of Charleston archives, but only in summary form of income and expenses in the contemporary newspaper press.) The first financial statement covers the period from October 1783 (just after the city's incorporation) to the end of August 1785 (*Columbian Herald,* 5 September 1785). It has no expense category for badges, which seems to suggest that no one was paid for making badges, which in turn suggests that they did not exist. Yet they must have, for the city reports an income of £257, 5 shillings from the sale of badges for 1784 and 1785. In the next financial statement found (for fiscal year 1785-1786, *Columbian Herald*, 7 September 1786), it was noted that £47, 5 shillings was paid out to make badges; and £302, 5 shillings came in. In this year, there is also an expense category for the city "purchasing Horses, Carts and Negro-Hire" that amounts to £257, 7 shillings. Obviously, if the city used hired-out Negroes, it must have obeyed its own laws, so those slaves it used must have been issued the tickets or badges. In the next year available, 1787-1788 (*City Gazette*, 4 September 1788), there was no expense category listed for badges, suggesting that no new ones were made, but the advertisement appearing in the press in January 1788 expressly stated that new badges were now ready. This financial period dates from after July 1786, when the stronger slave badge law went into effect, but despite the stronger penalties and more insistent language, badge sales went down. Only £112, 4 shillings and 6 pence came in. This drop in income must have been disappointing and infuriating for the city. Besides that, the record keeping and vigilance demanded by the stringent 1786 Negro law must have been extraordinary; so it is not surprising that the law was soon overturned.

The new ordinance, passed in 1789, had numerous clauses. No Negroes except licensed fishermen could sell items without permission; they were not allowed to take seats to sell except in specified places. Only fishermen could have boats; slaves could not congregate over a certain number except for funerals, stay out past certain hours, or buy liquor without their master's permission, etc. The procedure for fines was laid out, half "to the use of the corporation, and the other half to him, who shall sue for and prosecute the same to effect."[17]

Perhaps the most telling thing of all in this new 1789 law was the entire throwing out of all the strictures on hiring out slaves, strictures requiring slave badges (and free badges), restricting the number of slaves per white person, and registering slaves annually. The final clause of the ordinance states that the ordinance of 22 November 1783 and that of 26 July 1786, "be, and the same are hereby repealed. Provided nonetheless, That nothing herein contained shall extend or be construed to extend, to prevent the payment or recovery of monies due, and which may become due for badges, agreeably to the full intent and meaning of the said Ordinances until the first of January 1790." The date of this new law was 16 June 1789. It is interesting to note that in February of that year, the newspaper (*City Gazette*, 6 February 1789) notified citizens that badges were ready to be picked up; and a month later (*City Gazette*, 13 March 1789), with response apparently sluggish, the city noted that since so very few people had picked up their badges, it reprinted the ordinance in the paper. People were not obeying the law, so city government abolished the law four months later.

What this meant was that there was no longer a badge law in Charleston. Badges, called into being in 1783 (in a law that a 1785 newspaper article and a 1786 statute noted was often flouted) were no longer made by 1789, and only the retrieval of money coming from those in use continued until 1 January 1790. This may explain why slave badges from this era have yet to be found. In the first three years, many people did not obey the law. When the law was strengthened, it was abandoned three years after that. This also is the span, then, for the free Negro badges. Begun in 1783, the free Negro badge law died with the repeal in 1789, and was not mentioned in the statutes again. This at least resolves what happened to free Negro badges. "[I]t is impossible to determine dates of manufacture for free badges," one scholar believed due to the lack of dates stamped on them,[18] but the statutes show that free badges must date between 1783 and 1789. The reason there is no date on these badges is that the law did not call for it, and apparently, once bought or manufactured, the badge was good for life, with perhaps a fee for its renewal paid each year.

In the years following 1789, hiring out, no doubt, was still being practiced; it just wasn't regulated with badges, and it still proved troublesome. To try to aid this system without badges and the bookkeeping that it entailed, city government announced (*City Gazette*, 16 August 1791) that it had opened a "Universal City and Country Register Office," where people could hire slaves and owners could register slaves for hire, as long as the slaves had the "proper certificate of permission" from their owners. Then, on 17 August 1796, a new act was passed proclaiming, "that no owner, or other person, having the charge and government of negroes, or other slaves, shall permit any such slave to carry on any mechanic or handicraft trade of themselves, in any shop or otherwise, within the city." Slaves could not work as mechanics on their own, the penalty being one dollar a day for such activities; "nor shall any person whatever, hereafter put a negro, or other slave apprentice or otherwise, to learn any mechanic or handicraft trade of another slave, within this city, under the penalty of eighty-five dollars for every such offence." So no slave or Negro could be taught a mechanic trade by another slave.

> *Provided nevertheless,* That nothing herein shall extend, or be construed to extend, to hinder any mechanic, or handicraftsman, from teaching their own negroes, or other slaves, the trades which they respectively exercise, upon condition that they have, and constantly employ, one white apprentice or journeyman, for every four negroes, or other slaves they shall so teach and employ.

You could teach your own slaves your profession as long as you kept a certain ratio of white to black (one to four) in your shop, the quota now relaxed from the original 1783 statute that had required one white mechanic for every two slaves or negroes. The last line of the ordinance states, "That nothing ... shall be construed to prevent any owner of a mechanic slave or slaves, from hiring him to any free man who he shall please." No more ordinances on the subject were passed for the next few years; but the laws on the books obviously were not enough, for a new series of laws was soon enacted.

In 1800, the city passed "An Ordinance for the better regulation of Slaves, and for other purposes therein mentioned." The new law decreed:

> *Be it ordained by the Intendant and Wardens of Charleston,* That after one month from the publication of this ordinance, no owner, or other person, having the care and government of negroes, or other slaves, shall permit any such slave, whether male or female, to be employed on hire, out of their respective houses or families, without a ticket or badge, first had and obtained from the corporation of the city, to be given out by the treasurer, under penalty of forfeiting a sum not exceeding ten dollars, for each and every offense.[19]

So the law abolished in 1789 was now on the books again. Badges were back. Again there were fees for different categories, reconfigured from British currency to American:

> for every handicraft tradesman, three dollars; for every carter, drayman, porter, or day labourer, two dollars; for every fisherman, one dollar; for every house servant, or washerwoman, one dollar; for every huckster, or vender (male or female) of any article, of what description soever, six dollars: which said ticket or badge, shall continue for one year, and no longer, but may be renewed at the end of every year, on payment of the fees aforesaid.

These hired-out Negroes had to "wear the badge received from the city treasurer, on some visible part of their dress."

To make sure this was done,

> it shall be lawful for any person or persons whomever, to command any negro, or other slave, applying for hire, or working out, to produce his or her badge, and upon refusal, or not being able to produce one legally obtained, for the year in which the demand shall be made, immediately to carry such negro, or slave before any of the wardens of the city, who shall thereupon commit him, or her, to the workhouse, and cite the owner, or other person having charge of said slave, to appear before the next court of wardens, where the case shall be heard.

(This, in effect, put the same earlier laws back in place, minus some stringent requirements, such as the owner having to be notified in three hours time.) The statute continued:

> And if the said slave shall be convicted, such slave, or slaves, shall be publicly whipped, and may be confined in the stocks; there to remain at least one hour, unless the owner of such slave, or slaves, shall pay such fine as may be imposed by the court. And the court may adjudge any sum, not exceeding two dollars, to the person apprehending the said slave. And the owner, or other persons having charge of said slave, shall be further amendable for all such expenses as shall arise from the commitment and punishment of the said slave.

(These laws, again, are similar to the earlier ones, but with one main exception; slaves working without badges would just be punished for a finite time, not kept in jail for a year, and then sold.) Those illegally hiring a slave without a proper badge were to be punished, too, liable for "a sum not exceeding five dollars, for each day he, she, or they shall employ such slave, over and above the wages agreed to be paid such slave, for his or her work."

Next, feeling that "there are a greater number of slaves in the city than are necessary for the servile business, thereof," the lawmakers ordained, "that no slave, or slaves, belonging to any person, or persons, living without the limits of Charleston, except slaves belonging to orphan children; and even in that case, not more than four belonging to each orphan, shall be entitled to obtain a badge." This meant that slave owners who lived outside of the city limits of Charleston could not send their slaves to town to be hired out; only orphans beyond the city limits could do this. This prohibition did not extend to slaves "engaged in any public undertaking or employment," meaning slaves working for the city. Those breaking the law were liable to the same punishments as above. Furthermore, "no inhabitant of Charleston, shall be permitted to have more than six slaves to work out for hire, unless such inhabitant shall, for every slave or slaves, over and above the number limited, pay a threefold proportion for the badge or badges ... classified as aforesaid. " So if they did have more than the allowed number, they would have to pay three times more.

Finally, the city council decreed that no badge could be granted to a slave acting as a huckster, or vending any other article,

> where such slave or slaves, shall be under the age of thirty years *Provided*, that such restriction shall not debar any person from the selling of milk by any slave without a badge, or as a preclusion from the selling, or offering for sale any sort of grain, fruit, victuals or provision of any kind whatsoever, which the owner, or other person having care of such slave shall have sent, brought or received from his or her plantation or farms, or shall have reared or cultivated on his or her grounds within the city.

These amounts and prices had to be specified in a "ticket" from the owner, or controller. Perhaps the age was deemed necessary, to make sure the slave was responsible, but obviously younger ones could still sell articulated items if under control of the master. If the age of a slave could not be determined, then that was the task of the city treasurer. Badges were deemed so important that now anyone taking a badge out had to swear that the slave being licensed was his or her property, that they were residents of Charleston, or if orphan children, they hired out no more than four.

With so many new laws on the books regarding badges, and so much hinging on them, the lawmakers had to deal with the issue of counterfeiting, since surely that would be a temptation for many slave owners and slaves. To limit that possibility, the city council drew up severe penalties. Counterfeiters would be fined $20 for each offence; slaves were treated more harshly. Those slaves found counterfeiting

> shall be publicly whipped at the discretion of the court of wardens, not exceeding twenty stripes and may be put in the stocks, there to remain at least one hour, and may be also confined in the work-house, for any term not exceeding ten days. And if any slave, or slaves, shall presume to wear any badge which does not properly pertain to them, or which does not specify the particular nature of his, or her employment, such slave, or slaves, shall be publicly whipped, and may be confined in the stocks, there to remain at least one hour, unless the owner of such slave, or slaves, shall pay the sum of two dollars as an exemption for the punishment to be otherwise inflicted.

The laws made 16 July 1800 were obviously enforced and obeyed, for slave badges dated 1800 have survived. The laws were refined a bit later in 1801 to control "the exorbitant demands made by licensed porters, and other day laborers."[20] On 4 September 1801, the new law stated

> That from and after the passing of this ordinance, no licensed porter, or other day labourer, shall demand, or be entitled to receive any other than the following rates: For a full days labour, or the loading or unloading of the cargo of any vessel in which a porter or day laborer may be engaged, 85 cents. For half a day's labour, 42 d[itt]o, For a quarter of a day's labour, 25 d[itt]o.

In other words, not only did City Council control what the slave owner had to pay for the badge to allow his slave to be licensed out, it also now controlled what the slave could charge for his or her services. Lawmakers were obviously alarmed at slaves making more money than they turned over to their masters.

The law went on to decree:

> That if any porter or day labourer shall ask, demand, or receive any greater wages than ... herein ... specified, or as shall hereafter be established, such porter or day labourer, shall, if a slave, be carried before any one of the wardens, or other magistrate, who shall adjudge him to receive any number of stripes on the back, not exceeding twenty.

If free, the offender could be fined no more than five dollars. The council also set the hours for labor: "from sun rise to twilight in the evening, allowing one hour for breakfast, and one hour for dinner; except the months of June, July, August and September, when two hours shall be allowed for dinner."

The city marshal was empowered to "fix proper stands for licensed porters." Any one working out of an inappropriate spot could be whipped up to ten times. In 1803 Marshal James Browne released the locations he had picked to the press (*Charleston Times,* 11 November 1803). They were "No. 1, at the lower end of Tradd-Street, below the curtain line; No. 2, the north side of Beale's Wharf [near Boyce's Wharf today]; No. 3, fronting Mr. Cambridge's vendue store [on Exchange Street]; no. 4, the north side of the Exchange; no. 5, fronting Mr. Cochran's wharf [in the vicinity of modern day Cordes Street and North Atlantic Wharf]."

Many more restrictions, such as not shouting or singing obscene songs, were part of this law, as was the stipulation that no slave with a badge standing in his stand could refuse or neglect anyone asking him to work. Conviction could put the slave in the stocks for up to an hour, and give him up to ten "stripes." Finally, Council stated that it would decide on day rates for porters on the first Monday of December in each year, or on the first meeting after that date.

In 1806, City Council combined all these slave laws together, emending some and voiding others. It now declared that the laws abstracted above, including the one from 1789 (disestablishing the badge law), the 1796 law prohibiting slaves from being mechanics for themselves, the 1801 law setting wages for porters, and others (but not the 1800 statute re-instituting the badge) were repealed and voided in the points contradicting the current law. In 1808, the slave trade would be prohibited, and the city was now seeing an increase in slave sales; perhaps this 1806 law was a partial response to conditions.

The new law had many new clauses relating to badges and hiring-out practices. Clause VII took up the issue of mechanics. It stated:

> no owner ... of a slave or slaves, shall permit any such slave or slaves, to carry on any mechanic or handicraft trade, in any shop or other place within the city, in the name or on account of such slave or slaves, on pain of forfeiting one dollar for every day, that any and every such slave shall carry on any such trade as aforesaid; nor shall any person whatever put a slave as an apprentice, or otherwise, under the charge of another slave, to be instructed by the latter in any mechanic or handicraft trade within the city, under the penalty of fifty dollars for the first offence, and one hundred dollars for every repetition of the said offence. But nothing, herein contained, shall extend, or be construed to extend, either to prevent any mechanic or handicraftsman, from instructing or employing his own slave or slaves, in the trade by himself exercised, on condition, that every such mechanic or handicraftsman shall have, and constantly employ, one white journeyman or white apprentice, for every six slaves, so taught or employed by him; nor shall any owner of a mechanic slave or slaves be prevented, from employing him or them in his or her own lawful work, as he or she may please, or from hiring him or them to any free person, whom he or she shall choose, under such regulations as are set forth in this ordinance.[21]

So no slave could work for himself or for another slave. They could work as mechanics for their owners, and their owners could hire them out, if now there was at least one white mechanic, or even white apprentice, working for every six slaves, up from two (in 1751) and four (in 1783 and 1796.)

Clause X prohibited slaves from selling any article without a ticket, but a badge was not mentioned. Clause XI, on the other hand, decreed:

> Every negro or other slave shall be permitted to sell milk without a badge or ticket; and also such grain, fruit, victuals, and provisions of any kind whatever, as the owner, or other person having the care of such negro or slave, shall have sent, brought or received, from his or her plantation or farm, or reared or cultivated on his or her lands within the city, the same to be then offered for sale at the first hand, and the quantity and quality thereof, as well as the name of the negro or slave, offering the same for sale, to be specified in a ticket under the signature of the owner, or other person having the care or government of such negro or slave.

So a slave did not need a badge if he or she only sold products controlled by the master, and if what the products were and how much they cost were spelled out in a written document.

Clause XIII added other requirements. It declared:

> no owner, or other person having the care or management, of negroes or other slaves, shall permit any such slave, whether male or female, to be employed on hire, out of their respective houses or families, without first informing the city-treasurer, of the specific trade or employment, which he or she is to pursue, when working on hire, and without obtaining from him a ticket or badge expressing the same, and numbered, under a penalty of forfeiting twenty dollars, with costs, for each and every such offense. And for each ticket or badge, so to be obtained, the several sums following shall be respectively paid, viz. For every handicraft tradesman, three dollars; for every carter, drayman, porter or day laborer, two dollars; for every fisherman or fisherwoman, one dollar; for every house servant, or washer-woman, one dollar; for every seller of fruits and cakes, or of any article of what description soever, not prohibited, as aforesaid, fifteen dollars, which said ticket or badge shall continue, until the last day of December in every year, and no longer, and shall be renewed at the beginning of every year, on payment of the fees aforesaid.

Several things in this clause are worthy of note. Badges are now to be numbered, and records kept. (But the badges that have survived predating this law *were* numbered; so it seems that the laws caught up with the common practice.) Furthermore, mention has to be made by the owner/manager of the slave's occupation, and the keeping of these records on the city's part is required. The badges are said to expire at the end of the calendar year, making them no good for the next, and even dangerous, since fines are large for wearing the wrong badge. This obviously lead to their wholesale discarding and even destruction, which may explain why comparatively few are found and why some of those that have survived are damaged and bent in half. Also, it is interesting to note the price for those selling fruit (known mostly as a "huckster" in these early years) is $15. The high price is curious; perhaps those selling fruit and acting as hucksters for similar materials were freer agents; they could move about, could carry money, make change, and converse with others, black and white, slave and free. Perhaps, too, there was the concern, as earlier, that fruit sellers would set up anywhere and not just in the market and be a nuisance to traffic. (This expensive fee was soon reduced down to five dollars in 1813.)

These 1806 fees and laws were in effect for slave owners and managers with six or less slaves hired out. If a slave owner hired out more, he or she had to pay triple the amount for the right type of badge; fines were $20 for disobeying. (This provision would last unchanged until 1837, when the issue was taken up in City Council, and "an Ordinance to repeal so much of an Ordinance as requires a three-fold price for all badges over six, being engrossed, was ratified."[22]) In 1806, if one lived outside the city of Charleston, and paid "no city tax," one could not hire out slaves in the city limits, unless one was a special case, a widow (again added to the law) or an orphan. They could just hire out four. If slaves were hired out for public works, however, restrictions did not apply.

**1814 Servant, No. 718. (J. J. Lafar). A very crisp badge, it shows slightly different alignments in the stamping of "Charleston," "Servant" and "1814," and in the punching of "718."**

Now the city required not just payment but an oath:

> Every person, applying to the city-treasurer for a badge or badges, shall take before him the following oath, to wit, 'I, A.B. do solemnly swear (or affirm,) that the negro or negroes, (stating the number) is or are my property, or the property of C.D. a resident of Charleston or E. F. paying a city tax, in whose name or names (as the case may be) I do now apply, or the property of G.H. a widow, or of J.K. an orphan child, living without the limits of the city, and not have above four slaves now employed on hire therein, and that the employment of every such slave, when working on hire, is to be no other than such, as is now mentioned by me. So help me God.

The city treasurer was forbidden to grant a badge without the oath first being taken.

> And the city treasurer shall keep a register of all slaves, for whom he grants badges, together with their owner's names, and their respective ages and employments; and every badge granted by the city treasurer,

> shall express the number, as well as the specified trade or employment, to be pursued by any slave working out for hire.

Such logs would show how many slaves an owner did indeed have hired out, and they could be checked in case of loss of badges, suspected counterfeits or transfers of a badge from one slave to another. Such logs would be invaluable today to document slaves and the hiring-out practice, but not one scrap from one such record series is known. (Similar rosters, listing taxes paid by free blacks are extant, however, and "badge books" from the 20th century, showing the number of a badge attached to a vender's vehicle, have survived.) Whether the records were destroyed at the end of every year, burned in a fire, lost or carried away by souvenir hunters or destroyed by those hating (or covering up) slavery, is anyone's guess. (For more information, see the note on sources at the end of the volume.)

Once a badge was procured for the particular slave, he or she had "to wear the badge ... on some visible part of his or her dress." (An ex-slave interviewed in 1903, however, said slaves often just carried them on their person and produced them when asked. House servants, the law later stipulated, just had to have the badge and not wear it.) As in earlier laws, any person approached by a hired-out slave for services could demand to see the badge; if the badge was not produced, or if the badge did not match the profession the slave was working in, or was not for the current year, the person was "immediately to carry" the offending slave to the workhouse. Owners had to pay (or caused to be paid) a $20 fee and the costs incurred at the workhouse. If the slave owner had followed the law properly, the fine was only two dollars and expenses. If fines weren't paid within two months, the slave could pay the forfeit, receiving "at the public market, twenty stripes on the bare back. And it shall be the duty of the master of the work house, to give immediate notice to the owner of any negro or other slave, when brought to the work house as aforesaid, but, if the owner cannot be found out, to proceed, as the law directs, with regard to runaway slaves."

Clause XVII explained that those employing slaves

> without such negro or slave having a badge or ticket, duly obtained from the city treasurer, and correspondent with the work, in which such negro or other slave is employed, as aforesaid, shall forfeit and pay double the amount of such badge or ticket, with costs, for each day or part of a day, on which he or she shall employ such negro or other slave.

This punishment for *users* of slaves was much higher than the fee the actual slave *owners* had to pay. For if the owner allowed his slave to work out without a badge, he or she was fined $20 and expenses; those who actually employed the hired-out slave without a badge would pay significantly more. A person illegally hiring a fruit seller or huckster, for instance, if caught, would have to pay $30 *a day* for the offense (twice the appropriate badge amount—that for a fruit seller being $15.) It could be well over $100 if the slave worked out for just a week. Obviously the law was aimed not so much at the slave owner, as at those who would use a slave for his or her own purposes.

With fee structures as prohibitive as these, counterfeiting would be tempting, but again the laws addressed that issue:

> If any white person or persons shall counterfeit any badge or badges, he, she or they, shall forfeit and pay fifty dollars, with costs, for each and every such offence. And if any negro or person of colour shall counterfeit any of the said badges, he or she shall, by a warrant from under the hands of any two wardens of the city, be put into the stocks for one hour, and receive twenty lashes on the bare back, and shall moreover be confined in the work house for any term, not exceeding twenty days. And if any negro or other slave shall wear a badge, which does not properly belong to him or her, so wearing it, or which does not specify the particular natures of his or her employment, every such negro or slave shall be publicly whipped, by warrant from under the hands of any two wardens of the city, unless the owner shall previously pay the sum of two dollars, as an exemption from the punishment, that would otherwise be inflicted on such slave or slaves.

The city marshal was charged with fixing the proper stands where porters (as day laborers were called) could wait for work. Loitering in the wrong place could result in being whipped if a slave (one's owner paying a two dollar penalty could save the slave from the ten lashes). A free person of color could be whipped, too, or could pay a five-dollar fee to avoid that. Once engaged as a porter, if the slave did not leave his or her stand immediately and dawdled, he or she could suffer the same punishment just described.

Clause XX laid out the wages:

> for a full day's labour, which is to be from sun-rise to twilight in the evening, allowing one hour for breakfast, and one hour for dinner (except in the months of June, July, August and September, when two hours shall be allowed for dinner) eighty-one cents and a quarter; for half a day's labour, forty-three cents; for an hour's labour twelve cents and a half.

Furthermore, the next clause maintained,

> That if any person, hiring a porter or labourer by the day, furnished him with victuals and drink, he shall have a right, to deduct from his wages

> eighteen cents and three quarters for his meals in the morning, noon or evening, or six cents and a quarter for each meal so furnished.

If a slave or worker should demand or receive more than the allotted fees specified by City Council, then

> every such porter or day labourer, if a slave, shall be carried before any one of the wardens of the city, who, on conviction, shall adjudge him to receive any number of lashes on the bare back, not less than twelve, not more than twenty; but if a free man [of color], he shall forfeit and pay to the use of the city, a fine of not less than five dollars, and be confined in the work-house until the same is paid. And if any porter or day labourer shall refuse or neglect, to work for any person, such porter or day labourer ... shall, on conviction before any warden, of the city, receive at the work-house, or at the public market, a number of lashes not less, than twelve, nor more than twenty, unless the owner should previously pay to the city-treasurer the sum of two dollars for such porter or day labourer, if a slave, or unless such porter or day labourer, if a free man, shall previously pay to the city treasurer the sum of five dollars.

Of all these fines, some would go to the city treasury; but half could go to the person "prosecuting" or reporting the offender, "provided the offense be proved by the testimony of some other witness or witnesses, being competent and disinterested." There were other proscriptions against slaves, such as not smoking "segars," or walking with canes, and the master of the workhouse was obligated to give all the whippings without benefit of a fee or reward.

This then was the law for the next several decades, the 1806 law remaining unchanged for quite a while. It appeared verbatim in the digest of laws published by the city in 1818, with the following exception: It noted that on 1 February 1813, the fee for a fruit seller's badge was reduced. "Be it ordained," the statute declared,

> That from and immediately after the passing of this ordinance, the sum of Five Dollars shall be paid by every seller of fruit and cakes, or any article not prohibited by any ordinance, for a ticket or badge, to vend the same: and that every person violating this ordinance, by having a different badge from the one required, shall forfeit the sum of Five Dollars.[23]

Thus for about seven years, from 1806 to the beginning of 1813, fruit sellers' badges were significantly more expensive than others. This may suggest that those badges from these years might be harder to find.

Another class of laborers drew the attention of City Council in a meeting of 24 January 1814. In the *Courier* the next day, a note appeared stating that chimney sweeps now had to take out badges, "under the class of Day Labourers," i.e., those titled "Porter." The city marshal then gave word that "The owners of chimney Sweeps are hereby Notified, that unless they call on the City Treasurer for Badges, previous to the first day of February, the penalty will be rigidly enforced on all defaulters." Years later, sweeps would have a badge category all of their own.

**1815 Fruiterer &c, No. 74. (J. J. Lafar). Originally called "Huckster," the term "Fruiterer" came into use possibly by 1810.**

Attention then shifted back to hucksters or fruiterers, as they had come to be called in these years. On 19 October 1816, the *Courier* published a letter from someone who signed himself, "A Citizen." "Citizen" addressed his communication to the City Council, complaining of the practice of slaves in the market who bought fruit and grain, etc., that came in from the countryside and then sold it at a higher price, echoing "The Stranger" who criticized the same practice in the 1770s. "Citizen" suggested that Council

> publicly call in all the Huckster Badges, or in other words, badges issued by you, which give to those wenches the liberty to buy and sell—call them in up to the end of the present year, and never again to issue another, [and this] would, I conclude, be the most infallible remedy for this prevalent disease. By so doing, you will not only prove yourselves worthy [of] the title you bear, but at the same time the office you hold.

This complaint reveals two interesting things: (1) that women were mostly hucksters, or "fruiterers" as their badge now claimed ("Citizen" must have been more familiar with the older title); and (2) that slaves felt this badge allowed them to buy *and* sell.

The letter had its effect. For although there are no copies known of City Council meeting minutes of these years, on 6 November 1816, the following advertisement appeared in the *Courier*:

> *City Council*, Nov. 4, 1816. THE practice of allowing *Slaves,* who are holders of Fruiterer's Badges, to buy and sell grain, poultry, vegetable, or provisions of any kind, *thereby forestalling the Market*, being contrary to the true intent and meaning of the Ordinance passed for the government of Negroes, and other persons of color, on the 28th October, 1806, *Be it therefore, Resolved*, That from and immediately after the passage of this resolve, that holders of Fruiterer's Badges shall only be permitted *to dispose of Fruit and Cake*, as was, and is intended by said Ordinance. *Extract from the Minutes.* G. M. Bounthenau, C[lerk of] C[ouncil].

On the very next day (7 November 1816), the following communication appeared in the *Courier*:

> I am truly happy to observe, Mr. Editor, that the City Council have adopted a Resolution to put a stop to the infamous system of *Forestalling* in our markets. To such a pitch had this practice reached, that it was impossible for a citizen to purchase a pair of fowls, or a dozen of eggs, from a country boat—every thing having been previously promised to these *negro forestallers*, who immediately put an advance of near 50 per cent upon the articles thus bought. Council have now done their part, and it only remains for every citizen to set his face against the practice, by stopping and detaining any Negro found trespassing against the law; when we may reasonably calculate on a very considerable reduction in the prices of many articles of first necessity—CIVIS.

The writer called on citizens to be vigilant and catch those with fruiterer badges buying and selling in the market. Perhaps they were, for no new laws on the subject were passed in the next few years. Slaves continued to be hired out, and both blacks and whites grew lax, however. This is known from many of the documents that arose after the Denmark Vesey slave rebellion.

Vesey was an enslaved African American who ended up in Charleston as property of Captain Joseph Vesey who had purchased him in the Caribbean. Denmark must have been hired out by his owner, for he somehow got money to buy a lottery ticket; he won, and with his earnings, he purchased his freedom in 1799. In the summer of 1822, when whites heard rumors of a slave rebellion, Vesey was accused of being its leader. Whites panicked, held a trial in secret, and published a censored version of the proceedings. From this record, it is shown that many (at least five) of the slaves involved were hired out. In fact, one of them, William Garner, said being hired out made him "as good as free" (so, he argued in his defense, why should he participate in the plot? His defense did him no good, however, for he was important to the conspiracy, and although he managed to escape, he was ultimately caught and hanged in August.[24]) Jesse Blackwood was also high up in the plot. Instead of hiring himself out to make money for his master as his owner Thomas Blackwood, the man instead made contacts for Vesey among other slaves in the city. To keep his master mollified, other conspirators were asked to hand money over so Jesse could "pay wages to his master," who was president of the Planters and Mechanics Bank.[25] Jesse Blackwood was executed, too. Gullah Jack, a major conspirator, said to be a conjurer and native of Africa, was apparently a hired-out slave as well, as was Monday Gell. (They all met the common end.)

Many slave owners, who thus lost their slaves, revealed in court documents how much they depended on their hired-out slaves. Catherine Faber, seeking restitution by the State Legislature for her loss of her slave Polydore, told them that he had made $12 a month as an "excellent sawyer of lumber [and as] a ropemaker."[26] That was her household's only income. Other women also petitioned the legislature to make up the income they lost by the executions of their hired-out slaves. A 60-year-old man, William Sims, lost one slave by banishment and another by execution and was left wondering who would now support him in "the evening of my life."[27] In an odd twist, his banished slave Scipio would reappear near Charleston, with a forged pass he wrote himself. He was recognized and cornered in a yard on the neck, but he eluded his captors, making his way back to the city that had banished him (*Courier*, 25 August 1823).

In December 1822 (at the same time it entertained many of these petitions from those who lost their slaves), the State Legislature passed many new laws as a result of Vesey's revolt. The first law was "An Act the More Effectually to Prohibit Free Negroes and Persons of Color From Entering into this State and for other purposes." Another was specifically aimed at hiring-out practices. This law made it "altogether unlawful for any person or persons to hire to any male slave or slaves, his or their time: and in case any male slave or slaves be so permitted by their owners to hire out their own time, labor or service, the said slave or slaves shall be liable to seizure and forfeiture...."[28] (This seems to be a deliberate reaction to the slave Jesse Blackwood; and the law passed at the state level seems to be aimed specifically at controlling some of the actions of Charleston slave owners and managers.) Male slaves were singled out for this, with no mention of female slaves being forbidden their own time; whether it was assumed this would not happen, or because no female slaves were known to have participated in the Vesey insurrection cannot be ascertained.

The reputation of hired-out slaves had not been good from the very start: the first colonial laws spoke of that practice making the slaves lazy and allowing them to indulge in theft and drunkenness. In 1822, Thomas Pinckney noticed that many hired-out slaves were part of the Vesey conspiracy, so in his *Reflections Occasioned by the Late Disturbances,* he railed against "draymen, porters, fisherman, hucksters, butchers, barbers, & c."[29] He suggested that those in those mostly hired-out trades be replaced with whites. These white artisans agreed and petitioned the legislature, noting "the serious and alarming consequences arising from owners permitting their slaves to hire their own time, upon the payment of certain wages." The insurrection of Denmark Vesey, they added, had been part of the "machinations of this very class of our black population."[30] James Henry Hammond, who had coined the term "mudsill" to justify the need for a slave base upon which to build a civilized society, told an audience in 1849 that "whenever a slave is made a mechanic, he is more than half freed and soon becomes ... the most corrupt and turbulent of his class."[31] One hired-out mechanic in Baltimore eventually did become one of the most distinguished African American leaders of the 19th or any century. Frederick Douglass escaped Maryland for New England about ten years before Hammond's comment.

The "bad" reputation of mechanic slaves and hired-out slaves continued to the very end of slavery. In 1850, "Broad Street" expressed his opinion (in the *Courier*, 12 September 1850) that "slaves, by hiring their own time, become vagabonds and are not only unwilling, but they speedily become unfit for domestic servants." In 1864, none other than the Roman Catholic Bishop of Charleston, Patrick Lynch, in his pamphlet defending slavery, wrote that slaves "who hire their own time may be said to enjoy at least to some extent, the privileges of freedom," but freedom was not good for slaves, he argued, for "[i]t is generally found that they become idle and dissipated, and plunge into drunkenness and other vices."[32] Although the unfavorable reputation of hired-out slaves had been expressed from the beginning of the practice, it escalated, and became a political issue after the disputed Vesey insurrection of 1822. Like the decisive dates of BC and AD, or before and after the Civil War, the insurrection and the year 1822 became a landmark year in the history of the city of Charleston.

# CHAPTER 2

# 1823–1866: Laws of the Antebellum and Civil War Period

In 1823, citizens were still uneasy about the slaves, whether they were hired-out or not. One Charlestonian wrote the paper, "In times like these, all impudence should be checked in the bud" (*Courier*, 26 March 1823). Even street cries, which would become synonymous with the city and would be incorporated in the 20th century opera *Porgy and Bess*, were suspect. "The legalized audacity of the negros who hawk their wares, & c. about our streets, should no longer be permitted," the letter writer, "A Warning Voice," noted.

> The public cries should be regulated. The negro should be taught to announce what he has to sell, and to suppress his wit. A decency and humility of conduct should pervade all ranks of our colored population. "Who would have thought it," is the language of those who have no foresight. "Mocking is catching," says the proverb. So is every species of vice and folly. Banish insolence from our streets and highways in whatever way it may show itself.[1]

This uneasiness about slaves continued for years. In 1826, City Council amended the 1806 ordinance:

> *Be it ordained by the Intendant and Wardens of Charleston*, that badges or licenses for the purposes hereinafter mentioned be granted by the City Treasurer once in every year, to wit: in the whole month of January in each and every year, to such person or persons, as may apply therefor, and every badge or license shall be, and continue in force, for one year

> from the first day of January and no longer. Provided, nevertheless, that the City Treasurer is hereby authorized to grant badges or licenses to such person or persons as may not have applied within the said month, who shall notwithstanding, pay therefor, as though they had obtained licenses for a full and entire year, commencing at the period above stated.[2]

This was probably not new and was probably already being practiced: if a slave owner did not buy a badge in January, but in some later month of the year, he or she nevertheless had to pay for the entire year, with there being no prorated reduction. What was new was the next provision of the law:

> That from and immediately after the passage of the ordinance [it was ratified on 28 December 1826], the sum of two dollars shall be paid for a badge for every house-servant or washerwoman above the age of fourteen years, intended to work out within the limits of Charleston, and for every slave under that age, the sum of one dollar, under the penalty prescribed by the ordinance of the twenty-eighth of October, 1806.

So now the rate for a washerwoman or house servant had doubled from $1 to $2. If the slave was under 14, the fee remained $1. (What fee a 14-year-old was charged is not stated.)

This 1826 ordinance repeated the triple cost of hiring out more than six slaves, and again, it stated that no one outside the city of Charleston could hire out their slaves in the city, "*Provided,* however, that nothing herein contained shall extend or be construed to extend, to hinder the hiring of any slave or slaves, for any public work or employment, without the procurement of a badge." So, one living out of town could hire out his or her slave if the slave was used in public works, such as road building and the like. This slave did not have to wear a badge.

Clause IV was new. It stated that no one was "to take out in his, her, or their name or names, a badge or badges, for any slave or slaves belonging to another individual, except such person ... be the agent, attorney, trustee or guardian of the real owner of such slave or slaves." This trustee would have to declare the name of the owner; "every person so offending, shall forfeit and pay the sum of twenty dollars for each and every such slave, and all badges previously granted to such person, as well as all badges previously granted to the real owner or owners of such a slave or slaves, shall be and the same are hereby declared to be forfeited."

Another new provision forbade a transfer of "the badge procured for one slave for another slave," unless the slave belonged to the same owner, and that master took an oath to that effect at the city treasurer's. Failure to comply would bring a fine of $20 and the forfeit of the badge. All slaves having badges forfeited would need a new legal badge taken out before being allowed to be hired out again. Anyone could take a slave in this predicament to the workhouse where he or she would be kept until the $20 fine and the cost for the workhouse were paid. If the owner didn't pay within two months, the slave would be discharged, suit brought against the owner, and that owner forbidden to purchase any more badges until a year after that date.

To take out a badge under any circumstances, the owner had to take an oath, very similar to the one articulated in the ordinance of 1806; but now instead of just stating the number of the Negroes being hired out, the owner also had to state their names. In the final clause of the new ordinance, it was reiterated that of all fines collected, one half was to go to the informer, and the other half to the city.

There were no changes in the badge laws until 1830, when, apparently, some of the fear and anger against slave mechanics, implicated in the Vesey plot, abated. On 1 February 1830, the city of Charleston ratified a law stating:

> [N]o mechanic engaged in the exercise and pursuit of his particular trade or profession, shall be required to take out or obtain a badge or badges for his negro or negroes, in cases where such negro or negroes is or are hired by such mechanic to one or more individuals, carrying on the same trade as himself. *Provided*, That such negro or negroes be themselves of the same trade and are hired out in the capacity of mechanics, and that such hiring do not altogether, whether to one or more individuals, exceed the term of six months in any year; and *provided also*, that the number of negroes so to be hired shall not at any time exceed six.[3]

A mechanic could hire out his slaves to other mechanics and pay no badge fee, if in the same field, and if for just half a year. This would be a boon to wealthy mechanics, and it would cut into the ability of poorer mechanics, who did not own slaves, to compete. Mechanics would again start lobbying both the city and the state to change slave-hire laws.

This 1830 law also loosened other badge issues of the October 1806 ordinance. No longer was it "necessary for any negro to have a badge about his person, who may be hired by the owner to a white person as a house servant, or to reside on the premises of the latter in any other capacity, but the badge in such case shall be given to the person hiring to be kept by him or her as long as such hiring shall continue." House servants, by definition, were those in closest proximity to whites; by not wearing the badge, the servant could not be as free in the streets, and so possibly, would have to stay in closer relationship to the household or master, who, in turn, would control the slave's destiny, by having his or her badge in his or her keeping. The servant, perhaps serving meals at the table, or helping with children, would not have to wear a badge, and thus would make a more genteel appearance.

To show that only house servants were included in this category, the ordinance continued:

> That with the exception made ... all other negroes or slaves required by law to have badges, shall wear them about their persons and be ready to produce them when commanded thereto. And it shall be lawful for any person or persons to command any negro or other slave, applying for hire or working out and not embraced in the exception aforesaid, to produce his or her badge, and immediately to carry to the Work-House any one either having no badge or refusing to produce it, or producing a badge different from the work in which he or she may be employed on hire, or not producing a badge correspondent with and legally obtained for the year in which the demand is made.

The slave would have to stay there until the fine was paid. If the slave did have a badge, and just did not produce it, the fine would be $2. If the owner did not pay it within three days, then the slave would get "five stripes on the bare back and be discharged."[4]

In this decade, there were other changes to the laws controlling the slave hiring-out practice, and many of those laws were introduced in a new way. All laws regarding badges and hiring out, previous to this, were called "Badge" or "Negro" laws and codified and titled that way. In the decade of the 1830s, however, revisions came in the appropriation legislation, specifically laws passed early in the calendar year to supply the city corporation with operating funds.

The ordinance "to raise supplies for the City of Charleston, for the year one thousand eight hundred and thirty-two" is a fitting example. While all slaves residing in the city of Charleston were taxed ("one hundred and fifty cents" each; for every slave above ten in number, $3; and every slave above 20, $5), the only exception was made for those "negroes belonging to any mechanic, who individually pursues his trade and employs his negroes in such trade."[5]

The city hired many slaves directly, and the earlier 1826 law freed owners hiring their slaves to the corporation from taking out badges for them. Slave holders living outside Charleston could hire them out for public works, as well, and it was to tax this class that the 1832 bill included the following provision: "Every slave, working out or employed in the City of Charleston, whose owner resides without the limits of the said City, shall be subject to a tax of three dollars." (This would also include those slaves of widows or orphans outside of town who were allowed to hire out their slaves.) Besides them, many thousands lived just north of Boundary, the present-day Calhoun, Street and those who lived just across the street from the incorporated area and beyond out into the Charleston District could now be taxed by the City of Charleston if they hired out slaves there.

In 1833 and 1834, the City Council included all the above 1832 taxes and exceptions in its bills to raise operating funds;[6] but in 1835 and 1836, it changed. All slaves, no matter the number were just taxed at "one hundred and fifty cents," and now there was no exclusion from taxation of those slaves belonging to mechanics.[7] These bills were passed in March of those years, and in November 1836, a further appropriations bill had to be passed. "For City Contracts and Accounts, including City Badges and Lazaretto ... fifteen thousand two hundred and eighty-six dollars" was budgeted.[8] In November, the city began advertising for contracts, calling for official bakers, printers, and the like. Included among them would be the badge makers, who would be paid a few hundred dollars for their work.

When 1837 arrived it ushered in a year of change in the hiring-out laws. At the 24 January meeting, Joshua Lazarus and others petitioned City Council to repeal that part of the "Badge Law as requires a triple sum on the owners of slaves, working out over Six in number."[9] Lazarus was a prosperous businessman and banker, who would soon help bring gaslight to the streets and buildings of Charleston as President of Charleston's Gas Light Company. Obviously, he and the wealthy businessmen who joined in his petition were considered important. For at the 13 April meeting of City Council, a proposal to suspend the extra fees for hiring out more than six slaves came up for its third reading, and it was approved. One could now hire out as many slaves as one wanted.[10] But there had been a more important change to the laws just a month before. On 28 March, the City ratified "An Ordinance to raise Supplies for the city of Charleston for the year 1837."[11] In it, the taxes went up on a number of things, including slaves and their badges. Every slave under 12 years of age was now taxed at $1.50, while those over 12 were taxed at $2.50. The language in Clause VI was inexact, not specifying in which group those actually aged 12 belonged. But that slight oversight pales with the confusion caused by the next provision. "Every slave working out, or employed in the City," it ordered, "whose owners reside without the limits of the said city, shall be subject to a tax of five dollars, over and above, the cost of a proper badge."

The confusion stems from the fact that the law at this time forbade any slave owner living outside of Charleston to hire his slaves in the city of Charleston, except for those hired out for public works, and those did not require badges. City Council seemed to have now demanded badges and a tax for those slaves they said could not work legally in town. The only solution comes later in the ordinance, in Clause XV whose last line states that "licenses or badges taken out by non-residents shall be charged double," the amount paid by city residents.[12] Thus, with an aside, the City Council changed a long-standing proscription of hiring out of slaves of non-residents. Now, those living outside the city could hire out slaves in the area below Boundary Street. (The war between North and South—North and South of Boundary Street—would soon erupt; in a few years, there would be a great debate over badges on either side of that street.)

But in the meantime, those living North of Boundary Street and anywhere else outside the city, could pay double and have their slaves working on hire in the city (and also pay an extra tax of $5). What the badge fees were, however, also changed this year, an alteration called forth in the same Clause XV, ratified 28 March 1837. "In lieu of the sums now fixed by law," the new badge fees were:

| | |
|---|---|
| For every handicraft tradesman | 5.00 |
| For every carter, drayman, porter or day laborer | 4.00 |
| For every fisherman or woman | 2.00 |
| For every house servant or washerwoman | 2.00 |
| For every seller of fruits or cakes, or any article not prohibited | 5.00 |

The first category went up $2 from $3, and the next two categories doubled; now there seems to have been no prorating of the house servant fee for those slaves under 14, as called into being back in 1826. So nearly all fees for badges, except that for fruiterer which reduced from $15 in 1806 to $5 in 1813, went up.

Since these rates were raised in a tax bill aimed at supplying the city with funds, one can infer that the city had come to see these fees as a part of their annual budgeting process. (Indeed, as shall be shown, badges soon became a steady source of income for Charleston.) City lawmakers raised the rates to bring in more income, a response perhaps to the financial panic that hit Charleston in the early months of 1837. Cotton prices dropped precipitously and business ceased; there were fears that the banks in town would fail and would not have enough gold to cover the demands of those who wanted to convert their currency. Many businesses, including the collector of the port, demanded all payments in specie. The city needed to raise money in a year when citizens would have less income, and the mayor grew nervous over the increase in the new slave badge prices. The law had taken effect in March 1837, but most of the badges for the year had already been sold in January and February; all would have to pay these new higher prices come January 1838.

On 21 November 1837, the Charleston *Courier* printed the minutes of the 16 November Council meeting:

> The Mayor reminded council that the period was rapidly approaching for the annual issuing of Badges, Cart and Dray Licenses &c; and that,

> if no alteration was made in the existing rates, the Treasurer would be compelled to issue them according to the high prices established by the last Tax Ordinance. He was satisfied that a reduction could be made consistently with the public interests, and therefore recommended that measures should be taken for that purpose without delay.
>
> Mr. Wilson then introduced a Bill to establish the prices of Badges for Slaves working out on hire within the city; and also a Bill to establish the rates for Licenses for Drays, Carts, Wagons and other carriages driven for hire in the city, which were read a first time, and ordered to be printed, and read a second time at the next meeting.

That was on 22 November, and the minutes were dutifully printed in the paper on 29 November. To carry out the mayor's recommendations, "A bill to establish the prices of the badges for Slaves working out on hire within the city, was taken up and discussed, and referred to the Committee on Ways and Means."[13] What exactly happened in that committee is unknown; with few exceptions, the only minutes known to have survived from before the Civil War are those of the full council (and not its committees) printed in the press. One can guess, however, that nothing came of the bill; for, as will be shown in Part Two, the next year saw a great increase in badge income. Obviously, despite the mayor's concern, the prices were not lowered, and the badges brought the city more income. (A week before, on 16 November 1837, City Council, as it had in 1836, passed a bill to bridge funding into the next calendar year. In it, $12,000 were put aside for "City Contracts and Accounts, including City Badges and Lazaretto.")[14]

The year 1837 was a watershed year, then, for the badge laws. Despite the mayor's fears that they should be reduced, nearly all the fees doubled, and slave owners outside the city could now hire out their slaves, for double the fees. An extra tax was levied on them for the opportunity. And finally, there was no longer a triple charge for those hiring out more than six slaves.

In 1838, there came another small change, ratified on 22 April, less than a week before a catastrophic fire gutted the center business district and market of the city. Now, the fee for a badge for a slave mechanic or handicraft tradesman was raised $2, making these the prices for badges in the city:

| | |
|---|---|
| For every handicraft tradesman | $7.00 |
| For every Carter, Drayman, Porter or Day Laborer | 4.00 |
| For every Fisherman or woman | 2.00 |
| For every House Servant or Washerwoman | 2.00 |
| For every Seller of Fruits, or Cakes, or any article not prohibited | 5.00 |

> And Licenses or Badge taken out by non-residents, shall be charged double the above amounts.[15]

That these prices were charged is proven through entries in a ledger of the Horlbeck Brothers, architects and builders in the city of Charleston. There are notations in the year 1840, stating "paid Corporation for Badge for George, $14.00." This is under the entry for Mr. Joseph Palmer, of St. John's Parish, outside the city.[16] The Horlbecks would have used a mechanic; according to the 1838 rate hike, the fee was $7; doubling the fee for a license for a slave owned by someone outside the city would come to $14. On the same page of this journal is another entry under Mr. James Gaillard, of St. John's Parish, "paid Corporation for Badge for Tom, $14.00." Under both these entries are notations for clothes for slaves. Furthermore, there is the notation, "To one year services of Tom, ending 1 January 1841, at $10 per Month, $120.00." The calendar year usage aligns with the fact that new badges went on sale on 1 January, while both badges were bought 1 February 1840.

In this year, 1840, there was one small increase on the badge fee for fishers based on sex. Fisher badges for women could still be bought for $2, but now fishermen doubled to $4. Those living outside of Charleston, hiring out their slaves for double the badge amount, had to pay an extra tax. It was assessed at $7, up $2 from earlier years.[17]

In 1844, the city printed a digest of its laws, showing that many of these changes that had accumulated over the years since 1806 were now packaged into "An Ordinance to regulate Badges for Negroes working out on hire, and for other purposes," ratified 11 April 1843.[18] For the most part it just reiterated the laws with some shift in wording. The law affirmed that badges went on sale in January of every year and were good for that year only. One could buy them at any time after that, but there was no prorating; even if bought in December, purchasers had to pay the total fee. Those allowing their slaves to hire out without this registration were fined $20; the same penalty applied to those taking out a badge for a slave not one's own, either through ownership or agency, such as trusteeship, etc. Those who did this had the badge forfeited. Transferring a badge from one of the slaves in one's control to another was taboo, unless one registered it and swore to what he was doing. (It seems to have taken City Council permission, too, to transfer a badge from one owner to another; for on 22 April 1851, Henry Griggs would petition City Council to have a badge bought by B. Ellis transferred to him; the badge, it was explained was "taken out for a servant in February and [the servant] was purchased by [Griggs] 5th March."[19]) Slaves who had their badges forfeited could be taken to the workhouse and their owners fined $20. Such an owner could not take out a legal badge until he paid all expenses and a full year elapsed.

The oath a slave owner or agent had to swear altered a bit, too, to wit:

> I, A.B. do solemnly swear, (or affirm) that the negro or negroes, (stating the names and number), is, or are my property, and is or are of the ages

> respectively stated, or the property of C.D. (as the case may be,) and that the employment of every slave when working on hire, is to be no other than such as is now mentioned by me—So help me God.

The treasurer was told how to keep the register: slave names to be kept alphabetically, "with their respective ages and employments, together with their owner's names, in alphabetical order; and every badge ... shall express the number as well as the specific trade or employment to be pursued by any slave working out on hire." (The idea for this had come up at a City Council meeting on 31 May 1841, when the City Inquirer and Assessor suggested "the propriety of having kept in the City Treasurer's Office an Alphabetical Badge Book."[20]) Those hiring out slaves without badges would be fined double the badge price for the field of employment for every day the slave was employed. (Again, the city made the penalty greater for those illegally employing slaves than for the owners.) The slaves could be taken to the workhouse and punished as outlined in 1806. If the slave had a legal badge but did not show it, the owner could get the slave out for $2 and expenses; or if he refused to do this within three days, the slave could be punished with a corporal punishment decided by the mayor and then released. House servants hired to whites had to have badges procured for them but did not have to wear them. Counterfeit penalties for whites and blacks continued the same as they had in 1806. (The fact that the fines for counterfeiting did not go up at all in this era, along with there being any lack of mention of counterfeits being caught or fined, argues for the fact that counterfeiting was not being widely practiced.) Of the fines collected, one half would go to the informer, if any, and the rest to the use of the city.

In the later half of this decade, the laws remained pretty much the same, with the amount of taxes paid on slaves sometimes varying, sometimes prorated by age, and sometimes not. The extra tax on slaves with badges belonging to those living outside Charleston disappeared in these years.

In 1848, there was another addition to the badge laws. Although most slaves were owned by whites, some were owned by African Americans, and some slaves apparently were in control of other slaves. So the city had to make sure that these black owners and users of slaves were also included in their control. The law ratified on 14 March 1848 decreed:

> *Be it ordained,* that every negro or other slave employing on hire a negro or other slave without such last mentioned negro or other slave having a badge or ticket, duly obtained from the City Treasurer, and correspondent with the work on which such negro or slave is employed as aforesaid, may be taken up and committed to the Work House, and there detained until a fine of twenty dollars, and the expenses of the Work House, shall have been fully paid; but if the owner of said slave,

> so taken up and committed, or the person having the care and management of the same, shall, within, three days after being notified of such commitment, refuse or neglect to pay said fine and expenses, then such negro or other slave shall receive in the Work House such corporal punishment as the Mayor may direct, and be discharged.[21]

In 1849, the *state* changed its hiring-out laws too. After the Vesey insurrection in 1822, it had passed an act forbidding male slaves from hiring out their own time; those masters who allowed it could see their slaves seized. But now the law was altered (and softened) to read "that from the twelfth day of March next [1850], it shall not be lawful for any person, owning, or having in charge, any male or female slave, to permit such slave to hire his or her time, labor or service; and any person ... so offending, shall be liable to a penalty of Fifty Dollars," instead of having the slave seized entirely.[22] The law was now extended to females, too, apparently based on the findings of the Sumter, South Carolina, grand jury, which had pointed out this lack in the law, noting that women were often some of the worse offenders.[23] Half of the fine collected in these cases, the state law decreed, would go the informer, the other half "to the use of the District where the offence was committed." These somewhat relaxed new rules and penalties reflect a lessening of the fear citizens felt in regard to slaves and their individual liberties, a generation after Vesey.

There apparently was a softening in the enforcement of the laws, too, which many decried. A citizen, signing himself "Broad Street," warned the public in a letter to the *Courier* on 12 September 1850. He referred to the new law passed the year before by the Legislature, and said it was not enforced; indeed, it was a "dead letter." The annoyed man wrote:

> There are over 14,000 slaves in the old City, and there are by the city census less than that number of white persons. Making all allowances for mechanic employments, laborers, & c, is it not surprising that there are not servants enough for menial offices in Charleston? Nothing is more *difficult* than getting any servant, and nothing more impossible than getting *a good one*. In the New-York *Herald* you see half a column of servants desiring places. In our papers you see only a half a column of persons desiring servants.
>
> What! I ask is the cause of this in a community where blacks preponderate in numbers?
>
> The answer is, that the slaves by hiring their own time become vagabonds, and are not only unwilling, but they speedily become unfit for domestic service.

That was what the new law in the legislature, he believed, had been written to counteract. "So sensible was the Legislature of the necessity, that it passed both houses without a division: and yet it has completely failed. Not one slave less hires his time than before. What is the cause of the failure?"

"Broad Street" believed that the "penalty ($50) is not high as to defeat it. It is not because no one is pecuniarily interested," he reasoned, "for one-half is given to the informer.... The failure is attributable, I presume, to the indefiniteness of the Act. No one is specifically charged with its execution, and hence the old adage, 'what is everybody's business,' & c." "Broad Street" thought someone had to be in charge of enforcing the law, "Attorney General, Clerk of the Court, or any magistrate." It depended totally on informers to turn slaves and slave owners in. And informing "always odious, is more so, by reason of the generality of the practice complained of." So many people turned their backs to slaves hiring their own time, that an informer would be criticized for turning one in, he wrote. The only other solution he could see would be requiring "every slave to work one month on the streets, or any other public work for every month he is permitted to hire his time. This would correct the evil; for slaves, who have lived in idleness and pilfering, would be content, after becoming *acquainted with work*, to enjoy their idleness afterwards *at home*." He saw no end of self-hiring in sight. The only way to deal with it, he believed, was to make all those who broke the law work harder for the government. The weak law, apparently weakly enforced, stood unchanged until the end of slavery. But the public still continued to rail and demand changes in laws regarding slaves, slave badges and slavery. A big battle and the final major addition to the slave badge laws hinged on the territory of the Charleston Neck.

For many decades, Boundary (now Calhoun) Street had been the official northern limit of the city, and the dividing line had played a part from 1837 on in determining how much a badge cost for owners living south or north of it. Those thousands who lived north of that street paid no city taxes, did not have the advantages of gas lights except on public roads, and lacked other privileges of those who lived in the incorporated era. As revolutions raged in Europe in the last few years of the 1840s, there was a battle on the local scene between those residents of the Neck and those living in the incorporated area south of Boundary. There were heated letters to the editor and articles on whether on not the city should annex the area of the Neck.

The debate and lobbying had been going on for some time. As early as 1837 (the year those living north of the city were finally allowed to hire out their slaves), the mayor of Charleston, R. Y. Hayne, had gone on record saying the two sections should combine. "Connected as the City and Neck are with each other, in every thing which constitutes ONE PEOPLE," he had written; "it would seem that they must have a common interest in being united under ONE CORPORATION." One reason for this, if no other, had to do with the issue of police jurisdiction and slavery. "Our slaves ... when they find themselves excluded from the dram-shops and prevented from holding unlawful meetings in the City, have only to cross an imaginary line, and they are safe from pursuit," Hayne wrote.[24] All a slave had to do to escape city law was to cross Boundary Street. The newspapers noted this, too, for the *Courier* complained on 20 September 1845, that the Neck was "infested with ... grog shops [and] becoming the receptacle of stolen and ill-gotten goods."[25]

In 1840, Thomas Bennett chaired a meeting to discuss incorporating Charleston Neck. The immediate reason for this was "the present defective organization of the police" on the Neck, "and the absolute necessity of some immediate change." Hope lay in petitioning the state legislature for incorporation. This was a very charged issue, and the meeting resolved "That for the present the bill of incorporation be laid upon the table, and that a committee of thirteen be appointed to take into view our present defective police organization and to form, if possible, a new and efficient system of police for the government of Charleston Neck."[26]

Despite the trouble with police and drunk slaves, many residents of the Neck still wanted to stay free of Charleston and taxes, while others wanted to join. Many felt Charleston needed to enlarge to become "The Queen City of the South," and needed larger numbers and areas to promote itself. With time the debate grew spirited, some saying the Neck was nasty and dirty and needing improvement, others rebutting the argument entirely, claiming the Neck was healthier and cleaner than the city. While the war raged, the Neck continued, legally, a different entity. Resultantly, city directories often had two (or sometimes four) listings in these years; whites and free people of color would be listed for the city, and then the two categories would be repeated for the Neck. The 1840 City Directory specifically noted that streets were not numbered on the Neck, as they were in the city, and that, confusingly, two streets on the Neck bore names similar to streets in the city. After streets crossed Boundary, they got the designation "n," not for "Neck," but "North." The 1849 directory noted:

> Thirty years ago there were but a few houses beyond Boundary Street, except on King and Meeting Streets; now it is nearly as thickly settled as the City, and contains, probably, about 15,000 inhabitants.... Many of our merchants, and others engaged in business in the city, have their residences on the Neck, and the constant communication between them is so entirely uninterrupted, that a stranger would not for a moment suppose that there was any difference, but would naturally conclude that Charleston extended from South Bay to Line-street.[27]

To try to make it so, in January 1848, at a City Council meeting, it was decided that a committee should meet with the Commissioners of the Crossroads, which, enabled by the state legislature, had authority over Charleston Neck to discuss the "subject of licenses, badges, & c."

The Commissioners of the Crossroads asked the City Council of Charleston to deliver to them "the proceeds of 100 cart and dray licenses, and one third of the licenses for omnibuses and other carriages plying for hire." Apparently the Commissioners of the Crossroads felt that the aforementioned percentage of carts, drays, etc., that were licensed in the city actually worked in the Neck; this would provide them with some income, not possible any other way, since, as mentioned, the inhabitants of the Neck paid no taxes. The Commissioners also requested "that one fourth of all badges issued for Negroes working on hire be allowed as the proportion for the Neck."[28]

City Council received the proposal at the meeting of 27 January 1848, and a committee studied it. The newspaper put its report fairly succinctly:

> In submitting the proposition for consideration, the Committee would bring the attention of Council to the fact, that should it be deemed best to carry out or adopt this proposition, a large deficiency would exist in the ordinary current receipts of the Treasury, as will be seen by the annexed statement; and that it would, no doubt, be necessary to resort to some other source of taxation to supply this deficiency. However much it may be desired by Council to afford facilities and aid to the inhabitants of the Neck, in carrying out their system of municipal legislation, the Committee deemed it prudent that mature deliberation should be given to the question of contracting the present revenue derived by the city from taxation.
>
> The following amounts were derived by the city during the year 1847, from badges and licenses, as referred to by the Commissioners of Cross Roads, Charleston Neck, viz:—Dray Licenses, $3,260; Cart d[itt]o 1,140; Omnibuses, 250; Carriages and buggies, 390; Breaks,125; Badges, 13,343 [for a total of] $18,778.[29]

It is apparent now why the city looked askance at the proposition. A large amount of income was coming into city coffers from the sale of slave and vehicle badges, and the adoption of the proposition, submitted from the Neck, would reduce the city's share from about $18,000 to $14,000. So it is not surprising that "[a]fter the reading of the report, Council unanimously declined acceding to the proposition from the Commissioners of the Neck."

This refusal led to nearly a declaration of war by the Commissioners of the Neck. The very next issue of the newspaper reported the following:

> At a special meeting of the Board of Commissioners of Cross Roads, Charleston Neck, held at their Hall, this evening, the following preamble and resolutions were offered and unanimously adopted.

> Whereas, the Commissioners of Cross Roads, in their communications and proposals to the City Council of Charleston, respecting Badges and Licenses, have acted with a spirit of much moderation and great forbearance, which was the more apparent after Council had at first refused to appoint a Committee of Conference, although they themselves had proposed and urged the matter on the Board by a resolution of Mr. INGRAHAM'S. Although thus rejected, the Board, notwithstanding, again respectfully requested Council to consider the matter, and meet them in a spirit of amity and friendship; not from any fear but that the Acts of the Legislature would fully sustain them, but in a spirit of kindness which would promote the interests of both parties, and relieve the inhabitants of both City and Neck from increased taxation. The Committee of Council having received the proposals of the Commissioners, reported them to Council, and they were unanimously rejected. Be it therefore
>
> *Resolved*, That this Board cannot again ... offer any proposals to the City Council of Charleston, respecting Badges and Licenses, leaving the responsibility of having added double the amount of taxation on many persons of the City and Neck, where it properly belongs.[30]

So, blaming City Council for what they felt they had to do, the Commissioners of the Crossroads met "at their Hall" on 3 February 1848. "For the information of all persons concerned, and to correct any errors which may exist respecting the prices for Badges, and Licenses," they had published in The Charleston *Mercury* the following abstract from their minutes:

> Badges and Licenses are obtained at the Charleston Neck Guard House, from the hours of 9 o'clock, a.m. to 2 o'clock, p.m. daily, (Sundays excepted) at the following prices:

| | | |
|---|---|---|
| Badges—servants | | $2 |
| | Porters or Laborers | 4 |
| | Mechanics | 7 |
| | Fruiterers and Hucksters | 5 |
| | Fishermen | 4 |
| | Fisherwoman | 2 |
| Licenses for Vehicles | | |
| | Omnibuses | $40 |
| | Hacks or Carriages | 30 |
| | Cart or wagon, 2 horses | 15 |
| | Cart or wagon, 1 horse | 10 |
| | Dray with 2 horses | 15 |
| | Dray with 1 horse | 10 |
| | Carriages with 2 wheels | 2 |
| | Every kind of Vehicle used for exhibiting horses for sale | 25 |

> For the enforcement of these regulations, the following resolution was unanimously adopted by the Board: *Be it resolved*, That on and after the 8th day of February, instant, [1848] the Marshal be directed to take up and lodge in the Charleston Neck Guard House or any public Stable on Charleston Neck all carts, drays, omnibuses, and other vehicles, together with their horse or horses, mule or mules, for which licenses have not previously been taken out from the offices on Charleston Neck, and that may be found plying for hire anywhere between the northern boundary of the City [i.e. Boundary Street] and a line running from Cooper to Ashley River. The line, as located, includes Hampstead and the north Line of Line-street, and in the direction of the north line of Line-Street on to Ashley river. Such vehicles and animals to be retained in custody until the penalty of not less than $12, nor more than $20, and all expenses, be paid.
>
> Also, all negroes who may be found driving these vehicles, not owned by the owners of these vehicles, who have not taken out badges from the Office of the Neck. Also, all negroes who may be found working out on hire within the above mentioned line, and who have not taken out badges from the Neck Office, be committed to the Charleston Neck Work House and be there detained until the sum of $20 and all expenses be paid, for each and every offence.

What this now meant was that hired-out slaves who worked north and south of Boundary Street, or who crossed the street in their work, had to have two badges, one for Charleston and one for Charleston Neck. Furthermore, according to the City of Charleston statutes, all of those living north of Boundary, but having slaves working south of it, had to pay double the Charleston badge fees. (It is not known if this law was enforced.)

As for the Neck, "all fines and penalties imposed by these regulations ... shall be sued for and recovered before a Magistrate's Court or any other Court, having competent jurisdiction, to be appropriated to the uses and purposes of the Commissioners of Cross Roads." It was signed, "James Short, Secretary and Treasurer Board Commissioners of Cross Roads," the commission charged by the state legislature with control over the Neck.[31]

The members of the committee from the Commissioners of Crossroads, John F. Poppenheim, Theodore Gaillard, Oswell Reeder, and E. M. Whiting, had adopted a whole slew of rules regulating the Neck on 1 February, and as if to prove they were separate from the city, had a pamphlet printed showing their laws. Although not a legal part of the city it abutted, the Commissioners nevertheless felt enough kinship with the city to copy their laws almost verbatim. "All Badges, or Licenses for Slaves to be employed within the ... Neck," they wrote, "shall be granted by the Marshal or some other officer of the Board, in the whole month of January, in each and every year, to such persons as may apply therefor." Badges could be bought later in the year, but the fee would not be prorated. The fees were:

> For every handicraft tradesman, seven dollars. For every carter, drayman, and porter, or day labourer, four dollars. For every fisherman, four dollars. For every fisherwoman, two dollars. For every house servant or washerwomen, two dollars. For every seller of fruit or cakes, or any article not prohibited, five dollars.

Those hiring out slaves without paying the fees for badges would be fined $20 for every offense. Anybody hiring out someone else's slave would pay the same penalty, and the badges of the slave, and even other legal badges taken out by the owner of the same slave, would be forfeited. "*Furthermore*, no Badge or Badges shall in any case be granted to a slave or free person of color, with or without a ticket, unless the owner, agent or guardian of such slave or free person of color shall apply personally for the same."[32] (This particular provision regarding people of color taking out badges for slaves is a new wrinkle in the badge laws. After 1820, it was made much harder to free slaves, and those who were free were required to have a white guardian or responsible person in the community to vouch for them. The City of Charleston had added a law in 1848 stating that free people of color and slaves taking out badges had to follow the same laws as whites, but that law had not made the use of a white guardian necessary as this law on Charleston Neck did.) Other parts of the statute were very similar to the city's: badges were not to be transferred from one slave to another, even if owned by the same person, except if so registered in the record. If one ignored the rules, he or she had to forfeit the badges and pay $20. Those slaves with forfeited badges had to get new ones; offenders could be carried to the workhouse (on the Neck), detained, fined $20 and costs. If payment was not made within two months, the owner could be sued, and none of his or her slaves could be hired out for a year.

Like the treasurer in the incorporated city, the marshal "or any other officer appointed by the Board," was charged with keeping an alphabetical list of slaves, with their ages and employments, along with an alphabetical list of owners; badges were to express a number and category of work. (They neglected to state that the year had to be stamped on the badges, but archeological evidence shows that it was.) Those employing Negroes without badges could be fined twice the badge amount for each day they employed the Negro in a particular type of task. Similar to the slaves employed in the contiguous city, slaves on the Neck were to wear their badges "conspicuously about their persons," although house slaves, requiring badges, did not have to wear them. Slaves not wearing badges or with the wrong ones could be brought to the workhouse, and detained until a $20 fine and expenses were paid; if the slave did have a legal badge elsewhere, he or she could be freed for the fee of $2 and expenses. And if owners refused to pay, the slaves would be subjected to corporal punishment of a degree decided upon by the Board. Again, as in the city, those whites caught counterfeiting badges had to pay a $50 fine; slaves or Negroes doing it could receive 20 lashes and up to 20 days in the workhouse. Slaves wearing badges not theirs or not naming their profession could be punished at the workhouse or released when their owners paid a $2 fee. And finally, those who informed on the law breaker could get half the penalty paid, with the other half reserved for the "uses of the Commissioners of Cross Roads of Charleston Neck."

The Commissioners who did this were not uniformly liked by the Neck residents. In a meeting of 23 February 1848, angry residents elected a committee of five men who chastised the Board of Commissioners for naming people who did not live in the Neck to some offices. Among other things, this committee of five, consisting of Dr. C. Drayton, G. M. Kells, S. Bee, O. F. Folker, and C. P. Shier, resolved "that the *materiel of Charleston Neck* is ample to fill all offices, of profit and honor without borrowing." They suggested then that "those commissioners who have thus trampled upon the feelings and rights of their constituents can best serve the public good by vacating their seats."[33]

By the end of the year, many were angry and upset over the two armed camps on the peninsula, and the fact that those who did business north and south of Boundary Street had to pay double badge fees. The Commissioners of the Crossroads of Charleston Neck sent a communication to the City Council of Charleston on 29 December 1848, stating that:

> The Commissioners of Cross Roads of Charleston Neck, desirous of relieving their fellow citizens of Charleston and Charleston Neck from the burthensome weight of double taxation, on the Badges and Licenses, are again willing to meet the City Council of Charleston in a spirit of fairness and good feeling, and to agree on any measure consistent with justice ... to obtain this desired object....[34]

This was a good time, for new badges had to purchased come January. A committee of Council met with the Committee from Charleston Neck on 5 January 1849, and they forwarded the Neck's proposal to City Council. The proposals were: "1st. That the Badges and Licenses be taken out from the office of the place at which the parties who own the property reside." (So, for example, if one lived on the Neck and owned slaves who were hired out below Boundary Street, they would buy badges on the Neck; if the owner lived in the city and his or her slaves worked there or on the Neck, the badges had to be taken out in the city.) "2d. To allow the Badges to remain as they are at present, and to reduce the prices of the Licenses for Drays and Carts from $10 to 7.50, and the Omnibuses from $40 to $30, and Hacks from $30 to $22.50."[35]

This, then, would still allow for badges for Charleston, and those for "C. N," or Charleston Neck. One would pay for the badge in the part of the peninsula where he or she lived. It was a solution of sorts, and it was implemented, but no one really was happy with it. In her expense book, business woman Rebecca I. Moses, for instance, noted that she paid $26 for "City & Neck badges" in January 1848; the next year, she paid out $34 just for badges, and $32 in 1850. She lived north of Boundary Street, and this might have been the first time she had to buy such badges.[36]

Badges for hired-out slaves and their income, and licensing from drays and the income they produced, continued to be hot issues in the debate between the City and the Neck. In a public meeting at City Hall on 22 November 1849, C. G. Memminger, later treasurer of the Confederacy, rose and presented a number of resolutions. He declared that, one, "the people of Charleston are essentially one in feeling, in interest, and in devotion, to the public welfare; and that no private nor selfish interests should be permitted by a mere arbitrary line of separation, to secure for one side the benefits which have been produced by the burthens on the other," and two, "That the neck and City ought to be united under one Corporation." This prompted his third resolution that, "the Charter to be obtained should contain provisions to the following effect"[37]:

1. All debts of the City then in existence be charged upon the city property and paid by those liable.
2. All taxes levied upon the Neck for the following ten years go towards paying the proportional part of the expenses of the new corporation, with the balance be applied to expenditures and improvements on the Neck.
3. All land, slaves, horses, carts, etc. used in agriculture on the Neck be exempt from corporate taxes.
4. The Brick law, requiring structures be built of brick, not go into effect on the Neck for twenty years, except in wards where a majority of voters request it.
5. The Neck to be divided into four wards, each to have same number of aldermen as in city wards.

Those were the resolutions Memminger presented, and they were accepted with a few more resolutions: City property under lien to city creditors, once paid off, would be vested in all residents of the Neck and the city, and that the resolutions just passed should be sent to City Council, and if agreed upon, then City Council should petition the legislature to incorporate the city and Neck on these terms.

The city passed this petition and forwarded it, as recommended, to the state legislature, and that body made swift business of it. In the very next month, December 1849, realizing that "with the growing importance and increasing population of the part of the Parish of St. Philip, which lies to the north and west of Boundary, renders it necessary to provide ... a more efficient police, and in order to avoid a conflict of jurisdiction, it is expedient to unite the same with the city of Charleston." They therefore resolved: "*Be it enacted* by the Senate and House of Representatives, now met and sitting in General Assembly, the rest of the parish have a line drawn from the Cooper to the Ashley [Rivers] and that area to be divided, as suggested into 4 wards." The Senate and House ruled, (on 19 December 1849, effectively changing the city's charter), charging J. B. I'on, J. L. Nowell, James L. Petigru, H. W. Perroneau and G.N. Reynolds with drawing the lines and boundaries. The joining of the Neck and the incorporated area would go into effect soon:

> [F]rom and after the first Monday in September next, the authority of the several boards of Commissioners for the Poor and for the Main and Cross Roads, over the part of Charleston neck, between the present limits and the line hereinbefore mentioned, shall cease ... and the jurisdiction and authority of the City Council of Charleston shall be extended over [the Neck]."[38]

This date, falling after the end of August, the date for the end of fiscal year of the city, would bring Charleston Neck badges out of existence by the end of August 1850. All was set now, but many were still not happy. Articles on mass meetings and protests appeared in the paper nearly up to the September second date, with those for and against the union of city and Neck even putting forth their own candidates for mayor.

On 22 January 1850, John Poppenheim of the Commissioners of the Crossroads wrote the following letter to the City Council of Charleston:

> Gentlemen—The Legislature, at its late session, passed an act to annex a portion of the Charleston Neck to the City of Charleston. You are all fully aware that this legislation was in opposition to the wishes of a large majority of the voters of the Charleston Neck. After the passage of the act, it was published for general information, and referred to the people themselves, to determine by their votes, whether they would accept the terms of the incorporation. By the popular vote taken, a large majority still appeared to be opposed to the measure; and, consequently, it has devolved on this Board to test the constitutionality of the act of the Legislature.
>
> In coming to this conclusion, it had appeared highly advisable to this Board, that such arrangements should be made, by consent, as would enable the question to be finally settled at the earliest time practicable. It would be equally unnecessary and unwise, to allow the period specified by the act for its operation, to approach whilst the minds of

> the people of the Charleston Neck are affected as they now are, with an opinion of the unconstitutionality of the act; it might be, that unpleasant occurrence would reproach us, with not having adopted measures by which they could have been averted.

So, Poppenheim continued, he now sought cooperation of City Council "to allow this matter at once to be settled, by a reference to the Jurisdicial tribunals of this State. I have been informed that such an arrangement, if concurred in by you, would allow the case to be disposed of finally, at the sitting of the Appeal Court in May next."[39]

The City Council did concur, resolving that "the City Council will present no obstacle to impede an early reference to the proper Judicial tribunals, of the question of the constitutionality of the late act of the Legislature of the State, enlarging the corporate limits of the City of Charleston."[40] The case seemed to be on its way to the version of the State's Supreme Court, but there is no record of it ever having been argued there. Perhaps the $200 the City of Charleston paid to James Louis Petigru in April of this year "for professional services in Columbia, in relation to the annexation of the Neck to the City" might have something to do with that.[41] It all came to an end when the City Council resolved at its 1 October 1850 meeting "That all badges, cart and dray licenses for 1850, heretofore taken out, either from the City or the Neck, be considered as authorizing the holders to pass and repass without interruption through all the present City Wards."[42] And "Broad Street," who wrote the *Courier* on 12 September to complain that self-hire laws were not being enforced, noted, "All of Charleston is under one government; there is no '*City of Refuge*' [i.e., the Neck] for those who violate the laws of the land."

Despite the protests and all the turmoil, the union came about, and slave badges and licenses for the Neck, marked "C. N" or "Charleston Neck," vanished. In 1848, one had to have both Neck and Charleston badges if one's hired slaves moved north and south of Boundary Street, or just a Charleston or a Neck badge depending where one worked. From January 1849 until December 1850, either badge, Charleston Neck or Charleston, depending on where the owner lived, sufficed. After 1 January 1851, the Charleston Neck badge disappeared, all subsumed in the new legal entity of Charleston.

In 1848, the same year of the Neck debate, the City of Charleston began to issue badges in another category—chimney sweeps. (Since 1814, owners of chimney sweeps had been required to take out badges for these slaves working as day laborers.) Chimneys and their hazards had always been an issue in the city; just ten years before, a fire had burned down a large part of the central business district, and fire continued to be a problem every year, with many starting from chimneys. So the city tried to prevent fires with this new law. All sweeps cleaning chimneys now had to be licensed,

> and any free person who shall be employed in the sweeping of chimneys within the City without having first obtained a badge or license ... and every owner or other person having the care or management of any slave who shall permit such slave to be employed in the sweeping of chimneys within the City, without having first obtained a badge or license ... shall forfeit and pay the sum of ten dollars for each and every offence.[43]

The city treasurer would grant such licenses for the year and they would continue valid "until the first day of January, and no longer"; the fee of $5 had to be paid no matter in what month one purchased it. Those free persons and owners of slaves taking out such badges had to "give bond to the City Council of Charleston, in the penal sum of one hundred dollars, with one or more sureties, to the satisfaction of the mayor," before getting the badge. "Every chimney sweep shall wear suspended around his neck a crescent badge, with the number cut out thereof, to be provided by the City Treasurer." (None of these badges have survived, or none, to date, have been found or are known.) For every default, one had to pay the sum of $1. To assure quality control, should any chimney catch fire within two weeks of its sweeping, the owner of the building could furnish the number of the sweep, then he or his owner would be fined from $20 to $40. "The prices charged for sweeping shall be six and a quarter cents for each story, and no more." Again informers of infractions could split the penalty paid with the city. (To further enforce clean chimneys, the city fined people whose chimneys caught on fire.)

There was another issue linking fires and badges in these years. For a number of years, blacks, both slave and free, had worked efficiently and heroically in the Fire Department. Often, it seems, those slaves who hired their time came upon the scene of a fire and helped out. Apparently fearing that more and more slaves would desert their hired-out posts in time of fire alarms, in February 1846, City Council passed a measure "prohibiting the employment of Slaves in the Department, without a written permission of their masters." This, of course, was hard to do in a time of crisis, and the Fire Department felt the pinch immediately. In 1849, a committee petitioned the city to reverse its policy. This it did do, stating that the Fire Department could use slaves with badges to work out, *or* those who had written permission from their masters. Any slave with a badge now, it seems, could be used by the Fire Department.[44]

City Council turned its attention to more mundane issues in these years, too, seeing to the hiring of carts, drays and public carriages, declaring in 1855, for instance, that "each such cart, dray or wagon shall be provided with a badge containing the number thereof and marked *Private,* to be placed on the outside of each shaft."[45] The city set fees for wagons, carts and drays drawn by one horse or mule at $12; and $21, if drawn by two. Hacks and carriages with two wheels were licensed for $15, four wheels, for $30. Omnibuses, excepting line omnibuses, $40; and $56 was the fee for those drawn by four horses. Bread carts were $12.

These bread carts were the subject of an 1853 ordinance; each had to have a "tin badge from the City Treasurer ... affixed so as to be plainly seen at the rear end of the cart. " The treasurer was charged with providing tin badges marked "B.C." from number one on up. Each had to be renewed each year.[46] (None of these have been identified or are known.)

The other items eventually requiring badges in the city of Charleston were living creatures—dogs. In 1798, a law had been passed to require dogs running free to be muzzled, "so that he cannot bite"; a dog also had to "have a collar about his neck, with the owner's name engraved thereon, or otherwise plainly expressed." Dogs could be killed, and owners could be forced to pay a $2 fee.[47] The 1813 law fined owners of dogs going loose not less than $10. No Negroes, mulattos or free persons of color could keep dogs in any yard or lot unless the dog was secured and the dog had around its neck a collar "with the name of some creditable white person engraved thereon." (So, dogs belonging to blacks, like free people of color themselves, had to have white persons vouch for them.) Slaves breaking those laws were whipped at the workhouse with as many as 20 lashes, unless the owner of the slave paid the informer $5. Dogs being moved from one part of town to another had to be leashed. Butchers' dogs had to be secured to carts, and no dogs under any circumstances could be let into the market. Those killing dogs could be reimbursed 50 cents. The city marshal's own dogs "when employed or used by him, in catching or taking up hogs or goats," were above such laws, but they had to have a collar with the marshal's name engraved thereon.[48] In 1850, it was stated that "all dogs found going at large in the City of Charleston, except such as may wear such a Badge as the City Council may authorize the sale of, as provided for ... shall be liable to be killed by the City Police, or such person or persons as the Mayor may authorize and appoint for that purpose"; the owner of those dogs became subject to a fine of not less than $10, nor more than $20. The informer got half of the fee, the other half going to the city. It was then up to the city treasurer to "provide a sufficient number of Metal Badges, suitable for dogs, marked C.C.[Charleston Canine?] and numbered from one upward, and dispose of the same for the sum of Two Dollars."[49] Again, these were to be issued annually. One could, however, bypass buying a badge by instead paying a tax for the same amount.

All these and other badge laws were enforced up to and during the Civil War. As the war dragged on and inflation mounted, the price of badges escalated. The *Courier* of 23 January 1865 announced the new and exorbitantly high sums, all five times the price of what they were at the start of the war. A servant badge now went for $10; that of a porter cost $20. Fruiterers cost $25;

a mechanic's badge was priced at $35. Tellingly, there was no price listed for fishermen; perhaps it was considered too dangerous in the siege; or maybe slaves were not allowed near the harbor, suspected of giving aid or signals to the enemy.

Less than a month after these prices went into effect, Confederate forces evacuated Charleston. Yet the laws stayed on the books for almost a year. Not until the City of Charleston passed "An Ordinance in relation to Colored Persons, and offenses committed by them" on 16 January 1866, did the badge laws totally and officially disappear. "Whereas," the new statute ran:

> Slavery has been extinguished in this State by the action of the proper authorities, and all laws in referred thereto have become of no further force or effect:
>
> I. Therefore, *be it Ordained, by the Mayor and Alderman in City Council Assembled,*
>
> That all Ordinances, and parts of Ordinances and regulations which recognize the existence of slavery and define and enforce the rights and duties growing thereout, or which create and punish offenses against such rights, or against the public policy in reference to slavery, be and the same are hereby declared to be null and of none effect.[50]

With the stroke of a pen, a system that had started before the Revolution and had been made part of the city code at its incorporation, was ended. In the dust were tens of thousands of slave badges, and the laws regulating them soon followed them into obscurity.

## *Key Points in the Development of the Slave Badge System*

1690 Slaves leaving their plantation or domain need a ticket.

1712 Slaves not allowed to hire their own time.

1721 Persons hiring a slave required to have a certificate, note or memorandum.

1751 Slave owners outside the city, with a few exceptions, cannot hire out slaves in town.

1764 Hired-out slaves required to wear a ticket or badge.

1783 With city's incorporation, annual nature, categories and prices of badges regulated. Badges for free people of color also mandated.

1789 Slave and free people of color badges no longer required.

1800 Badge laws, for hired-out slaves, reappear.

1806 Badge laws codified; an oath needed. Fees tripled for more than six slaves hired out.

1816 Laws defined so fruiterers cannot buy material, only sell it.

1822 In response to Vesey's rebellion, state legislature increases penalty for slaves hiring their own time.

1830 In some instances, mechanics need not take out badges for their hired slaves. House slaves not required to wear their badges.

1837 Limits on the number of slaves one can hire out abolished. People out of town allowed to hire out their slaves in the city for a double fee and surtax.

1848 Negroes hiring slaves included in the laws. Badges for Charleston and Neck issued. Chimney sweep badges issued.

1849 State legislature relaxes its strict law of 1822 re slaves hiring their own time. Badges for either Charleston or Charleston Neck must be worn by hired-out slaves.

1850 Until City and Neck join in September, badges from Neck or City must be worn by hired-out slaves. Dog badges issued.

1865 Last badges issued.

1866 All slave-related laws, including badge laws, abolished.

## *Slave Badge Designations and Prices by Year*

| *Occupation* | *1800* | *1806* | *1813* | *1826* | *1837* | *1838* | *1840* | *1865* |
|---|---|---|---|---|---|---|---|---|
| Mechanic | 3.00 | | | | 5.00 | 7.00 | | 35.00 |
| Porter | 2.00 | | | | 4.00 | | | 20.00 |
| Fisher (woman) | 1.00 | | | | 2.00 | | | N/A |
| Fisher (man) | 1.00 | | | | 2.00 | | 4.00 | N/A |
| Servant | 1.00 | | | 2.00* | 2.00 | | | 10.00 |
| Fruiterer/Huckster | 6.00 | 15.00 | 5.00 | | | | | 25.00 |

*1.00 dollar if under 14.

*Note:* The terminology that appeared on the badges is discussed at length in the following chapters. Briefly put, most badges carried the titles above. The term "Carpenter," a type of "Mechanic," was used through at least 1813; "Fruiterer" replaced the term "Huckster" by around that time as well, being used possibly as early as 1810. "House Servant" was used only in the year 1800, it being replaced by "Servant." No designations by sex or age are known to have appeared on badges.

*Above:* 1800 Fisher, No. 14. (Ralph Atmar, Jr.). Like many others, this badge, possibly the earliest one known, was folded, broken, or purposely damaged at the time of its discard. *Below:* 1833 Servant, No. 16. (J. J. Lafar). Statutes demanded that badges had to be worn. Apparently, this servant made four holes to attach it to his or her shirt, jacket, or hat.

A

*Above:* Free Badge, No. 307. Rarest of the four free badges known, this is the only one in silver. *Below:* Dog Badge 1850, No. 290 (top), and 1852, No. 297 (bottom). The 1850 badge, with owner-added center holes, was made and issued in June of the year and is the earliest one found. The 1852 badge is the only other Charleston Canine badge known. Both were made by William Rouse.

B

*Above:* 1802/1803 Mechanic, No. 88. (Charles Prince). This is one of three similar badges known showing the remnant of the year "1802" broken off, with the later date "1803" then stamped on the front. (Courtesy of the Rivers Collection.) *Below:* 1807 Servant, No. 20. (Charles Prince). Because of an advertisement for another badge (a number 20, Porter, also from 1807), this large octagonal badge helps prove that badges were numbered consecutively within various categories.

*Above:* 1800 Fisher, No. 14 (left). 1800 Mechanic, No. 177 (right). (Ralph Atmar, Jr.). These badges display some early categories. All occupations except Carpenter have been found. *Below:* 1801 Mechanic, No. 27 (left). 1802 Porter, No. 116 (top). 1803 Porter, No. 480 (right). (Charles Prince). Although all are round, Prince used different diameters for different years and occupations.

D

*Above:* 1811 Servant, No. 180 (top). 1812 Servant, No. 426 (mid-left). 1813 Porter, No. 86 (mid-right). 1814 Porter, No. 78 (bottom). (J. J. Lafar). The 1811 badge design is the only one known featuring the reverse scallop. 1812 shows the first diamond-shaped badge. 1813 features the only perfect octagon, patterned after R. Atmar's 1800 badge, but larger. 1814 is the first square badge. *Below:* 1810 Fisher, No. 24 (left). (J. J. Lafar). This is the earliest known badge by Lafar. With no 1808 or 1809 badges having been found, it is not clear if Lafar made badges earlier than 1810. 1821 Fruiterer, No. 48 (right). (J. J. Lafar). Note the "&c". Lafar was the only badge maker to add this designation. Earlier badge makers used the term "Huckster," and later ones used "Fruiterer" only. It shows the confusion arising from the term, for a "Fruiterer" sold more than fruit.

E

*Above:* 1815 Mechanic, No. 56. Front (left) and back. (J. J. Lafar). The "Robt. Cheevers 251 E. Bay" badge. It is the only badge known to bear a name and address. *Below:* 1848 Servant, No. 433 (top). 1848 Porter, No. 21 (middle). 1849 Servant, No. 184 (bottom). (Charleston Neck Slave Badges). Charleston Neck badges are very scarce. The two from 1848 show different sizes and occupations; their maker is unverified. The 1849 badge was made by William Rouse in his typical diamond design. Rouse also made the 1850 Neck badges (not shown).

F

*Above:* 1832 Servant, No. 1994 (top). 1835 Servant, No. 1654 (mid-right). 1841 Servant, No. 641 (mid-left). 1844 Servant, No. 2150 (bottom). (John Mood). These badges by the same maker show two different sizes, with the later ones being smaller. *Below:* 1836 Servant, No. 531 (top). 1842 Fisher, No. 46 (mid-right). 1847 Porter, No. 618 (mid-left). 1861 Fruiterer, No. 77 (bottom). (William Rouse). The 1836 is the largest one Rouse made, simiar to those made by Lafar and Mood. The 1847 badge is the only square badge he made, and the 1861 is his smallest one.

G

*Left:* 1856 Servant, No. 1093 (very top). 1859 Porter, No. 990 (top). 1862 Servant, No. 1618 (mid-right). 1863 Servant, No. 44 (mid-left). 1864 Porter, No. 336 (bottom). (William Veronee). The 1856 and 1859 badges have unclipped corners. Starting in 1862, many of Veronee's badges were front- and back-stamped, showing the reuse of badges from one year to the next. *Bottom, left:* 1865 Servant, No. 13. (William Veronee). This was stamped on the back of an 1864 Servant badge, No. 541. Very few 1865 badges were made; there are only two known at this time. *Below, right:* 1848 Charleston, SC, Servant, No. 163. (Counterfeit). No authentic badges bore the state name or were of this design. This badge would have been recognized as an obvious forgery in 1848, so it must have been made later, possibly created for the tourist trade.

*Right:* 1855 Porter, No. 69. (William O'Connor). This was the only year that O'Connor made badges. They are the crudest-made badges from all known years.

H

# Part Two

## The System: Annual Recapitulations of Income and Expenses and a Guide to the Badges

"Barbers are supported in idleness & ease by their negroes who do the business; & in fact many mechanicks bear nothing more of their trade than the name."[1]

—Timothy Ford, 1786

# Chapter 3

# 1800–1810

Chapter 1 demonstrated the fact that badge and licensing laws regulating the hiring of slaves were part of the colony's codes of law before the Revolution. Badges had to be worn in some manner, proclaimed the law of 1764; and there were categories with different prices paid for different badges by 1783. In the latter year advertisements began to appear in the newspapers stating that the badges could be picked up at the treasurer's office. Soon the city was reporting in these papers the sums of money paid for making the badges. Although a few free people of color badges are known, not a single slave-hire badge from this era has yet to surface or be identified. So that means that the oldest surviving slave-hire badges date from the year 1800.

The law calling these badges into being was passed 16 July 1800. It said that it would not come into effect for another 30 days; so hired-out slaves had to have badges by the middle of August 1800. City records on the sale of badges have not been located, so there is no other evidence, other than the badges themselves, to help document their history—or so researchers believed. With no mass of pre–Civil War financial records from the city available, the only other possible sources available are the newspapers; and indeed, they have yielded a rich lode of materials to help document the entire slave-hiring process. For nearly each year in the period of 1800 to 1865, published recapitulations of the city's income and expenses have been found at the end of the fiscal year, which came about on the last day of August. Some of these summations extend back to 1783, the year of Charleston's initial incorporation. These published accounts, with other information available for a few other years, along with newspaper advertisements on badges and badge makers are previously unused sources of information that have proven useful in reconstructing Charleston's economic history and civil policies.

To present gross statistics and render technical descriptions of the badges themselves is the best way to document the system, but to present such information in a readable and non mind-numbing way is a challenge. To make the lumps of raw data more digestible, the information has been broken up by decade. Within each decade are presented three types of reports: (1) the financial data (and any other historical information available) from the newspapers, or elsewhere; (2) a description of the badges and what is known of their makers; and (3) a table summarizing the findings. With this data, it is possible to estimate how many slaves were hired out in a given term; for a few years, one can even document how many slaves were hired out in each category. (This information was published by the city of Charleston for two fiscal years, 1849-1850 and 1850-1851. A formula derived from those statistics allows for the estimates for the number of badges sold each year. An explanation of this formula is included in the appendix.) This can impact our perceptions of slavery; for in knowing what percentage of urban slaves in the city of Charleston had different lives from others in servitude (some often acting as their own bosses), one can posit yet another facet to the lives of those enslaved. Furthermore, the number of slave badges either made or sold each year may be of interest to collectors to help gauge the rarity of the particular item. The detailed descriptions of the badges are for collectors, museum curators and possible purchasers. Unfortunately, many frauds have been perpetuated in the past, and many counterfeits are still being sold, often for large sums of money. So information on the appearance, shape and text on the badges is given for each year, and those patterns that emerged over the decades are noted, as well.

Something that complicates each year's statistics is the disparity between what the statutes demanded and the how the city operated fiscally. Badges were generally put on sale on 1 January of each year, but the city closed its financial books on the 31st of August. (It appears this may not have been the case for the early years of the 19th century, however, as will be shown shortly.) This means that for those years when this practice was in effect, say, 1850 for instance, data from badges bearing the calendar year 1850 appear in two different fiscal years. Income from 1850 badges sold from 1 January 1850 through 31 August 1850 would be included in the 1849-1850 fiscal report (spanning 1 September 1849 through 31 August 1850). Income from badges sold from 1 September 1850 through 31 December 1850, would be reflected in the 1850-1851 fiscal year statement (1 September 1850–31 August 1851). This explains the difference in the summations below; financial data is given in fiscal year units (1799-1800, 1800-1801, etc.) while data on the badges themselves is given in calendar year units (1800, 1801). To cause less confusion, and to try to align such dates, the fiscal year spans are also designated by the date of the badge sold primarily in that span. Badges bearing the date 1850 were put on sale, as noted, on 1 January 1850—the fifth month of the fiscal year; most badges were sold in January, February, March and April. So the majority, probably 80 to

90 percent or so of those badges marked 1850 were sold in the 1849-1850 year; this explains why, to clarify matters, the fiscal year date (1849-1850) is linked to the 1850 badge date in the summations of each chapter. Annual summaries not from contemporary sources, but based instead on estimates or calculation, are presented here in *italics.*

## *1800-1801 (1800 badges)*

On 1 September 1800 (in the *City Gazette and Daily Advertiser*) the city published an "Abstract Statement of Receipts and Payments of the City Corporation, from the 1st of September, 1799, to the 30th of August, 1800, inclusive" for citizens to read. Income categories included taxes, city rents, tavern licenses, fines, fees paid by Sullivan's Island residents for the lazaretto, sale of fugitive slaves, etc. The city also recorded amounts paid out for building the lazaretto, paying the city guard, purchasing wood and candles, making doors for the work house, paying scavengers to clean the streets, and very significantly, noting that Ralph Atmar, Jr., was advanced $100 "on account [of] city badges." He is the first person known to make badges.

As previously stated, the law re-establishing the use of slave-hire badges did not go into effect until the middle of August 1800, just a few weeks before the city closed its financial books on the last day of that month. Thus the city would not have made a significant amount of money in these few weeks from the sale of these badges. In fact, *no* income is reported in the recapitulation of city finances for this period, noted above, the only notation being the $100 paid out to Atmar to make badges.

No income was reported because no income was made. It appears that the badges were not even ready by the end of the fiscal year. The *City Gazette* of 18 August 1800 noted, just as the Badge Law went into effect, the following:

> City Badges: The City Treasurer hereby gives notices that on Monday 1st of September next [the beginning of the 1800-1801 fiscal year], he shall begin to deliver out Badges, and continue to do so until the third Monday in said month, on which day, and after the law will be strictly enforced against every defaulter. W. Roach, city treasurer.

Although the ordinance called for compliance to begin in August, it did not start until September, the new fiscal year, so no income could have come in for the 1799-1800 fiscal year. On 3 September, the following was appended to the above notice in the *City Gazette*:

> Denomination and Price of said badges, are as follows: Huckster, not under thirty years of age, six dollars per badge. Mechanic, three dollars.

> Porters and cart and dray men, two dollars. Washers, Fishers and Hired Servants, one dollar.

These indeed were the categories and prices established by the ordinance. The terms used in the press give a clue as to what the words on the badges were: "Huckster," "Mechanic, "Porter, "Washer," " Fisher," and "House Servant" or "Servant."

This advertising of badges in September, at the beginning of the fiscal and not the calendar year, would be continued for the next few years. This, then, raises the question: what would the badge date be? If badges for 1800 (no doubt bearing the year "1800" on them) did not go on sale until September 1800, were 1800 badges sold only until January 1801? Or were badges marked 1800 sold for 12 months, until the end of August 1801? This latter scenario may have been the case; the subject is further discussed below.

Before going on to that, however, it might be best to first pay attention to another item mentioned in the recapitulation of the city's 1799-1800 budget. The city, according to the report, "received net profit on East Bay-Street lottery, lst class tickets [$]2,570.88; and 2nd class, [$]2,000." It states how much was taken in, but not who won it, but this we know from history. The winner was to have a profound impact on the whole slave badge system in the coming years, and on slavery and the city itself—slave Denmark Vesey. (With his winnings, he would buy his freedom, and thus begin his march into the history books.)

While Vesey began to enjoy his newfound freedom, the city went about its business. On 31 August 1801, the *Charleston Times* carried the information that the city had brought in $4,192.66 and sold 2,116 badges, "issued to the owners of Slaves working on hire within the city, expense of making said Badges deducted." For the first time, it is stated how many badges were made; if 2,116 badges were made and sold, at least that many slaves were hired out in the city of Charleston from September 1800 through August 1801. The 1800 census reports that there were 9, 819 slaves in Charleston. More than one-fifth of the entire slave population in the city of Charleston in this year was hired out, meaning that many had more autonomy, or freedom of movement, or more skills than ever thought previously.

The amount of money brought in ($4,192.66) is very high in comparison to the amount brought in the next fiscal year.

### *1801-1802 (1801 badges)*

On 25 July 1801, before the new fiscal year beginning in September 1801 began, the following advertisement appeared in the *Charleston Times*:

> Contracts for City Badges. The Committee on Contracts, will contract for delivery of 2,500 badges, by the first of September next, to be made of copper, or tin. Proposals to be left with the City Treasurer, on or before the first of August next, who will furnish a pattern of the Badges. David Alexander.

This advertisement reveals much: the city expected about 2,500 badges would be sold in the next 12 months or so, and that contracts were awarded to those who submitted them, the winner probably being the one with the lowest bid. According to the ad, the city treasurer had not yet decided what the badges would look like or even of what metal they would be made. (Archeological evidence demonstrates that the choice was copper; if tin was used for badges before 1800, this might explain why none have survived, tin not being as resistant to corrosion and disintegration in the soil.)

Another thing this advertisement (and another one soon to be published) suggests is that there seems to have been a mixing of accounts across the fiscal year. The advertisement calls for the contract for badges to be given in August; and an advertisement in the *Times* on 20 August 1801 states that Badges for 1801 are ready. This is an odd piece of information, for it has been 1801 for many months now. What badges have been for sale all these months? Did they read 1800? (It seems likely that they did, and that no matter the calendar year, the badges sold bore the date of the fiscal year in which the sales began.)

Another point of confusion also arises from the date. If 1801 badges are being sold in August of 1801 for the rest of 1801 and on into 1802, in what fiscal year will the income be reported? Since the fiscal year extends only to the end of August, the income for all the badges being sold in this month will be recorded in the 1800-1801 fiscal year. Although people would buy a badge in August 1801 to use for the next 12 months, the income from that sale would turn up in the fiscal year ending in just a few weeks.

This indeed seems to have been the case, for the newspaper reported that at the end of the fiscal year 1801-1802 that 2,373 badges had been sold. Although this is a higher number than reported the year before (and very close to the 2,500 badges ordered), a lower amount of money, only $2,453.22 ("expense of making said badges deducted") came into the city coffers (*Charleston Times*, 3 September 1802). If the figures for this year and for the year before are to make any sense (less badges sold the previous year—2,116—but almost double the amount of money—$4,192.66), one explanation might be that badges sold in August 1801 for the fiscal year 1801-1802 showed up as income for the 1800-1801 fiscal year. There seems to be no other way to explain the apparent disparity, other than there perhaps being a misprint in the press. Despite the confusion in the dollar amounts, some things are certain: more than 2,000 badges were made, bought, sold and worn in each of these two years.

One who wore an 1801 badge was a fisherman named Anderson, who, according to the newspaper (*City Gazette*, 29 December 1801), had one in his possession when he "absented himself."

### *1802-1803 (1802 badges)*

On 23 August 1802, the *Charleston Times* carried the following advertisement:

> City Badges, for the year 1802. The City Treasurer gives notice that on Wednesday, the first day of September next, he will be ready to issue Badges to the owners of such Slaves as are working out on hire within the city; when all persons concerned are requested to deposit their old badges at this office, and take out new ones, conformably to law. W. Roach, city treasurer. *City Treasurer's Office. 23 August 1802*

Again, badges will follow the fiscal year, i.e., badges bearing the date 1802 will go on sale beginning 1 September 1802 (the beginning of the fiscal year 1802-1803), and will be in effect until the end of August 1803. (It is assumed that these badges will all bear the date 1802.) But suddenly, there is something new. The treasurer asks that all badges be brought back before new ones are given out. This may help explain why there are so few known from these years—apparently many old ones were turned in. (What is even more surprising, however, is that there are at least a few badges from this era that have two concurrent years stamped on them. A mechanic badge in the Rivers Collection bears the date 1803 on it, but just beneath it, one can just make out the top of other numerals—1802.) It appears that the city, when taking badges in from previous years, in a few instances at least, had the badge maker snap off the early year (placed on the bottom of the badge) and punch the newer year on it. (See color plate on page C of insert.)

At the end of the 1802-1803 fiscal year, on 1 September 1803, the *Charleston Times* stated that only 449 badges "were issued to the owners of slaves working on hire, within the city"; the income reported was only $655.38, "minus the expense of making said badges." Most other income categories of this year reported in the paper tally with the year before, so this falling off in numbers is very puzzling. It could mean that people, seeing that they could get by without buying badges, began to abandon the practice. This theory is bolstered by the following advertisement which appeared in the *City Gazette* on 3 October 1803, a month or so after the 1802-1803 fiscal year ended:

> Notice. To the owners of Slaves working out on hire, and to those in the habit of hiring them. The City Marshal gives notices to the owners, &

> c. of Slaves working out on hire, who have neglected to take out badges for the same, that he shall on Monday, the 10th of October, inst. proceed according to law in such cases, against all defaulters: and that no one may plead ignorance thereof, the ordinance is re-published for the information of those concerned—James Browne, City Marshal.

Since so few were sold, badges from this year 1802-1803 fiscal year (probably bearing the date 1802) should be exceedingly rare, but there are some 1802 badges known—and several more showing that "1802" was snapped off and the next year stamped above it.

### *1803-1804 (1803 badges)*

It seems that the ad quoted above must have had its effect, for in this following fiscal year, the number of badges (badges probably bearing the date 1803) sold increased up to 1,574 (*Charleston Times*, 1 September 1804); the income, minus the expense of making the badges came to $2,769.23. Something else that could have prompted this rise in sales, other than the marshal's declaration to enforce the law, was a sort of employment office for slave hire that opened up in October of 1803. On the 20th, the following advertisement appeared in the *Courier:*

> Intelligence Office. GEORGE C. BAILEY, No. 26, CHURCH STREET, BEGS leave to inform his Friends and the Public, that he intends, for the accommodation of the Citizens, to keep an INTELLIGENCE OFFICE, for persons wanting Employment, and also for the hiring out of Negro Servants.

For every white person's name entered in his register, Bailey was to be paid $1.

> For every Negro's Name that is entered in his Book for Hire, the Owner is to pay a Quarter of a Dollar only. As the benefit of having such an Office in this City, must be apparent to every person, he will not say much on the subject; because any person wanting a Servant of any description, will be able at once to know where to apply for the same; and any person wanting a situation for themselves, will know where is the most proper place to make their situation known, which will save them the expense of advertising in the Newspapers.

If anyone did not see the wisdom of this, Bailey noted, "THESE INTELLIGENCE OFFICES have been found of very great utility in London, for these many years past."

Indeed, people so liked the idea that on 9 November 1803, the editor of the *Courier* (despite the point raised against newspapers) praised Mr. Bailey's Register Office. The editors wished him success and hoped the public would not hesitate but immediately make it the place to "hire or let out Negroes. There are few cities in America and we believe not one in Great Britain, of equal consequence of Charleston, without an office of the kind—and Mr. BAILEY being the first to establish one here, deserves immediate encouragement, and in case of future rivalship, a decided preference."

Perhaps for all these reasons, then, the number of badges sold this year went up. As noted, some of the 1803 badges started out as 1802 badges, having the newer year stamped on them.

### *1804-1805*
### *(1804 badges from 1 September to 31 December 1804; 1805 badges from 1 January to 31 December 1805)*

In fiscal year 1804-1805, 1,354 slave-hire badges were sold, bringing in $2,035 *(Charleston Times*, 31 August 1805). Instead of following the pattern for the years before, with the badges for this fiscal year bearing all one date, something else happened. It appears that badges marked 1804 were sold only from 1 September 1804 through the end of the year, and 1805 badges were sold from 1 January 1805 at least through the end of August 1805. The availability of these badges marked 1805 was noted in the *Courier* on 8 December 1804, saying that City Badges for the year 1805 "for such slaves as are working out on hire in the City" would commence being issued by the city treasurer "on the first Monday in January next."

This shows a change in the process, a change that continued from this point on. If this were the case, then badges going on sale by September 1, 1804, would have 1804 stamped on them, but by December, new badges marked with 1805 were put on the market to carry on into the next calendar year. This would mean that badges bearing the date 1804 might have only been sold in August, September, October, November and into December, for five months instead of the usual 12; this would mean that badges bearing the date 1804 would be fewer in number than those of other years. Indeed that seems to be the case, for no badges bearing the date 1804 are known to the authors. (More relating to this peculiar year is given in the 1805-1806 recapitulation, immediately below.) This would explain the lack of badges for this year, and it would make enforcement easier in the coming years, if badges worn matched the calendar year.

### *1805-1806 (1806 badges)*

Statistics for this fiscal year are not very satisfying, showing just dollar amounts, and no gross number of badges sold (*Charleston Courier*, 3 September 1806). For the first time, however, the city treasurer made tallies of the badges bought from 1 September 1805 through 31 December 1805, (which would bear the date 1805) and the badges sold from 1 January 1806 to 31 August 1806 (which would bear the date 1806). The 1806 badges were advertised as being ready in the *Courier*, on 23 December 1805. This would tend to support the theory that now the process was different, that badges bearing two different calendar years were sold in one fiscal year. Also arguing for this shift is the fact that when the new slave badge law of 1806 was passed, it, for the first time, specified that badges were good for the period of January through December. Earlier statutes previously stated that badges lasted until the end of a year, possibly meaning a fiscal year. The figures given show that only $13 came in for the months of September, October, November and December 1805. (If a similar amount had come into city coffers from September through December of the year before, that would clearly explain why no 1804 badges have survived—there being so few made or sold with that date.) Many more were sold in the next eight months of the fiscal year: $1,375.25 came in for the months January through August 1806, for a total of $1,388.25. *By using a mathematical formula, it is suggested that approximately 821 badges were sold in this period.*

Since there is no definite data present in the newspapers from this point onward for the gross number of badges sold for particular periods, one must now rely on mathematical estimates. The numbers derived using this formula are *estimates* only, and will be valid *only* if the same percentage of badges in particular categories were made and sold each year, as were made for the year for which that information is known. This hardly seems likely, but nevertheless, this is the only statistical means available to derive information.[2]

### *1806-1807 (1807 badges)*

When the fiscal year (1 September 1806 to 31 August 1807) was tabulated, it continued a downward trend regarding income, with only one cumulative financial total of $1,140.75 reported, with no breakdown by months and no gross number of slave badges made or sold. This happened despite the raising of the price for the fruiterer badge up to $15 in October of 1806. *The estimate of badges sold totals 556.*

The newspapers noted when 1807 badges would go on sale (*Times*, 17 December 1806) and tell of one badge holder, or at least of one who should have held a badge. On 25 June 1807, the following advertisement appeared in *the City Gazette and Daily Advertiser*: "Ten Dollars Reward. Absented herself on Wednesday last, my Negro Wench, Charlotte, about 18 years of age, slender made, her complexion a yellow cast; is well known in the city as a day worker...."[3] On 17 April 1807, Sancho, with a Porter's badge, number 20, also ran away—a very crucial bit of information, as will be shown shortly (*Times,* 17 April 1807).

### *1807-1808 (1808 badges)*

The dwindling trend continued, escalating radically this year, for the Charleston *Courier* of 3 September 1808 reported only $702.94 brought in for this fiscal period. This decrease in badges bought and sold could either mean that attention to the law grew even more lax, or that the economy was in trouble, as indeed it was with the coming of the war of 1812 with England. With the Trade Embargo Act passed by the US Congress in 1807, American ports were closed to export-import trade. All classes of businessmen, planters, merchants, slaves-auctioneers and the like experienced a drop-off in business. There was now less money to spend, and less need to employ slaves. But badges were sold; advertisements for the 1808 badges did appear (*Courier,* 11 December 1807). *Perhaps as few as 342 badges were sold.* With this low numbering, perhaps it is no surprise to report that no badges from 1808 are known to the authors at the time of publication.

### *1808-1809 (1809 badges)*

The availability of these badges was made known in an advertisement in the *City Gazette,* stating that 1809 badges were ready on 12 December 1808. But the numbers of badges sold declined even more from the year before. On 1 September 1809, the *City Gazette and Daily Advertiser* announced that the income for badges was $618.94, with no expenses noted. *Mathematical estimates suggest only 302 badges selling.*

### *1809-1810 (1810 badges)*

In the *City Gazette* of 27 December 1809, badges for 1810 were advertised; and a bit later, in the *Courier* of 18 January 1810 the following appeared: "The City-Marshal PARTICULARLY notifies to those concerned, that after the last of the present month, he will rigidly enforce the *Ordinances*, respecting

*Cart* and *Dray Licenses*, and *City Badges*." This may have had an effect on the badge-buying public for the numbers went up this year. At the end of the fiscal year, the published report (*City Gazette and Commercial Daily Advertiser*, 1 September 1810) showed $1,344.88 in income; the non-rounded figure suggests that this is the income minus expenses. *Estimates suggest that perhaps 656 badges were sold.*

As for the badges themselves in this time period, much is known. It might be prudent, however, to first discuss the general nature of all Charleston slave badges before remarking on the particulars of this first decade.

All known badges are copper. All have holes in them to enable the passing through of a string or ribbon to help the bearer wear the badge visibly, as required by law. (Some slaves apparently drilled extra holes to make sewing badges onto garments easier.) All also have a particular number and a category; and all of them, but for the first year known (1800) have a geographic locator expressed—"Charleston," "C. N" or "Charleston Neck." Every time "Charleston" appears, it is an arc at the top of the badge. Some badges from 1800 through 1828 have their maker's mark on the back.

The words and numbers impressed on the copper tags were done in several ways—*engraved, stamped* or *punched*. In *engraving*, the craftsman would "write" in the metal, carving out numerals as if writing with a pen. In *stamping*, the badge maker would use a die, several letters in a three dimensional format, like letters from a typewriter, on a metal plate. When stamping that into the metal (similar to how a notary public impresses a piece of paper with a seal, consisting of raised letters), the whole plate would make an indentation in the blank badge (the same way the notarial seal impresses the page, making a circle with information in the center). The letters "Servant" for instance would be impressed into the metal, but they would appear to be framed in a rectangle for the rectangular metal plate with its raised letters would make an indentation in the blank copper. Finally, some information could be *punched*; instead of having a whole word like "Servant" as part of a die, a single letter "S" or number "9" would be hammered into the soft metal.

As for numbering, with so few badges from the early years surviving, conjecture rules. As the system started, badges may have been numbered as they were sold. (All badges found have numbers on them, despite the fact that it was only in 1806 that the statute declared this to be necessary.) Early on (in 1800 and 1801, at least), if the first badge sold was to a servant, for instance, it might have been engraved with the number 1; if the second one sold was fisher, the fisher badge might have been engraved with the numeral 2. Later, probably by 1803, badges could have been numbered in each category, meaning that the first porter badge sold was numbered 1, and the second porter sold was numbered 2, with the same thing holding true for each category.

This certainly seems to have been the case by the year 1807 (and for all the years following). Proof comes from a Servant badge numbered 20 for the year 1807 which exists in a private collection. But there was another badge with that same number, but in a different category, for that same year. In the 17 April 1807 issue of *The Times*, the following advertisement appeared:

> Ten Dollar Reward. Run away from the Subscriber about two months ago, his fellow SANCHO—He is about 28 years of age, of a yellow complexion, and about five feet seven inches in height. Had on when he went away a light mixture round Jacket, and white woolen Overalls, edged with blue; he has also his Badge as a Porter No. 20, by which means he gets work about Gadsden's Wharf, as he was seen there last Monday...."

Peter S. Bee noted at the end "If he returns of his own accord he will be forgiven."

Peter Bee had a slave named Sancho who ran away in about February 1807, with a low number Porter Badge 20, bought probably very early in January of that year. And so, with an extant badge from a different category ("Servant") with the same number and the same year, one can infer that numbers in each category started at one and went upwards.

It has been difficult to make this match in other years; most badges are lost, and those that exist are locked away in museums or in private collections, there being no one place where all known badges can be compared and seen. Yet it is obvious that from a certain point, this process of numbering each category from one onward continued for all the years that the badge system was in effect. To date, the most common categories have been found to have the highest numbers on them; while the expensive badges in categories that few slaves could fill turn up with relatively low numbers. The highest number found for a servant so far is 2878 (an 1861 badge); servants were the most common (2,400 made in 1849-1850 and 3,500 in 1850-1851 will be explicated below). As for other categories, John Bennett wrote of seeing an 1843 porter badge with the number 1375; the highest other porter badge known to the authors is 1283, from 1847. (1,400 were made in the 1849-1850 fiscal year, and 1,600 in the next.) The highest number known for a mechanic badge (in 1858) is 450; this matches nicely with the number made in 1849-1850 (400) and 1850-1851 (600). The highest fruiterer found to date is 161 (from 1859); 180 were made in the fiscal year 1849-1850, and 500, a very high number, were produced in 1850-1851. (This increase in the number of badges from the 1849-1850 fiscal year to the 1850-1851 year was due to the Neck being joined to the incorporated city of Charleston and the number of slaves hired out above Boundary Street now being included in the city's badge laws.) The highest known fisher badge is 136 from 1824 (150 were made in the 1850-1851 fiscal year, with only 100 the year before); and the highest number known for the very skilled carpenter (a subcategory, apparently, of mechanic) is 69, from 1813. The lack of any fruiterer or fisher badge bearing a high number shows, then, that no badges made in small amounts display high numbers, while those badges that were common *do* display high and low numbers. This, in turn, would suggest, that badges with low numbers were made and sold early in that year, while those with high numbers were sold later. This appears to have been the case from 1807 on, and may have started as early as 1803. Only with more knowledge from more badges can such a claim be confirmed.

The following are descriptions of the earliest known badges:

## *1800*

The earliest documented badge, as stated, dates from 1800. It is octagonal, with all sides nearly uniform, with a hole on the top side to allow for suspension by a thread, ribbon or leather strap. This badge bears three lines of text: the year 1800 is stamped on the bottom, the particular occupation is stamped in the center; and the number, "No. 14" for example, is engraved on the top line. "Charleston" does not appear on the badge. (Since this is the lowest badge number known to the authors, this, in turn, may be the earliest badge known, period.) Several badges from this year have surfaced; no doubt more are around and will be found. Fishers, Mechanics, House Servants, Porters and a Huckster have been unearthed. Atmar was the only one known to have used the term "House Servant"; all others who followed preferred the shorter term, "Servant." Atmar also always stamped his name on the back of his badges right under the hole.

From the 1800 statute, the badges (and their prices) were: handicraft tradesmen, in these years called either "Mechanics," or "Carpenters," $3. Carter, drayman, or porter, or day laborer labeled "Porters" on the found badges sold for $2. Fisherman, titled "Fisher" on the badges, cost $1, as did the "Servant" or "House Servant" badge for hired servants, washer women and maids; and every "Huckster" or vender (male or female) badge was $6. In 1813 when the price for this category of badge would change, the law would refer to it as a seller of fruits and cakes; the change of name on the badge could have come in some time before.

The maker of these badges, as revealed in the newspapers of the time, was Ralph Atmar, Jr. (1767–1809). He was a goldsmith and engraver, and the fact that he got this city contract is a testimony to the fluid times in which he was living. (Or perhaps it is testimony to the fact that his father was a messenger to the House of Representatives and his position figured into getting his son the contract.)[4] Ralph Atmar, Sr., the badge maker's father, had petitioned General Benjamin Lincoln to capitulate to the British when they besieged the city in 1780. But then he, his wife and his two children were banished for not taking the oath of allegiance when the British took control. Ralph Atmar, Jr., the future badge maker, was 14 at the time; he and his parents and his sibling went to Philadelphia, eventually returning to Charleston, where in 1792, he married. He advertised himself as a "Jeweller, Silver Smith and Hair worker" the next year. He had a brief partnership with James Monk and also took up the art of engraving. After the partnership dissolved, he advertised himself as R. Atmar, Jun. at 95 Broad Street, in October 1800; his shop was "nearly opposite the New Church."[5] He was looking for a goldsmith to work with him in his shop, and also wanted an apprentice, perhaps both needed now that he had the city's business in making badges.

## *1801*

The badges for 1801 are different from those from 1800. For one, they are round versus octagonal; and their maker is different. Charles Prince made them; the name "C. Prince" appears stamped on their back. Prince was a tinman, as the phrase went, and not a silversmith. (The granting of the contract to a tinman, coupled with the City Treasurer considering tin as a possible metal for the August 1801 badges, again leads credence to the possibility that pre–1800 badges and some made in the years for which no badges have been found might have been made of tin.) He also served as lamplighter for the city of Charleston, and was a Methodist who owned no slaves, as far as can be ascertained. The fact that another badge maker in the coming years would be a Methodist and that Methodists were some of the more enlightened religious groups in the city at the time, often favoring abolition of slavery and advocating a Christian attitude to slaves, is intriguing. Those making badges for slaves, objects that would give slaves a better life, were often of a religion whose teachings advocated just that.

Prince was not just in a different profession from Atmar; he also made his badges differently the first few years. They are round and of varying diameters and circumferences. Those with smaller dimensions are found on his "mechanic" and "servant" badges; the "porter" is quite large. This could be helpful perhaps, for someone in need of a porter could with a glance see the large round badge and deduce the slave was a porter or drayman or day laborer, and hail the slave from across a street. (An illiterate person could tell the difference, too.) Prince also was the first to stamp "Charleston" on his badges. It appears on the first line; the second line has the letters "No" stamped, followed with a numeral or numerals engraved. It appears Prince followed the same practice begun the year before: he, or someone else, would pull the badge with the proper profession on it, (stamped on the third of four lines) and then hand engrave the number as the fee came in. The lowest number known for this year is a 27 "Mechanic"; the next one found is 36, a very large "Porter." "Fishers" and "Hucksters" badge sizes may fall between the large porter and smaller servant and mechanic. Prince made badges from 1801 through at least 1807, marking them all with his name. The order is: first line: "Charleston" (stamped); second: "No" (stamped) and numeral (engraved); third: Profession (stamped); fourth: "1801" (stamped).

## *1802*

These badges are round, as the year before, varying in size, also as before. A fairly low number, 72, a servant badge exists;[6] the large Porter 116 is illustrated on page D of color insert. The order of information is as follows: first line: "Charleston" (stamped); second line: "No" (stamped), numerals, determined at the time of the paying (punched); third line: occupation (stamped); and fourth line: 1802 (punched).

As noted earlier, there are some surviving badges that show the practice of re-punching them with new years. A 23 August 1802 advertisement in the Charleston *Times* asked owners to bring in old badges before getting new badges. One 1802 Mechanic badge reveals the tops of the number of 1802, showing that the part of the badge with those numerals was snapped off and the year 1803 was punched in the blank area left. The badge, buckled by stamping and punching and use, offered resistance to the punching of the new year on it; the badge maker had to punch the numeral zero twice, making it look like an 18003 (see page C of color insert). A servant badge, number 335, and another mechanic badge, number 137, also show this practice.[7]

## *1803*

Charles Prince continued the round design in 1803. On some of his badges, on the bottom line, "1803" was hand-punched. Others have the year stamped. Some dies differ, too, showing that there were many changes and little uniformity in this year. The order of text was: "Charleston" (stamped); "No." (stamped) and numeral (punched); Occupation (stamped); "1803" (stamped or punched).

## *1804*

As stated earlier in this chapter, it appears badges bearing this date may only have been sold for a few months and so that may explain why they are so scarce. The authors have not seen or handled an 1804 badge, and no image of one has surfaced. In this same short period the next year (September through December 1805), only $13 in income would be generated, so the number of badges produced for 1804 could be quite small.

### *1805*

The 1805 badges that have surfaced are eight-sided. "Charleston" is on the top line (stamped); the second line has "No." (stamped) with a numeral (hand-punched); the occupational terms on the third line are stamped; and the year "1805" (on the fourth line ) is also stamped. The maker of the actual "1805" stamp used to mark badges this year was a sub-contractor to Charles Prince. Court records at the South Carolina Department of Archives and History show that silversmiths Peter X. and later badge maker J. J. Lafar charged Prince $2.50 in December 1804 for making the "1805" stamp he would use for his badges (Charleston district Common Pleas Judgment L10018, 1808, No. 141 A).

### *1806*

1806 badges vary a bit from those of the year before. They are eight-sided this year, larger than the 1805 badges, and are more elongated. The number of the badge is hand engraved instead of punched. First line: "Charleston" (stamped); second line: "No." (stamped) and numeral (engraved); third line: occupation (stamped); fourth line: "1806" (stamped). They are similar to 1807 badges. The just-cited court case between the Lafars and Prince shows that the Lafars made the "Porter," "Fisher" and "1806" stamps that Prince used in marking his badges this year.

### *1807*

These badges, still made by Charles Prince, are octagon shaped and also slightly bigger than 1805. They have a slightly elongated look. Along with 1806, they are largest eight-sided badges found to date. Again, "Charleston," "No," the occupation, and the year (all in the same order of the preceding years) are stamped, while the individual badge number is hand engraved. In early 1807, the Lafars charged Prince for numbering 92 badges. This suggests that other numbers on badges later in the year might have been engraved by someone else. They were paid for their labor, while Prince had the city contract. One badge wearer this year was a "Negro woman named Louise of the Congo Nation"; she ran away with "a round basket with cakes and an hucksters badge" (*City Gazette*, 23 September 1807).

## *1808 and 1809*

To date, no badges from these years have surfaced. Figures reveal (*Courier*, 3 September 1808) that at the end of August 1808, the city had only collected $702.94, so the number of 1808 was small; *estimates put it at 342.* In 1809, the City collected less, only $618.94, *with the estimate of badges sold being 302.* So this very small number of badges made might account for them not being known; or it could be that badges from this year were made of an inferior copper and deteriorated quicker than others, or perhaps they were made of another metal, such as tin. The only thing that can truly be said with certainty about these badges is their rarity. The next known badges, from 1810, were made by a different maker than Charles Prince. When Prince stopped making them and the next maker started will perhaps only be known when (and if) badges from 1808 and 1809 appear.

## *1810*

This year ushers in a new badge maker, who might have begun making them a year or two before, but with no badges from 1808 or 1809 found, there is no certainty. The badges are marked on the back, "Lafar." They are octagonal and close to the size of the 1805 badges, but their shape is not uniform: the eight sides are not of equal size, instead the badge is more similar to a square with the corners cropped on the diagonal, making for four sides of one size and the cropped four sides smaller. All the information, except for the numerals of the badge number, is stamped; the badge numerals are engraved. The order of the text differs from the work of Charles Prince: the first line is "Charleston" (stamped); the second is "1810" (stamped); following that on the third line is the occupation (stamped), and the fourth and final line contains "No" (stamped) with a numeral (engraved).

The maker of these badges was John Joseph Lafar (1781–1849), son of a dance instructor, Joseph Lafar, and Catherine Bouillat. John Joseph and his brothers, Peter and John, were born in Charleston and all worked as silversmiths; later their cousin, David P. Lafar, a cooper, joined them in their shop. From 1805 through 1807, Lafar, even before he got the city contract, was already involved in making stamps and numbering badges for Charles Prince. Lafar, unlike Prince, owned slaves and also served as City Marshal from 1818 to 1830.

Other titles of his included Messenger of the Council, Keeper of the Exchange, and Justice of the Peace. He also was of a martial bent, as well, being a Second Lieutenant in the Charleston Regiment of Artillery. He died of consumption in 1849 and was buried in the Huguenot church graveyard on Church Street.[8]

In summary, in the first decade of their renewed use, badges and their making evinced a certain fluidity, suggesting that the system was new (it was reintroduced in 1800 after an eleven-year hiatus) and was being made up as it went along. In the first year, the city name does not even appear, and the names of categories vary. Sometimes the handicraft tradesmen are called mechanics, sometimes carpenters. There is no standard shape; octagons, elongated octagons, and circles of various sizes appear and disappear. The shapes shift from year to year, even when made by the same craftsman. Sometimes data is stamped, sometimes it is engraved, and sometimes punched. All these changes suggest that the system was new and was evolving. (The advertisement for the 1801 badges fairly admits this, saying that the city treasurer has not decided between copper and tin; and that he will furnish a pattern in August, not described or stated to be known in July.) In the early years, it appears that badges were sold on the fiscal year, meaning that badges sold from 1 September 1801 through August 1802, for instance, likely bore the date 1801. This practice changed by January 1805, when badges numbered that year were made available. And in 1806, the new statute specifically stated that the badges were to be used from January through December of a particular year. The whole process, and the badges themselves, would become more standardized in the next decade.

Recapitulating the above years, the first documented period of the slave-hiring process can be tabulated in this way (*Italics* are used to show estimated numbers):

| *Fiscal Year* | *Badge year* | *# of Badges* | *Income less expenses* | *Expenses* | *Maker* |
|---|---|---|---|---|---|
| 1799-1800 | | | | 100.00 | |
| 1800-1801 | 1800 | 2,116 | 4,192.66 | | Atmar |
| 1801-1802 | 1801 | 2,373* | 2,453.22 | | Prince |
| 1802-1803 | 1802 | 449 | 655.38 | | Prince |
| 1803-1804 | 1803 | 1,574 | 2,769.23 | | Prince |
| 1804-1805 | 1804† | ? | ? | | ? |
| 1804-1805 | 1805 | 1,354 | 2,035.00 | | Prince |
| 1805-1806 | 1806 | *821* | 1,388.25 | | Prince |
| 1806-1807 | 1807 | *556* | 1,140.75 | | Prince |
| 1807-1808 | 1808 | *342* | 702.94 | | ? |
| 1808-1809 | 1809 | *302* | 618.94 | | ? |
| 1809-1810 | 1810 | *656* | 1,344.88 | | Lafar |

*2,500 called for in the press.

†This period was only from 1 September 1804 through 31 December 1804; a year later, only $13 came in from 1 September 1805—1 December 1805.

"Badge year" denotes the predominate badge sold during the fiscal year.

# Chapter 4

# 1811–1820

### *1810-11 (1811 badges)*

The *City Gazette and Commercial Daily Advertiser* noted that 1811 badges would be ready for pickup soon on 27 December 1810. This was the newspaper that had a contract with the city of Charleston to print all official notices; it would have (and probably did) print the annual recapitulation of income and expenses in September of 1811, but copies from that year have not been located. To come up with an estimate, a figure half way between the previous and next fiscal years has been used as income, and it, in turn, was used to determine the number of badges sold, a statistically valid procedure, but one whose results may not be totally reliable. *Estimates put the income at $1,807.13 and the number of badges sold at 881.*

### *1811-12 (1812 badges)*

The *City Gazette and Commercial Daily Advertiser* (1 September 1812) reported that "City Badges issued to owners of Slaves working out on hire" brought in $2,269.39, this probably being income minus expenses. *It is estimated that 1,106 badges sold.*

In this period, R. W. Cleary advertised for his runaway slave "Sam, a fisherman by trade, but [who] frequently worked as a laborer, as he had a laborer's badge" (*City Gazette*, 18 May 1812). Sam would have worn an 1812 Porter's badge. Another slave in this category sporting a similar badge was "a Negro fellow Mingo ... well known around town as a Porter, for which has a Badge, No. 192." His owner asked "that no person ... hire him or enable him to get out of the state" (*Courier*, 22 May 1812). Pompey, "a painter by trade ...

constantly employed working out, being furnished with a badge" was also advertised for by his owner, George Cross.[1] Pompey would probably have had an 1812 Mechanic's badge.

### *1812-1813 (1813 badges)*

The treasurer noted he was "ready to issue out Badges" for the year 1813 on 24 December 1812 (*City Gazette and Commercial Daily Advertiser*). There was a slight falling off of income this year from the one previous, with badge income later noted as $2,025.84 *(City Gazette and Commercial Daily Advertiser*, 1 September 1813). Although less money was brought in, more badges were probably sold, because in February, the price for fruiterer badges was reduced from $15 down to $5. *Estimates put the number at 1,227.*

Edward Johnson's slave, Belinda, "about 5 feet 2 inches high, thick set, [who] smiles when spoken to, and is very plausible in her conversation, [and who] rolls in her walk," ran away, with an 1813 badge (perhaps a servant's), numbered 57 (*City Gazette*, 24 May 1813).

### *1813-1814 (1814 badges)*

On 22 December 1813, the *Courier* noted that badges for 1814 would be ready the first Monday in January. On 2 September 1814, it reported that the city showed receipts of $2,208.80 in the category of City Badges, issued to hired-out slaves. The less than a rounded dollar amount suggests that expenses have been deducted (or amounts from fines added, or both). *Perhaps 1,338 of these "City Badges" were sold.*

### *1814-1815 (1815 badges)*

Just as the badges for 1815 went on sale, the city treasurer placed an advertisement in the papers under the title, "City Badges for 1815." It read:

> I DO hereby give notice to owners or representatives of such Slaves as are or may be working out on hire within the City, that I shall commence issuing BADGES for the year 1815, on the first Monday of January next, Wm Roach, City Treasurer [*Courier*, 2 January 1815].

Roach also advertised for Cart, Dray and Hackney Carriage Licenses simultaneously.

In the recapitulation of receipts and payments "of the City Corporation from the 1st of Sept. 1814 to the 31st Aug. 1815," the amount for "City Badges issued to the owners of Slaves working out on hire" was given $3,134.21 (*Courier*, 2 September 1815). This is a step up from the year before. *It is estimated that 1,898 badges were sold.*

Someone who broke the badge law this fiscal year was "a Negro Wench named Mary, about 30 years of age, belonging to the estate of James Toussiger." She "Absented Herself ... without the smallest provocation.... [and] has frequently been seen about the city huxtering [sic] without either badge or ticket" (*City Gazette*, 20 October 1814). At about the same time, Sarah Solomon's slave, Hester, ran away. "As she has taken her badge with her, it is very likely she may say she is hired out" (*City Gazette,* 21 October 1814). These events happened in the part of the 1814-1815 fiscal year when the slaves were wearing 1814, not 1815, badges.

### *1815-1816 (1816 badges)*

At the end of the 1815-1816 fiscal year, $3,255.40 income was reported, another step up from the previous accounting period (*Courier*, 2 September 1816). *As many as 1,972 badges may have been sold.*

### *1816-1817 (1817 badges)*

Business continued to improve. "City Badges, for one year" brought in $3,561.32 in income (*Courier*, 2 September 1817). More income meant more badges sold; *estimates peg the number at 2,157.* It was during this fiscal year, that several articles of interest appeared in the newspapers concerning badges. On 19 October 1816, the *Courier* published a letter from "A Citizen" who complained about those with huckster or fruiterer badges buying up goods in the market and then selling them for more. As explained in greater detail in Chapter 1, City Council soon prohibited this practice.

All was probably back in order when the following advertisement appeared in the *Courier* of 27 December 1816:

> City Badges for 1817. I DO hereby give Notice to the Owners or Representatives of such Slaves, as are or may be working out on hire within the city, that I shall commence issuing Badges for the year 1817, on Thursday, *the 2d day of January next.* Wm. Roach, City Treasurer.

Later in this fiscal year, on 11 June 1817, the *Courier* published a breakdown of a census the City of Charleston took on June 1. It broke down white males, white females, slave and free colored males, and slave and free colored females for each of Charleston's four wards. The slave population totaled 11,515. Since an estimated 2,157 badges were sold in the fiscal year overlapping the June 1 census, it can be suggested that 18 percent of slaves were hired out in the city of Charleston in this period.

**1817 Servant, No. 121. (J. J. Lafar). In most odd years of this era, Lafar's badges were diamond-shaped.**

### *1817-1818 (1818 badge)*

In this fiscal report, the committee on finances reported both income and expenses; $3,792.60 came into the city; and $280.25 for "City Badges for 1818, [was] paid for making sundry badges through the year" (*Courier*, 5 September 1818). The less than a rounded dollar amount for income, then, is puzzling, since all badges cost even dollar amounts. Perhaps fines collected by the city for badge infractions are reflected. *An estimated 2,297 badges were sold in this period.*

### *1818-1819 (1819 badge)*

The city collected slightly less this period for badges, but paid out a bit more, reporting $3,702.44 in income and $296.50 in expenses (*Courier*, 5 September 1819). *Projections infer that 2,243 badges were sold.*

### *1819-1820 (1820 badge)*

A slight slump in receipts occurred in this fiscal year. "City Badges issued to owners of Slaves working out" brought in $3,383.94, and $310 was "paid for making them this year" (*Courier*, 4 September 1820). *Reflecting the lower*

**1820 Servant, No. 160. (J. J. Lafar). Lafar used this particular order of information in this year and in 1826.**

*income, it is suggested that only 2,050 badges might have been sold.* The U.S. census showed there were 12,652 slaves in the city of Charleston in 1820. If the suggested number of 2,050 slaves being hired out is correct, 16 percent of the slave population could have been wearing badges.

As for the badges surviving from this era, they are quite uniform in appearance compared to the ones made before, perhaps due to the fact that some of the experimentation had passed. Another reason for the growing conformity is due to the fact that one person, silversmith John Joseph Lafar, or his shop, was the creator of all of them; the previous period from 1800 to 1810 saw at least three different makers.

### *1811*

The badge that appeared in 1811 began an evolutionary process. Lafar took a square piece of copper (before they had been round or nearly octagonal) and scooped or scalloped its four corners to give it a slightly different look. It is similar to the 1810 badge, technically an octagon, but really a square badge with corners cropped on a diagonal to make eight sides. The corners of this 1811 badge, however, were cut curved towards the center, not straight. All the lines of text and the year "1811" were stamped, while the individual badge number was hand-engraved. The order of the text was: "Charleston" (stamped); "1811" (stamped); occupation (stamped); and number, the abbreviation "No" (stamped) and then a numeral (engraved).

### *1812*

This year introduced the first diamond-shaped badge, which would eventually become the predominant design for the entire period up to 1865. Squares, with corners clipped or not, having a hole punched in a corner, would appear diamond-shaped when suspended by a string or ribbon on the wearer's clothes or body. Again, the city name, the category name, and the year are stamped, as is "No." The order of the information is different from 1811; it is: "Charleston," number ("No." and numeral), occupation, date. Each individual badge number is hand-engraved.

### *1813*

In 1813, Lafar went back to the octagon shape used by both of his predecessors, Atmar and Prince, but his badges were larger than the former's and smaller than the latter's. Lafar, as did Prince (and probably Atmar), used the term "carpenter" for the handicraft tradesman category; this may be the last year that this term is used, for no badges with this term have been found after this year. All instead bear the term "mechanic." (It is possible that this may also be near the point in time when the term "huckster" vanishes. A mention of a huckster badge worn by a runaway dates from 1807, but an 1813 badge with the alternative term "fruiterer" has been found; and in 1813, the laws were revised, and the fee for this category "seller of fruits and cakes" was raised to $15.) Further archeological finds will prove or disprove this theory. One thing that is not in doubt about this year, however, is *that its badges are the last to have any of its numbers engraved.* All subsequent years feature badge numbers individually punched. The order of information this year is "Charleston" (stamped), date (stamped), occupation (stamped) and "No" (stamped), numeral (engraved).

### *1814*

Another pattern began this year, when Lafar issued square badges. From this date forward through 1829, the even-numbered years (1814, 1816, 1818, 1820, 1822, 1824, 1826, 1828) would feature four-sided square badges with the hole for the ribbon or string punched not in a corner, but in a spot equidistant from the ends of the top side. This way the badge, when worn, would not look like a diamond, but a square, two sides parallel to the ground, two sides perpendicular to it. The badges bearing the odd-numbered years in this era (1815, 1817, 1819, 1821, 1823, 1825, 1827, and 1829) tend to be diamond-shaped. The four-sided square pieces of copper have their corners more pronouncedly clipped, and the hole to suspend the badge is punched in a corner, making the badge hang by a point of the diamond, with another corner pointing to the ground. This, of course, would be very useful for the public, affording all an immediate visual cue in determining whether or not the slave was wearing a badge appropriate for the year. Lafar, the maker of these badges, also served as a law enforcer, the city marshal, in many of these years. Not only was he making badges, but was also making his job as marshal easier to carry out!

There is another change that begins this year, one that also varies with the odd and even years. In *most* of the even years after 1814 (1816, 1822, 1824, 1828), the date is under "Charleston" and above the occupation, while the individual badge number is on the very bottom (1818, 1820 and 1826 show slight variations). On most of the odd years, however, the number of the individual badge is now between "Charleston" and the occupation, and the date (1815, 1817, 1819, 1821, 1823, 1827, 1829) is on the very bottom. (However, 1825 is different.)

The order of text for 1814, a slight variant from the following even-numbered years, is "Charleston" (stamped), "No" (stamped) and numeral (punched); occupation (stamped); "1814" (stamped).

## *1815*

Badges from the odd-numbered years, as just explained, were diamond-shaped, with the lines of text following the "odd year" format: "Charleston" (stamped), "No" (stamped) with numerals (punched), occupation (stamped), "1815" (stamped.) Badges from this year have been found in varying thicknesses of copper. Thicker copper badges stood (and stand) a greater chance of survival in the soil, and they would have been harder for slaves or taxpayers to bend or destroy.

One of the most unusual badges found is from this year. It was discovered in January 1995, and when the owner was cleaning it off, words appeared on the reverse: "Robt. Cheevers, 251 E. Bay" (see page F of color insert).

Badges were sold to owners or managers of slaves, but slaves themselves wore them. Records of the wearers and owners were made in the city treasurer's office (at the Exchange Building, at the foot of Broad Street at East Bay, in these years) so the badge, if found, could have been traced and returned to the owner, making the owner's name on it unnecessary. If the owner did not need to engrave his name on it, would the wearer?

Research suggests that this might have been the case. In fact it appears the engraver might have been the slave and not the slave owner. A few white Cheevers can be found in city records in the early 1800s. A Richard Holmes Cheevers, drayman, for instance, lived earlier, dying in 1803,[2] and in the 1850s, there existed a free woman of color named Peggy Cheever, who mentioned a granddaughter Margaret, Margaret also having been the name of the white Cheevers' daughter.[3] In the list of free people of color taxpayers included in the city's published list of 1860, there is a Joseph Cheever, owning $1,000 worth of real estate.[4] Around 1815, however, there were no Cheevers listed in the directory. (There is a death record for an Oliver Cheevers, drowning at age 40 in 1819, but nothing else is known of him.) Since slaves were not listed in the directory (free people of color were), it would suggest that a Cheevers in 1815 would have been someone lacking both a permanent address and a free status. There is nothing conclusive one way or another, however, about the name. But the address leads to interesting and suggestive things.

Street numbers in Charleston have altered and shifted radically over the years, so no link to the present day 251 East Bay Street can be inferred. There was no directory published for Charleston in 1815, but one did appear in 1816, meaning that the data was probably compiled the previous year. The directory lists a Patrick M'Gann (sometimes referred to as McGann) living at the address in question (251 East Bay).[5] He must have rented, for there is no deed recorded in his name for that property, or any other. McGann was a watchmaker, and earlier court cases show him in debt for various things, such as watches and watch keys. A 1799 document referred to him as a silversmith.[6] In any case, as a watchmaker or silversmith, he would have been, in the parlance of a day, a mechanic. And the badge engraved with the address "251 E Bay" *was* issued to a mechanic, but certainly not McGann himself, for he was a white Catholic from Ireland.[7] Any slave of his in the trade, or one hired to him to help in the shop, however, would have worn a mechanic's badge, and such a mechanic could have been skilled in engraving in tiny areas such as the back of a slave badge. So did McGann, as a mechanic, own a slave that he hired out as a mechanic, or did he hire a mechanic slave from someone else?

McGann was not a wealthy man; he would die in the workhouse, and census entries for him would reveal no slaves in his household in this era.[8] And besides, wouldn't a slave owned by McGann carry his (McGann's) name, and not a name like Robert Cheevers? And if a slave he hired *was* named Robert Cheevers, wouldn't that mean the slave was owned by a white Cheevers in 1815?

Not necessarily. If a slave signed his name Cheevers, it could mean that he was once owned by a Cheevers, but no longer. For proof of this theory, that slaves did not necessarily carry the names of their current owners, one just has to just look to the Denmark Vesey trial record published seven years later in 1822. At least five slaves in that record carry different last names from the last names of their owners, even though the preponderance of the slaves *do* have their owner's name attached to them, if a surname is mentioned.[9] So, a slave named Robert, owned long-time by a Cheevers, perhaps that drayman who died in 1803, could have passed into Patrick McGann's hands or, more likely (since McGann owned no slaves), the slave could have been hired by him. (And, in fact, there are records of this Richard H. Cheevers selling mulatto slaves.)[10]

Reinforcing this theory is the fact that McGann was intimately associated with a woman who hired out slaves. That she was once a slave herself and was once owned by McGann is an extra bit of fascinating history.

She first appears in the legal records as a mulatto female slave named Bash (with her two male children, George and Angus) sold by Benjamin Moore to Philip Lewis on 19 November 1795 (the sale would not be recorded until August 1805).[11] Then, in 1798, Lewis transferred ownership or all his "right claims and titles to these premises" to Patrick McGann. Jervis Henry Stevens, who would always stay involved with this woman, Bash, witnessed that transfer to McGann. (And interestingly enough, a man named Alex Shivas, similar sounding to the name Cheevers in this era of unregulated spelling, also witnessed part of the transaction.)[12]

Seven years later, the relationship between McGann and Bash changed and was no longer one of master and slave. For on 30 July 1805, Patrick McGann and a woman called variously Barshaba, Barsheba and Bashaba Cattle, Cattel, or Catell or Catel, jointly sold slaves together. She was illiterate and just made a mark, while McGann signed his name.[13]

There is no doubt that this Bashaba Cattel is the same female sold to McGann; for just a week or so later, McGann, in an odd transaction dated August 1805, sold a "Mustizo woman named Barshaba together with her two male children George and Angus" to Jervis Henry Stevens, the same fellow who witnessed the earlier sale of Bash to McGann.[14] It is relevant to note that all these transfers of Bash or Bashaba to a variety of people were recorded all on the same date. Obviously at this date, an attempt was being made to set her record straight and clear up her legal status. (What is interesting, too, is that when Cattell sold slaves with McGann in July 1805, she was still technically a slave herself. It appears she was the true slave owner, and not McGann; he never sold a slave, other than Cattell herself, alone, but always with her as a partner.)

One can guess why it was necessary to clear up her status. Sometime after this, she is free. An 1812 document shows Patrick McGann acting as trustee for Barshebe Catel in selling slaves; she makes her mark; he signs.[15] In 1814, McGann, "trustee for Barsheba Cattell by and with the consent of said Barsheba," sells another slave.[16]

The most telling and poignant document, however, is Barsheba's will and codicil or addition to it made Christmas Eve and Christmas, 1818. She calls herself "a free colored person of the city of Charleston," and mentions a slave named Bob. As conveniently as possible after her death, she requests that her executors sell Bob who apparently is valuable (as a mechanic slave would be) for the benefit of "my friend Patrick McGann, and my daughter Jane Rebecca McGann, share and share alike." She also mentions a slave named Nancy, and directs her executors to receive the wages of "the said wench," showing that

Cattle did, indeed, make money off her slaves by hiring them out. As her executors, she appointed the same Jervis H. Stevens, who witnessed her sale to McGann in 1798, and who once owned her, as well. (He also was Sheriff of Charleston; interestingly enough, the other executor she named, but who did not serve, was Lionel Kennedy, Esquire, who in a few years would serve as one of the judges at the trial of Denmark Vesey.) In her codicil, she directed some of her silver (perhaps silver made by McGann) be given to her daughter and should her daughter die, she directed that her estate go to McGann. McGann and Stevens became her executors, when her will was probated 3 February 1819, meaning she was dead by that date.[17] (McGann would not die until 1834.)

Does this mean that the slave she called Bob in her will was Robert Cheevers who engraved his name on a 1815 mechanic slave badge? Not necessarily. There is no definite proof, but the facts are very suggestive: McGann was a watchmaker and repairer, whose common-law wife sold slaves and who hired out slaves she owned; she held a slave called Bob; and when her estate was inventoried by the court in July of 1819, it noted "An old Negro Man, Robert" whom they valued at only $125. (Her Negro woman named Nancy, whom in her will Barsheba said was 38 years old and worth $550, was listed at only $230.)[18] Any slave hired to McGann by Barsheba Cattel would probably have been a mechanic; such a slave would very likely have known how to engrave, and maybe to show his own worth, now that he was aged, he sat down and carved his name and address of McGann's shop in 1815. This also agrees with the those John Bennett interviewed in 1903 who said slaves were proud to wear a badge.

### *1816*

These badges follow the "even year" description given in the data for 1814: "Charleston" comes first, then "1816," Occupation, and "No" with numeral. Only the badge numeral is punched; all other information is stamped.

### *1817*

The badges are diamond-shaped with text on four lines as follows: "Charleston," "No" with numeral, occupation, then "1817." Everything is stamped but for the punched numeral.

### *1818*

The even years between 1814 and 1828 feature square-shaped slave badges. But this year is slightly different with the text. On 1818 badges, the first line

**1818 Mechanic, No. 94. (J. J. Lafar). In most even years of this era, Lafar's badges were square-shaped. Only in this year did Lafar put data in this particular order.**

**1819 Servant, No. 728. (J. J. Lafar). This is the largest diamond-shaped badge Lafar made, in the same year he became City Marshal.**

is "Charleston"; under that is the occupation; next comes "1818"; and finally the individual badge number, configured, as always, with "No" followed by a numeral (all stamped, but for this punched numeral). Nearly all other "even year" badges in this era follow the pattern of "Charleston," year, occupation, and then "No" and numeral. Lafar seems to have been tripped up in his own method this year.

### *1819*

This follows the "odd year" formula, being diamond-shaped. (For an explanation, see the text under section "1814.") But this is the largest diamond made by John J. Lafar. The order is "Charleston" (stamped); "No" (stamped) and numeral (punched); occupation (stamped); "1819" (stamped).

### *1820*

This year follows the "even year" formula, but again, as in 1818, there is a variation. (Again, see the description under "1814.") Under "Charleston" (on the first line) comes occupation on the second line; "No" with the badge numeral is on the third line, followed on the bottom line with the year. All are stamped, except for the punched badge numeral. (The 1826 and 1859 badges would follow this pattern.)

Tabulated, the period from 1811 to 1820 looks like this (with estimates in *italics*):

| *Fiscal Year* | *Badge Year* | *# of Badges* | *Income* | *Expenses* | *Maker* |
|---|---|---|---|---|---|
| 1810-1811 | 1811 | *881* | 1,807.13 | | Lafar |
| 1811-1812 | 1812 | *1,106* | 2,269.39 | | Lafar |
| 1812-1813 | 1813 | *1,227* | 2,025.84 | | Lafar |
| 1813-1814 | 1814 | *1,338* | 2,208.80 | | Lafar |
| 1814-1815 | 1815 | *1,898* | 3,134.21 | | Lafar |
| 1815-1816 | 1816 | *1,972* | 3,255.40 | | Lafar |
| 1816-1817 | 1817 | *2,157* | 3,561.32 | | Lafar |
| 1817-1818 | 1818 | *2,297* | 3,792.60 | 280.25 | Lafar |
| 1818-1819 | 1819 | *2,243* | 3,702.44 | 296.50 | Lafar |
| 1819-1820 | 1820 | *2,050* | 3,383.94 | 310.00 | Lafar |

"Badge year" denotes the predominate badge sold during the fiscal year.

# Chapter 5

# 1821–1830

## *1820-1821 (1821 badges)*

The financial report for the fiscal year running from September 1820 through August 1821 was published in *The Southern Patriot*, 1 September. It stated that "City Badges issued to owners of Slaves working out" brought the city $2,736.16; no expense category is noted. *It is estimated that only 1,618 badges were sold this year, less than the year before and the year after.*

## *1821-1822 (1822 badges)*

This year included the summer of the Denmark Vesey slave rebellion, trial, and hanging. For some reason, the books were closed on the 29th of August 1822 instead of the 31st (*Charleston Mercury*, 2 September 1822). The amount brought in was $3,424.28, with the cost for making the badges, *2,074 by estimation,* being a very low $17.50. (Perhaps a plethora of badges were carried over from the year before.) As discussed in Chapter 1, some of the slaves in the rebellion were hired-out men who abused the practice and actually used their time to aid the conspiracy. The fact came out in the trial, and as a result, the City Council petitioned the State Legislature for help. The aim was to somehow help the city reduce the number of slaves in town. Specifically targeted were "the Domestics, handicraft persons and all those who hire themselves out or are hired by their owners."[1] The only real result coming from the state legislature was a new *state* law forbidding any hired-out slave to be in charge of himself; i.e., a slave could not be hired out to just bring in money for his master; he now had to be controlled by someone else.

For this fiscal year, there are other records extant that help document the slave-hire practice and its abuse. Scratch copies of City Council minutes exist in manuscript, these being the notes that would be copied over in a fair hand, and added to the permanent record. Other than these and some fragments from the mid–1830s, no other antebellum manuscript minutes are known to have survived.

These minutes show people petitioning City Council for relief of fines meted out to them for slave badge abuse. The 10 December 1821 minutes show Mr. Otis Mills "praying to be relieved from the payment of a fine of $16 incurred by his employing 4 negroes, who had no Badges to work out." Council rejected his plea; as it did that of Mrs. Mary Ramsay, who, on 17 December, asked that the "fine incurred by her servant selling fruit without a Badge be remitted" (City Council Minutes, 10 and 17 December 1821). At the 12 February 1822 meeting, Council did remit the fine incurred by John Burbaum [?] for his Negro working without a badge; but it rejected similar petitions from D. Fogartie, Frances Smith, Rebecca Jackson, and Joseph Winthrop. On 26 March, Council received petitions from a Mr. Addison and Marks Lazarus for slave badge violations, the latter for "hiring out a small Boy without a Badge." Their pleas to have their fines revoked were rejected. Lydia Bryant told City Council on 19 April that she had hired a Negro to Mrs. Bell "for stated Wages ... requesting to be informed if it is requisite for her to take out a badge." It was.

The city remitted half the fine, that part owed it (and not the informant) when Robert Buttes petitioned for relief on behalf of Mary Gatton's Negro working without a badge (3 June 1822). At the 27 August meeting, while still paying out charges incurred in the trials of Denmark Vesey, City Council heard the petition of Mary Roddey asking for the refund of the fine she paid for her Negro working out without a Badge. It was referred to the Committee on Relief, whose actions are not known. These records afford a glimpse of the day-to-day use and abuse of slave badge laws.

A slave who wore a badge this year was a "Negro Girl CLARINDA, about 17 years of age, yellow complexion, about 5 feet high, round face, good set of teeth, is very talkative, and well known in this city. She was bought from the estate of Axon some time ago; resorts [to] certain houses in the city and suburbs; has badge No. 176." Clarinda's 1822 badge was probably marked "Servant" (*Courier*, 11 April 1822).

## *1822-1823 (1823 badges)*

The *City Gazette* for 12 September 1823 reported on income and expenses of the past fiscal year in the city. "Funds of the City Corporation from the 1st September, 1827, to 20th February, 1823, taken from the Books of the Late Treasurer," showed income for badges of $392; expenses for making additional 1822 badges, $30.75; and $298.75 for making 1823 badges. After the treasurer's death and a new person began occupying the position, the records began at 21 February 1823 and continued until the end of August. In that period, $1,740 came in from badge income and an extra $140 had to be paid out to continue making 1823 badges. All in all, in this fiscal year, $2,132 came in as income and badges cost $469.50. *It is estimated that only 1,261 badges were sold and that number of slaves was hired out,* a great decrease of 40 percent from the year before, suggesting that the Denmark Vesey rebellion, and fear of those slaves who hired their time, might have had an impact on the practice in the year after the dramatic events. (Disputing this, however, is the fact that several 1823 "Servant" badges are known that have numbers in the 1700s; this would suggest that many more badges than the formula suggests were made. The formula, as explained in the appendix, is based on the percentages of badges sold in various categories for a later fiscal year; these percentages were not necessarily the same each year.)

One slave who had an 1823 badge was "Mary, a washerwoman on the Green. Her badge is No. 471," her owner stated in an ad seeking her return (*Courier,* 26 March 1823).

### *1823-1824 (1824 badges)*

Figures for this year show a bouncing back in the hiring-out practice; $183 came in for badges from 1 September 1823 until the end of the calendar year. $5,496 came in for the next eight months (January through August) of 1824, for a total amount of $5,679, the largest amount for any fiscal period to date. The city paid out $23.62 for the making of additional 1823 badges (most likely from September through December 1823); and for badges made in 1824, it paid $453.50, the total expense being $482.12. The newspaper (*Courier*, 4 September 1824) states that the money was paid out to J.J. Lafar; thus, for the second time a specific badge maker is named in the city's financial reports. *Mathematical estimates suggest that 3,440 badges were made in this period, a great step up.* On 7 August 1824, the *Courier* published a census for the city of Charleston in which it noted there were 13,858 slaves in all four wards of the city. (There were 12,357 whites and 1,698 free people of color counted.) The numbers suggest that 24 percent of slaves were hired out. One reason that the number of slave badges sold and slaves hired out may have risen this year is that there was a boost in the local economy, with cotton prices rising from an 1819 depression.

### *1824–1825 (1825 badges)*

Lafar continued as badge maker this year. He was paid $5.62 for additional 1824 badges he had to make. He was then paid $466.25 for badges he made for the year 1825. The city's total expense then was $471.87; and its total income was $5,397, the figure being the sum of the amount that came in for badges from 1 September to 31 December 1824 ($165) and for the first eight months of 1825 ($5,232). Although the city did not report on a definite number of badges sold *(estimates set the figure at 3,269),* it is still possible to see the gross amount has nearly tripled from some of the first years in the century. Lafar also made some extra money for making tin badges this year, tin apparently being for the cart and dray badges (*Courier*, 5 September 1825). This was a banner year for cotton, and the city thought it was on the verge of a new economic boom.

### *1825-1826 (1826 badges)*

The numbers seem similar for this year as the year before, as reported in the press (*Mercury*, 2 September 1826). From 1 September 1825 to the end of the year, the city brought in $155 for slave-hire badges; and from 1 January 1826, through 31 August, another $5,300 came in, totaling $5,455, with the city paying out $461.87, with no badge maker being articulated. (From the extant badges, with his name stamped on the back, it is obvious that Lafar was still making them.) *Estimates suggest that 3,304 badges were produced and sold.*

**1826 Mechanic, No. 336. (J. J. Lafar). This duplicates the exact order of the 1820 badge.**

### *1826-1827 (1827 badges)*

According to the financial records for this fiscal year (*Charleston Mercury*, 1 September 1827), income was $171 for the last four months of 1826, and $7,077 for the first eight months of 1827, for a total of $7,248, an enormous increase of $1,622 from the year before. By referring back to the statutes, one can explain this growth. For on 28 December 1826, just as the new 1827 badges were to go on sale, the price for servants badges doubled, at least for those servants over 14 years of age. Information available for subsequent years, and the high numbers of servant badges found, testify to the fact that there were more "servants" sold each year than any other category. So it makes sense that since this large category doubled in price, that the amount coming into the city coffers would increase. If all else remained the same, this might mean that there were about 1,600 servants hired out this year, which may be likely, as it is known that 2,400 servant badges would be made in the year in 1850. *(The estimate for badges sold this year is 3,314.)* For expenses, $8.12 was paid out to cover badges made in the closing months of 1826; and $459.37 for "copper Badges; and 26.50 for tin badges for Carts and Drays" was paid out in the later period. The total expenses for slave badges for that fiscal year was $467.49.

### *1827-1828 (1828 badges)*

Income for this period was $158 and $6,579 in the two periods; and expenses were $9.37 and $437.50. This would make this year's totals $6,737 in income and $446.87 in disbursements (*Charleston Mercury*, 29 August 1828). *It is estimated that 3,080 badges were sold.*

### *1828-1829 (1829 badges)*

No financial year-end report has been found for this period. *But by splitting the difference between the two known years, estimates suggest that income was $7,151, and in consequence, 3,270 badges were sold.* The newspapers tell of one slave who had a badge this fiscal year: Eve, described as "tall and thin, of a yellowish-black complexion, and bloated appearance in the face; [she] was dressed in black—small gold bead rings in her ears, and a string of gold and coral around her neck." She "took advantage of a badge" and was absent for four months before her owner at 65 Broad Street, advertised for her (*Courier*, 30 September 1828).

### *1829-1830 (1830 badges)*

The income reported for badges was composed of $586 for the period September through December 1829, and $6,979 from January through September 1830, amounting to $7,565, an increase from the newspaper reports of September 1828, especially in the first four months (Charleston *Mercury*, 3 September 1830). Expenses for these two categories were $19.87 and $424.11, respectively, for a total of $443.98. (A slightly different category of expenses is listed this year: $216 was "paid for painting numbers on tin," suggesting a different way of marking the cart and dray badges.) *Estimates suggest a total of 3,459 badges were produced.* The fourth federal census was taken this year, counting 18,721 slaves in the city. If 3,459 slaves were hired out, that would mean that 18 percent of the slave population was in this category.

As for what the badges looked like, as explained in the section under the description of the 1814 badges in the previous chapter, they followed an odd/even year pattern.

### *1821*

The 1821 badge was diamond-shaped, starting with "Charleston" on the top line, followed by "No" and the numeral on the next line, occupation on the third line of text, and then "1821" on the last line. All data was stamped except for the badge numeral, which was punched.

### *1822*

The badges this year were similar in shape, text and execution to the 1816 badges; first line, "Charleston (stamped), second, "1822" (stamped); third, occupation (stamped); and fourth, "No." (stamped) and numeral (punched).

### *1823*

**1823 Servant, No. 229. (J. J. Lafar). Note that Lafar stamped his name on the front; this is the only year that he uniformly used his initials, "J.J.," as well as his last name.**

1823 badges follow the odd-year pattern, being diamond-shaped and having the lines of text and numerals as described in the 1821 badges. Yet these, the first made after the Vesey affair, are somewhat different. Badge maker Lafar stamped his name "JJLafar" on them, instead of the usual "Lafar" seen in the earlier years. The designation, oddly enough, appears on the front side of 1823 badges, under the year, and not on the reverse. This makes the badges from this year carry five lines of text, with Lafar's name on the

**1824 Porter, No. 469. (J. J. Lafar). Lafar has stamped his name on the front, but with no initials. The same holds true for 1825.**

bottom. As to why suddenly Lafar put his name on the front of the badge, one can only guess. Did it have to do with a show of force to hired-out slaves, showing them that the sheriff was somehow monitoring them through the badges they wore? Possibly, or it could have meant nothing. For although Lafar was sheriff of Charleston (and a City Council member), he played no great role in the Denmark Vesey rebellion, at least according to the official reports published, which do not mention his name. He did play a small role perhaps in events leading up to it: in January 1821, he warned black minister Morris Brown that he could no longer hold a school for slaves, since it was against the law. This prompted one leader of the insurrection, Monday Gell, to redouble his efforts.[2] In 1823, Servant badge no. 471 was worn by a washerwoman on the Green named Mary. Her owner offered a $5 reward for her return in the 26 March 1823 *Courier.*

### *1824*

The badges from this year have just "Lafar" (not "JJLafar") stamped on the front, on the bottom line. All are square, with "Charleston" first; then "1824"on the second line; occupation on the third line, and "No" on the bottom, followed by the numeral. One odd 1824 "Mechanic" badge, however, with "JJ Lafar" stamped on the front, similar to 1823 badges, is known. Again, as with all the badges in this decade, all data is stamped but for the punched badge numerals.[3]

### *1825*

This follows and ends the pattern of the Lafar stamp being on the *front* of the badge—as always on the very bottom. This year, they are diamond-shaped and follow the pattern exactly of the year before, which is a variation on the odd-year theme.

### *1826*

1827 Servant, No. 646. (J. J. Lafar). A typical diamond shape for odd years in this era.

The badges are square. The placement of the lines is: "Charleston"; occupation; "No" followed by the badge's numeral; and then "1826," a variation on the arrangement of text and numbers on most badges from the even years from 1816–1828. "Lafar" appears on the back, as it did before 1823.

### *1827*

These badges follow the pattern of the 1823 badges, but "Lafar" is stamped on the back. The order is "Charleston" (stamped), "No" (stamped) and numeral (punched), occupation (stamped) and "1827" (stamped).

### *1828*

The badges, as expected, are square and follow the pattern of even years of this decade, except for 1818, 1820 and 1826. The one notable thing is that it is the last time that "Lafar" is stamped anywhere on it (all on the back this year). Although Lafar continued to make badges, he no longer marked them with his name.

1828 Servant, No. 918. (J. J. Lafar). This is the last year Lafar used a square shape (and the last time he stamped his name on the back).

### *1829*

Badges are diamond-shaped. The lines of text in order are: "Charleston"; "No" with numerals; occupation; and then "1829." All are stamped but for the badge numerals, which, as is the pattern, are punched.

**1830 Servant, No. 1531. (J. J. Lafar). All workmanship shows this to be Lafar, but he did not stamp his name on the back.**

### *1830*

The shifting from square to diamond shape in alternating years is now over. The 1830 badges are diamond-shaped like the year before; the only difference between this year and 1829 (other than the date) is the placement of the badge number, for now the badge number is on the bottom line and the year "1830" is on the second line. This pattern of switching positions between odd and even years will now be followed through 1834. So, the order is "Charleston," "1830," occupation, and "No" with numeral on the bottom line.

The figures for this decade look like this (figures in *italics* are estimates):

| *Fiscal Year* | *Badge year* | *# of Badges* | *Income* | *Expenses* | *Maker* |
|---|---|---|---|---|---|
| 1820-1821 | 1821 | *1,618* | 2,736.16 | | Lafar |
| 1821-1822 | 1822 | *2,074* | 3,424.28 | 17.50 | Lafar |
| 1822-1823 | 1823 | *1,261** | 2,132.00 | 469.50 | Lafar |
| 1823-1824 | 1824 | *3,440* | 5,679.00 | 482.12 | Lafar |
| 1824-1825 | 1825 | *3,269* | 5,397.00 | 471.87 | Lafar |
| 1825-1826 | 1826 | *3,304* | 5,455.00 | 461.87 | Lafar |
| 1826-1827 | 1827 | *3,314* | 7,248.00 | 459.37 | Lafar |
| 1827-1828 | 1828 | *3,080* | 6,737.00 | 437.50 | Lafar |
| 1828-1829 | 1829 | *3,270* | *7,151.00* | | Lafar |
| 1829-1830 | 1830 | *3,459* | 7,565.00 | 443.98 | Lafar |

"Badge year" denotes the predominate badge sold during the fiscal year.

*Extant 1823 badges with higher numbers suggest that more than 1,261 badges were made.

# Chapter 6

# 1831–1840

### *1830-1831 (1831 badges)*

The 1830-1831 fiscal year saw $119 being brought in for the last four months of 1830 and $6,561 for the months of January through August 1831, totaling $6,680. Expenses were $7.25 and $366, (for a total of $343.25) without the tin dray and cart badge category being mentioned, although there are notations for cart and dray owners buying additional badges (*Courier,* 2 September 1831). *Estimates suggest that 3,054 badges were sold in this period.* One slave who should have but did not wear a badge was Nance, described as "stout, has a flat nose, large mouth, and full projecting eyes." She absconded from her owner, J. Henry, on 14 February 1831. "It is believed," Henry advertised in the paper (*Courier*, 15 March 1831), "that she is harbored by some person washing clothes, as she is a remarkably good washerwoman, and has no badge."

### *1831-1832 (1832 badges)*

The fiscal statement shows income "to City Badges, for 1831, received this amount, 4 months, $181; to city badges for 1832, received this amount, eight months, $7472." Together that makes income $7,653. On the other side of the ledger, there is "City Badges for 1832 for making Copper badges, 266.10" (*Courier,* 1 September 1832). *Perhaps as many as 3,499 slave-hire badges were sold.*

### *1832-1833 (1833 badges)*

In 1832, the city started to advertise for contracts to be submitted by those interested in making the badges for the next year. Before this period, the city had been placing advertisements in the paper in November for various other contracts; in 1828 and 1830, for instance, it had advertised for blacksmiths, printers, butchers, and bakers seeking contracts with City Council, the ads appearing under the signature of William Roach, Clerk of Council. (An earlier ad to solicit contracts had appeared decades before in 1801.) The following appeared on 1 November 1832 in the Charleston *Courier*:

> CONTRACT: PERSONs desirous of Contracting with the City Council for making, lettering, and numbering about three thousand Copper Badges, and finding the necessary Copper: also for finding tin, making, painting and numbering about 280 badges for Carts and Drays, will send in proposals jointly and separately, addressed to the Committee on contracts, and to be left with the subscriber previous to the 10th of November next. WM. ROACH, Clerk of Council, Oct. 29.

City Council apparently let the contracts by 19 November: John C. Millar was announced as city baker and Henry J. Harry, city blacksmith. Isaac Holmes was named to supply the City Institutions with wood, and John J. Lafar was named "to make the City Badges" (Charleston *Courier*, 20 November 1832).

When the city accounts were printed in the *Courier* on 2 September 1833, the amounts showed "City badges for 1832, 131.00; for 1833, 7,208.00"; and "City Badges, for 1832, paid for making Additional Badges, 5.95. City Badges for 1833, paid for Copper Badges, 219.90." In total, the amount this fiscal year came to $7,339 in income, and $225.85 in expenses; "about three thousand were made this year" the paper stated, *and statistical estimates come close, pegging the number* ***sold*** *at 3,356.*

## *1833-1834 (1834 badges)*

On 18 November 1833, the *Courier* announced that John J. Lafar won the contract again with City Council. The income column published in August of 1834 showed $206 received from September through December 1833; and $7,515 for the first eight months of 1834. Total income thus was $7,721, while expenses were $240.66, the city paying $1.80 for additional badges for the final months of 1833; and $238.86 for copper badges from January through August 1834 (Charleston *Mercury*, 30 August 1834). Since this number is higher than the number for the year before when approximately 3,000 badges were called for, one can deduce that more than 3,000 were made this year. *In fact, it is estimated that 3,530 badges were sold in this fiscal year.*

### *1834-1835 (1835 badges)*

Fragmentary City Council minutes show some of the petitions of citizens regarding the badge laws in this fiscal year. Charles A. Magwood prayed for relief of a fine at the 6 October 1834 meeting; William Gayer, Susan M. Cleary and G. H. Rumph did as well at the 23 December 1834 meeting; the city agreed to relieve these and many other fines imposed at the 13 January 1835 meeting. On 10 February 1835, John Robinson, Charlotte C. Keith, Phebe Lewis, Sophia Price and Mrs. Snowden petitioned for "relief under the Badge Law." All were granted their wish except for Mrs. Snowden; the Committee on Relief asked to be excused from ruling on her request.[1] Sarah Fuller asked for relief at the 11 March meeting, which was granted 24 March. Mary King, Sarah Webber and Sarah A. Glen petitioned for the same thing on 7 April 1835; the fate of their request is unknown.

Earlier in the fiscal year, at the 18 November 1834 meeting, council had given the contract to make city badges to John and Peter Mood; they turned around and did this quickly, having the 1835 badges ready by the 23 December 1834 meeting when they asked to be paid $199.50 for the badges they made. City Council approved. Tabulating the fiscal year, the City reported that it brought in $119 for badges in the tail end of 1834; and $7,553 came in from 1 January to 1 September 1835, for a grand total of $7,672. Making the badges cost the city $3.60 for the tail end of 1834 and $199.50 for the first eight months of 1835, totaling $203.10 for the fiscal year (Charleston *Mercury,* 4 September 1835). Again, it can be seen the number of badges sold is probably over 3,000. *3,508 is the number estimated sold.* In the collections of the Charleston Museum, there is a receipt for slave badges sold in this fiscal year: "Recd July 20th 1835 of A. Wallace Esq.," it begins, "nineteen dollars for Badges for 1835 for Sam, Lisbon, Jenny, Charles, Bill, Frank, Harriet and Eliza." It is signed H. Maxcy, T.M.

### *1835-36 (1836 badges)*

On 6 October 1835, Moses Jacobs petitioned Council for "relief under the Badge Law." The Committee on Relief's ruling is not known.[2] A month or so later, on 10 November 1835, the City Council placed an advertisement:

> Persons desirous of Contracting with the City Council for making, lettering and numbering 3,300 Copper badges, and finding the necessary Copper; also for finding Tin, making, painting and numbering about 300 Badges for Carts and Drays, will send in proposals jointly and separately, addressed to the Committee on Contracts, and to be left with the Subscriber, on or before the 14th of November, inst.

Again it was signed William Roach, Clerk of Council (*Courier*, 13 November 1835). By 17 November, William M. Rouse had been selected, perhaps because of his low bid (*Courier*, 18 November 1835). When the city next published its fiscal report (Charleston *Mercury*, 2 September 1836), it showed income of $1.95 for badges for the remaining months of 1835, and a step up, $8,105, for the next year's first eight months (totaling $8,106.95). It paid out $188.49 "for making copper and tin badges" for the end of 1835 and the first eight months of 1836. *Estimates are that 3,707 badges were sold.*

### *1836-1837 (1837 badges)*

The expenses and income were quite similar for this fiscal year as the year before. Badges brought in $151 for the last four months of 1836 and $7,990 through August 1837, totaling $8,141. (In this year the figures for carts and drays are now given, too: $166.50 in income for 1836, and $4,126.50 for 1837, for a total of $4,293.) All in all, this was a profitable year for the city, since total expenses for badges in 1837 was $135.20, a step down from the year before, perhaps because the badges were now getting smaller and using less copper. (Rouse made his badges smaller in 1837 than he had in 1836.) Also, there is no amount listed for making extra badges for the last four months of 1836, suggesting enough, and possibly extras, were made at the beginning of the year. In September or October of 1836, as fragmentary City Council records show, Miss Sarah C. Wakefield petitioned for relief under the Badge Law. On 1 November 1836, reporting on her petition, and those of others, the Committee on Relief agreed to their requests.[3]

The availability of the badges for this year was advertised in the Charleston *Mercury* on 13 January 1837:

> CITY BADGES FOR 1837: THE subscriber hereby gives notice that Badges for 1837, are now ready for delivery. They can in no case be delivered to a Negro, with or without a Ticket. Edward Roach, City Treasurer.

*Perhaps as many as 3,722 badges were sold. The figure may be lower, however.* It was at the end of March of this year, as explained in Chapter 2, that City Council raised rates for badges; most of the badges had been purchased by that time, but all those purchased between April and the end of August would have cost more, so if gross income was the same as the year before, as it nearly is, the gross number of badges sold was probably less.

From City Council minutes published in the newspapers, another detail emerges. On 6 June, Benjamin Cohen, guardian of Benjamin Walker, petitioned City Council "praying relief under the badge law." It was referred to the Committee on Ways and Means, and since these records are not known, neither is the result of his petition (Charleston *Courier*, 22 June 1837).

## *1837-1838 (1838 badges)*

William Rouse again was the choice for the City Council, he being announced to "make the Copper and Tin Badges." (City Council declared him the contract winner in its meeting of 16 November, reported in the *Courier* on 21 November.) When the fiscal year was closed at the end of August, it was reported that the amount for city badges for 1838 was $12,176. For the last months of 1837, it was $146 (Charleston *Mercury,* 1 September 1838). The total comes to $12,322, an enormous step up from the year before.

This could have been expected, and indeed it was. As noted, in March of 1837, City Council raised the cost of mechanic badges from $3 to $5, and doubled the price of porter badges (from $2 to $4) and that of fisher men and women (from $1 to $2). Furthermore, it now opened up slave hiring to those slave owners who lived outside of Charleston, for double the price of what those living in town had to pay. These increases had so worried the Mayor that just before the year 1838 began, he had warned City Council that something should be done. They referred it into committee, but on 1 January 1838, the new prices and opportunities for non-residents went into effect. The mayor need not have worried, for obviously the hiring-out practice was ingrained behavior; the city reaped a great profit from these increases, and even increased another badge price (for mechanics, from $5 to $7) in April of 1838, by which point most 1838 badges might have been sold.[4] For badges for 1838, the city paid $188.35, there being no separate entry stated for 1837. (For the next year, the dollar amount would be almost exactly the total dollar amount for this year, and it would be estimated that 3,730 badges would be needed.) *According to mathematical interpretations, 3,972 badges were sold in this period. But this does not take into account that some badges would have sold for double the amount, now that those out of town could pay those prices to hire out their slaves. So the number 3,730 may be about right.*[5]

(Carts and drays brought in $309.50 in the last months of 1837; and $4,810 for 1838, for a total of $5,119.50.)

## *1838-1839 (1839 badges)*

In the *Courier* of 1 November 1838, John Rogers, Clerk of Council, advertised for persons "desirous of ... making, lettering and numbering 3,730 COPPER BADGES, and finding the necessary copper. Also for finding tin, making, painting and numbering about 450 BADGES for Carts and Drays." William Rouse got the contract, reported City Council on 12 November 1838 (*Courier*, 14 November 1838). The accounts published the following August (Charleston *Mercury*, 30 August 1839) showed $12,122 coming in for the 1839 months, and $169 for 1838, altogether totaling $12,291. (Carts and drays brought in $303 for 1838 and $4,550 for 1839, totaling $4,853.) The amount listed as "paid for making" the badges was $178.75. According to City Council minutes of 11 February 1839, $176.25 had already been paid for making 1839 badges by this date, showing that, indeed, the lion's share was already spent in the early part of the calendar year (*Courier*, 14 February 1839). *There may have been 3,852 sold, according to estimates, very close to the 3,730 ordered; and again, the number sold should really be smaller, based on the double-priced badges being sold to those out of town hiring out their slaves.*

### *1839-1840 (1840 badges)*

A few months after closing the previous fiscal year, an advertisement appeared for making badges for the coming year, 1840. John R. Rogers, Clerk of Court, advertised for someone to make, letter and number about 4,000 copper badges, and to find the copper and tin, and make, paint, and number about 450 badges for carts and drays (*Courier*, 2 November 1840).

Experiencing a shortfall of income at the beginning of the fiscal year, City Council discussed funding and reported on "probable receipts," i.e., what it thought income for the city would be for that year. $12,000 was budgeted as income from badges (*Courier*, 16 September 1839).

The city actually did better than projections. At the end of the fiscal year it was reported that $197 came in for the badges for the rest of the year 1839; $13,372 followed in 1840, totaling $13,569. (For carts and drays $192.50 and $4,395.50, totaling $4,588, came in in these respective time periods.) The amount of $230.25 was paid for making the badges (Charleston *Mercury*, 5 September 1840). *Estimates suggest that 4,194 badges might have been sold in this period. Again, once allowing for a smaller number based on some double-priced badges, this estimate is right on target with the 4,000 badges called for.*

The 1840 census stated that there were 14,673 slaves in the city of Charleston for this year; if in fact all the 4,134 badges estimated sold this year is accurate, that would mean that about 27 percent of Charleston's slaves were hired out, living lives or carrying on tasks for others other than their masters.

For this year, and others following, data regarding badges is available from City Council minutes, published in the newspaper. At the 13 February 1840 meeting (reported in the *Courier* on the 15th), it was reported that on 6 February, a Negro was in court for not having a badge on his person and was fined

$2. A slave working without a badge on the 8th had his owner fined $20, half of which went to the city treasury (and the other half, presumably to the informer). Another slave without a badge, probably not in his possession, was fined $2 on 19 April (*Courier*, 29 April 1840). In May, a Negro (or his owner) was fined $10 for no badge (*Courier*, 14 May 1840), and several more in the same condition were arrested on May 15, 18, and 21, with fines ranging from $10 to $20. "These badge cases resulted from taking the census of Ward No. 2." Apparently someone vigilant, working on the 1840 Federal census, noted the breaking of law and reported it, probably getting himself half of the fines. Eight more "slaves were taken up working without badges, but not yet decided," later minutes report. That was followed by a long list of at least 15 more cases, some marked "fine remitted," others only having their "City part remitted," and still others remitted in full (*Courier,* 4 June 1840). At the next meeting on 16 June (reported in the *Courier*, 19 June 1840), Catherine Paget, obviously knowing that there was great latitude in fines, prayed "relief from a fine imposed for a servant working out without a badge." Marshal [Solomon] Moses reported a Negro woman hired with no badge, fined $10 by the Mayor, and a Negro man hired with no badge, fined only $5. Six more slaves with no badges were reported in the 17 July 1840 *Courier*, each case fined $10. Edward Sebring at this meeting petitioned City Council, "praying that the double-tax, as a non-resident, assessed on his negroes, mechanics, working in this city, may be reduced to a single tax, they not working out on hire."

In these years, following the new pattern that had emerged at the end of the previous decade, slave badges sported a different look. All were diamond-shaped, and for the first few years, the only difference from year to year, other than the particular date, was the placement of the badge numbers and the year numbers.

**1831 Servant, No. 939. (J. J. Lafar). Lafar has swapped the location of the stamped date and punched numerals of the year before.**

### *1831*

Lafar's diamond-shaped badges presented information with "Charleston" on the first line; "No" with numeral on the second line; occupation on the third line; and then date. All data was stamped, except for the punched slave badge numerals.

## *1832*

The text order on these badges was "Charleston," date, occupation, "No" with numeral. Again, except for the punched badge numerals, all other information was stamped.

They came from the shop of Peter and John Mood, who would lose the contract the next two years, but they would get it back at the end of 1834, for the 1835 badges. The Moods, Peter and John, were sons of an earlier silversmith, Peter Mood, Sr. (1766–1821), and they continued in partnership until about 1841. Their shop had a sign of crossed spoons, and soon they diversified, advertising themselves as "Wholesale and Retail Dealers and Manufacturers of Silver and Gold Ware." It appears they suffered a financial catastrophe when one of their employees got the head clerk inebriated, took his keys and stole all the inventory, leaving John to start over in business "with no capital but an honest name, skillful hands and an abiding trust in God." Peter, leaving the business, went to New York.[6]

Once again Charleston had a Methodist slave badge maker. As noted earlier, Methodists were known for their stand on the slavery issue; many favored abolition, and the church had a significant outreach into the slave population, teaching religion, if nothing else. Mood personified much of this. Born a Lutheran (and like many of their number, a member of the German Friendly Society), Mood, according to family tradition, was so moved by a Methodist service that he converted and brought the rest of his family as well to the church, eventually naming a son after the Methodist Bishop Francis Asbury. When Asbury visited Charleston, it is said that Mood and his family met with the Bishop and prayed over the problem of slaves and blacks in South Carolina; they decided to break the law and secretly teach black ministers to read and write. Mood, aside from his silversmith duties, was also a Methodist minister, serving as an itinerant preacher from about 1824 to 1830. In 1832, he organized a Sunday school for black children and maintained it personally for years, not backing down even when threatened with being tarred and feathered. His sons were also involved with educating blacks, serving the Methodist Church and doing what they could to ameliorate slavery, even standing up to attacks for their beliefs. John Mood's father-in-law, it is said, died on the West Coast of Africa returning freed slaves to the continent from which they were stolen. In the same vein, John Mood's son, Henry, once told a story of how he and his father were walking through the streets of Charleston when they saw a slave on the auction block making the Masonic sign of distress. Henry told his granddaughter how his father had sent him off to find others to help him buy the slave. (The granddaughter grew up to become the only South Carolina novelist to win the Pulitzer Prize for fiction.) Julia Peterkin, in her era, too, would be chastised for her too-human treatment of and empathy for blacks in her books and stories. It is quite intriguing then to see that such a man opposed to slavery would be in charge of stamping out slave badges that, once in the hand of a slave, could make his or her life better. There is no proof or even suggestion that Mood did anything to subvert the law (as he did in teaching blacks to read), but the possibility is tantalizing.[7]

### *1833*

The badges this year reverted to the 1831 pattern; "Charleston" was on the first line; then came "No" with its punched numerals; occupation followed. The last line bore the date "1833." Lafar was the maker.

### *1834*

This year, the pattern copied the 1832 shape and text layout exactly, the only difference, of course, being the calendar year. This was Lafar's last year as a badge maker.

**1834 Servant, No. 1464. (J. J. Lafar). This is the last year Lafar made badges.**

### *1835*

On 19 November 1834, the *Courier* announced that a contract went to John and Peter Mood, Jr., "to make the City Badges." These badges by the Moods are diamond-shaped, and they have data in this order: "Charleston," the badge number, occupation, then date. All information is stamped, except for the numeral which is hand-punched. It is important to note that from this point onward, the abbreviation "No" for "Number" disappears from the badges, and only the numeral itself appears. 1835 badges are the same shape and size used by Rouse the next year; it may be that he had leftover badges from the Moods. When Rouse made more badges the following year (1837), they were smaller.

### *1836*

The badge contract was awarded to William M. Rouse; his diamond-shaped badges for this year used a different typeface: there are small dots (.....) on his badges around the stamped occupations. Rouse also spelled differently from his predecessors. He spelled mechanic with a final "k" as some of the early statutes did; his badges for 1836, 1837 and 1838 all use the final "k." He swapped the order of date and number that the Moods had followed (see 1835), and stamped all his information, except for the badge number which he punched. The first line of text was "Charleston"; the second was "1836"; the third, occupation, then badge number. Rouse would continue to make badges to the end of the decade, their sizes growing smaller and smaller, either by design, due to the increased price of metal perhaps, or an increase in profit margin (or both).

William Madison Rouse was a silversmith, the son of a well-known Charleston leather man, shoemaker and tanner. The family had many slaves. In 1831, he won a medal for making an excellent set of spoons, while apprenticed to Silversmith John Ewan. The apprenticeship was for four years, and in 1834, when he was finished, he apparently went to work for himself, soon winning the city contract for 1836. He advertised making silver tea sets, but more often than not, in later years, listed himself as a jeweler, still staying in Charleston during the Civil War siege of the city, moving his store to 211 Meeting Street, the corner of Burns Lane. He would become a watchmaker, and later the keeper of St. Michael's clock, a position paid for by the city. Rouse made more slave badges than any other maker, manufacturing thousands within his particular years. He lived on in Charleston until 12 September 1888, dying at 76. He is buried in Magnolia Cemetery.[8]

### *1837*

Made by Rouse, these badges are diamond-shaped, and the order of information is "Charleston," badge number, occupation, then date. Data, but for the punched badge number, is stamped.

### *1838*

The badges for this year resemble those from 1837, but the lines bearing the date and the badge number are reversed from the year before.

### *1839*

These badges follows the 1837 pattern, all made by Rouse.

### *1840*

Badges from this year are just like the ones from 1838, bearing information in this order: "Charleston," date, occupation, and finally, the badge number.

**1840 Porter, No. 148. (W. M. Rouse). the difference is very noticeable in Rouse's dies and punches from those of his predecessor's. A maker's tools served as a "signature" of sorts.**

The following is a summation of these years (again, *italics* denote estimates):

| *Fiscal Year* | *Badge year* | *# of Badges* | *Income* | *Expenses* | *Maker* |
|---|---|---|---|---|---|
| 1830-1831 | 1831 | *3,054* | 6,680.00 | 343.25 | Lafar |
| 1831-1832 | 1832 | *3,499* | 7,653.00 | 266.10 | Mood |
| 1832-1833 | 1833 | (abt 3,000*) *3,356* | 7,339.00 | 225.85 | Lafar |
| 1833-1834 | 1834 | *3,530* | 7,721.00 | 240.66 | Lafar |
| 1834-1835 | 1835 | *3,508* | 7,672.00 | 203.10 | Mood |
| 1835-1836 | 1836 | (3,300*) *3,707* | 8,106.95 | 188.49 | Rouse |
| 1836-1837 | 1837 | *3,722* | 8,141.00 | 135.20 | Rouse |
| 1837-1838 | 1838 | *3,972* | 12,322.00 | 188.35 | Rouse |
| 1838-1839 | 1839 | (3,730*) *3,852* | 12,291.00 | 178.75 | Rouse |
| 1839-1840 | 1840 | (abt 4,000*) *4,191* | 13,372.00 | 230.25 | Rouse |

*Number of badges estimated, in press, to be made.

"Badge year" denotes the predominant badge sold during the fiscal year.

# Chapter 7

# 1841–1850

## *1840-1841 (1841 badges)*

The City advertised for bids to make 3,800 copper badges, and 450 tin badges for carts and drays in the *Courier* (2 November 1840.) City Council expected less income this year, perhaps due to the downturn in the economy; cotton was selling at the lowest price in 20 years. Council estimated at a meeting on 28 September 1840, soon after the beginning of the fiscal year, that the income from badges would be $10,000, and the cost for making them would be $226 (*Courier*, 30 September 1840). Members should have been happy at the end of the year when they surpassed their estimates in income. The total for income was $12,255, there being no separate totals for different calendar year portions (Charleston *Mercury*, 6 September 1841). The same holds true for expenses; only the total figure, $169.80, lower than what was estimated, is listed.

Some funds came in for fines. A slave caught working out for hire without a badge prompted a $10 fine in November (*Courier*, 12 November 1840). It was assessed, the newspaper stated a day earlier, against "Mr. Cannon's negro...." On 17 March 1841, the Recorder fined two owners/employers $10 each for slaves working without badges; on the 19th, the fine he imposed was $20. There were other cases on the 15th and 17th as well; and ten more "slaves belonging to different owners [were] detected working out without Badges ... to be decided on Thursday next, 25th, inst." (*Southern Patriot,* 24 March 1841). Those ten, Kit, Tilda, Charles, Dick, Alick, Charles, James, Prince, Rachel and Richard, were "fined by His Honor the Recorder $10, each, and amount paid. Five other cases of servants working out, not yet decided" (*Southern Patriot,* 5 May 1841).

Despite this income over projections, council members were not happy with the final income reported at the end of the fiscal year. At the 30 August 1841 meeting (*Courier*, 2 September 1841), they noted that total city expenditures exceeded income by $7,260. Expenditures, they stated, "would have been within the income, if the amount received for Taxes, Badges, etc., had been the same as the last year, of which we had no reason to doubt, but contrary to our calculations, we have received from these sources $10,000 less this year than the last." At first one may sympathize with this supposed sudden downturn in income, but the council members apparently conveniently forgot that at the beginning of this fiscal year, they had only budgeted $10,000 in income. (Besides, in actuality, badges were down just about $1,000 from the year before—and taxes down about $4,000, for a total of $5,000 or so, not the $10,000 they lamented.)

The 1841 badges were made by John Mood; it appears the paper mistook his name, confusing him with family member Henry, who was announced as "to make City Badges" in the 19 November 1840 Charleston *Mercury. Estimates suggest the number of badges sold this year to be 3,908,* very close to the 3,800 badges estimated.

## *1841-1842 (1842 badges)*

This fiscal year brought in $12,345 to the city coffers from the sale of slave badges, while carts and drays brought in $315 for the tail end of 1841, and $3,615 for the beginning months of 1842, for a total of $3,930. The expense for making badges was $132.90 (Charleston *Mercury* 3 September 1842). William M. Rouse got the contract for this year *and may have made 3,842 badges, according to estimates.*

There were not too many badge infractions reported this year in the City Council minutes; one of the few was noted in *The Southern Patriot* on 21 April 1842. At a meeting James M. Walker, Esquire, petitioned council on behalf of Mrs. Catherine Theus, "praying to be relieved from a penalty for her servant working out with a servant's badge in place of a Drayman's badge." The servant badge had cost her $2, but a drayman's or porter's badge was more expensive, it being $4.

On 14 April, the executors of Mrs. Lydia Jane Waring noted in their account book that they had to pay $22 regarding the slave Portius, $20 being paid in penalty for working with the wrong badge, $2 for exchanging the badge.[1] This account book details several years' worth of transactions regarding hired-out slaves and shows how financially rewarding it could be. Most of the slaves were house servants, costing the executors $2 a badge; Billy, a mechanic, once cost them $7. Although they often seemed to flout the law, apparently sometimes buying new badges in the middle of calendar years, on the anniversary of the previous purchase, instead of doing it all in the beginning of the year, they nevertheless paid attention to it. They paid out up to $22 a year for badges for slaves named Portius, Philip, Sander (Cassandra), Dorcas, and others. They made notations for costs accrued, for slave care, laying in, clothing, medicines, and room rent, but slaves brought in more money than they cost. July 1841, for instance, shows the following income: Cash for one month's wages from Philip, $5.50; from Sander, $7.50; from Portius, $10 ("two dollars being deducted in consequence of sickness"); Violet, $6; and Dorcas, $3.93. The next month shows $34.34 "Cash from Southern Wharf for four months hire of Frederick." In 1842, slaves were bringing the estate income from $28.50 to $32 for some months. Meanwhile wages for slaves hired out to plantations only brought $50 a year. The account book shows not just scrupulous accounting, but scrupulous care taken of slaves who, in turn, rewarded the estate and heirs handsomely.

### *1842-1843 (1843 badges)*

Early on this fiscal year, City Council addressed the issue of those avoiding paying monies due the corporation. "On the subject of slaves," it noted, "a large number are entirely omitted and the means of discovering the deficiency extremely difficult and uncertain." Looking at what records they had to rely on, they looked to the badge books. "Occasionally the number of Badges furnish a check or development, but only to a limited extent." Obviously, every person wearing a badge was a slave and all those slaves should be taxed; perhaps 20 percent or so of slaves wore badges, so this was helpful, but not enough. It was recommended that the City now add other data; it was suggested that "slaves be returned by name and probable age, as the best mode of discovering or correcting any omission." Ways of detecting free people of color who avoided taxes were discussed, too (*The Southern Patriot*, 6 October 1842). Many were still being caught. On 26 September 1842, Mrs. C. Cleary petitioned City Council "to be relieved from the penalty for her servant working out without a badge" (*The Southern Patriot*, 28 September 1842), and in December, Thomas Mortimer sought relief "from a fine for his servant working out without a badge" (Charleston *Courier*, 1 December 1842).

W. M. Rouse continued to make the badges this year, according to the *Courier* (16 November 1842). The total amount brought in amounted to $13,178 (with carts and drays earning $170 in the last four months of 1842, and $4,340 for 1843's first eight months, totaling $4,510). The cost for the badges came to $143.85 (Charleston *Mercury*, 31 August 1843). *Estimates project that 4,101 badges were sold in the period.*

## *1843-1844 (1844 badges)*

The 23 November 1843 issue of the *Courier* stated that John Mood got the contract "to furnish badges" for the upcoming calendar year. In January of the new year, advertisements appeared, stating that E. Roach, City Treasurer, "hereby notifies those concerned that he has commenced issuing BADGES, for the present year. They can in no case be delivered to a negro with or without a ticket." The tax ordinance was extracted as well, showing the fees for particular badges: handicraft tradesmen, $7; porter, carter and drayman, $4; fisherman, $4; fisherwoman, $2, and sellers of fruit and cakes, etc., $5. Finally, it was noted that "Licenses or Badges taken out by persons residing without the limits of the city, shall be charged double the above amounts" (*Courier,* 9 January 1844). At the end of this fiscal year the city had brought in $13,737 and spent $151.20 (Charleston *Mercury,* 30 August 1844). (Cart and Drays brought in $260 in the first four months of the fiscal year and $4,860 in the next eight for a total of $5,120.) *Perhaps as many as 4,275 badges were sold.*

## *1844-1845 (1845 badges)*

There was a bit of a downward trend in this period. The city took in $12,347 for badges for the fiscal year spanning 1844 and 1845; carts and drays brought in $5,290 (Charleston *Mercury,* 29 August 1845). The city paid out $143.44 to the badge maker, who was William Rouse (Charleston *Courier*, 23 November 1844). *Rouse made as many as 3,843 badges for the city to sell.*

**1845 Servant, No. 1784. (W. M. Rouse). A typical design with clipped corners.**

For some reason, Benjamin W. Warren had requested that City Council "refund one half the cost of a badge, taken out for his servant, August" (*Courier*, 30 September 1844).

## *1845-1846 (1846 badges)*

The downward trend continued, with the annual report (*Courier*, 2 September 1846) showing a total of $12,133 coming in (and carts and drays bringing in $4,940, a slightly lower figure, too). It cost the city $131.85 for the badges. No advertisement or report on award of the contract in the papers has been found for this year, but archeological evidence suggests Rouse kept the contract and produced badges similar to the year before. *Approximately 3,776 may have been sold,* almost exactly the number of badges to be called for the next year.

### *1846-1847 (1847 badges)*

In November 1846, the city again advertised for proposals (*Courier*, 5 November). It was assumed "at least 3,775 Copper Badges," and "about 365 [tin] badges for carts, drays and omnibuses" would be needed. W. M. Rouse was announced as winning the contract (*Courier*, 24 November 1846).

In April of 1847, John Chalk petitioned to be relieved of the fine he was levied for a slave working without a badge (Charleston *Courier*, 7 April 1847). He was referred to the Committee on Relief, which ruled next month that he be relieved only of the half due the corporation. At the same meeting, W. M. Pelot, on behalf of J. M. Verdier, asked "to be relieved from the payment of a fine for an alledged violation of the Badge Ordinance." And as for Mrs. Huard's petition, "the Committee asked to be discharged from the further consideration of the case" (Charleston *Courier*, 19 May 1847). S. W. Lawton asked for relief, too (Charleston *Courier*, 3 May 1847). In June (*Courier*, 3 June 1847), three more Charlestonians, Charles E. Crawley, James Harrol and M. N. Venning, asked relief for the same thing. All had the city portion of their fines remitted at the next meeting; the Committee on Relief decreed the same for the earlier case of Pelot, on behalf of Verdier, recommending that "the portion of the fine due to the Police office only be imposed" (*Courier*, 18 June 1847).

When the fiscal reports were made (Charleston *Mercury*, 2 September 1847), it was shown that $13,401 came in for twelve months (carts and drays totaling $5,505). The cost for making badges was $157.90; *this paid for the 4,171 badges the city may have sold.* Apparently more were sold than expected.

Because of what was to happen the following year on the Charleston Neck, there is more data available on badges in this fiscal year. Information comes from an article that appeared in the Charleston *Mercury*, 29 January 1848, in which figures were shown for the calendar year of 1847, apparently January–December. (The reason for making an accounting of these items was due to the debate of whether or not to incorporate Charleston Neck with Charleston.) The figures show that the city received income in the following amounts for the following badges and licenses: Dray licenses, $3,260; Carts, $1,140; Omnibuses, $250; Carriages and Buggies, $390; Breaks, $125; and Badges, $13,343. The closeness of this calendar year amount to the fiscal year amount ($13,401) suggests that calendar year totals and fiscal year totals might have been about the same.

## *1847-1848 (1848 badges)*

This year followed the same pattern as the year before; the city advertised for someone to make at least 3,775 copper badges, and about 365 badges for carts, drays and omnibuses (*Courier*, 8 November 1847). W. M. Rouse again got the contract "to furnish City Badges"; he was listed separately for "City Licenses for Carts, &c." *(Courier*, 30 November 1847). The total that came in from badges *(an estimated number of 4,277)* was $13,741; $5,340 came in from Carts and Drays. $189.20 was paid out to make badges (Charleston *Mercury*, 2 September 1848).

Although there are census figures for the city of Charleston for the year 1848 (compiled by the city itself), it would be unwise to determine the percentage of hired slaves to the slave population based on this census, since historians have concerns over its accuracy, particularly in the number of slaves in the city.[2] According to the 1848 census, which seems to have taken pains to prove that there were more whites in the city of Charleston than blacks, there were only 10,772 slaves in the city; if 3,775 badges were sold, as suggested in the paper, that would bring the percentage of hired slaves up to 35 percent, the highest ever known; and if the mathematical estimated number is true, it would mean that 39 percent of the slaves were hired out, which certainly seems far-fetched.

As for activities reported in City Council minutes, in March of 1848, J. Hume Simons petitioned, "asking to be refunded amount twice taken out for badges" (*Courier*, 15 March 1848). This might be due to the fact that in February, for the first time, badges had to be worn by slaves working out for hire on the Neck as well. Unfortunately, there are no known reports for monies brought in on the Neck.

## *1848-1849 (1849 badges)*

This year the Committee on Contracts let the contract for badge making to two different people: the *Mercury* of 29 November 1848 reported that W. M. Rouse would furnish badges, but John Mood would "furnish Tin Badges." (The information is confirmed by the City Directory for Charleston for 1849, listing those two under the heading for "City Contracts.")[3]

In February 1849, there was an application from T. Gaillard "to be refunded the amount of 2 badges, twice taken out by error." It was granted and referred to the city treasurer to certify the claim (*Courier*, 8 February 1849). It is possible again that this duplication might have arisen from the fact that badges were also issued on the Neck this year. No figures regarding these sales are known.

In August the fiscal report showed $13,750 coming in for badges for the city of Charleston, and $6,080 coming in for carts and drays. The cost of making badges was $164.60 (Charleston *Mercury,* 31 August 1849). *Estimates suggest 4,279 were sold.*

## *1849-1850 (1850 badge)*

For this fiscal year, and a period almost overlapping it entirely, there is a wealth of information for the City of Charleston, but not the Neck.

The 28 November 1849 *Courier* stated that, again, the contract for making badges was split; it reported that W. M. Rouse had been selected to make the tin badges for carts and drays, and that a newcomer, [D. H.] Deveaux was chosen to make the copper slave badges. But from other evidence, it appears the *Courier* muddled and reversed the names.

In September (*Courier*, 27 September 1849), Newton Pierce petitioned Council for relief for a fine imposed for a slave working out without a badge. The Committee on Relief at this meeting ruled on the petition of Thomas G. Gantt, trustee and agent of the estates of Mrs. S. Gantt, and for Mrs. E. Thompson. Gantt stated that in February of 1849 (which would have been in the previous fiscal year), he moved from the city to the Neck, so he felt that the taxes he paid on three dogs and 14 slaves should be remitted. (Since being on the Neck, he did not have to pay taxes.) Three of the slaves he moved to the Neck lived and slept there, and worked in the city with city badges. The Committee ruled against him, however, noting that taxes were levied on property, including dogs and slaves, living in the city as of 1 January, so he was still liable for the fees. "In relation to the slaves referred to as sleeping on the Neck, but working in the City under City Badges, such are likewise subject to taxation under the Ordinance, which declares that 'every slave within the City, or employed within the City, though his or her domicile may be without the city, shall be liable to a tax.'" So, the petitioner was out of luck.

Reporting on all the income and expense at the end of the fiscal year, the newspapers noted $13,290 in income from badges, and $173.62 spent to make them. *It is estimated 4,135 badges sold.* And for the first time, the cost for making dog badges ($42) was stated (*Courier*, 2 September 1850).

Extra, overlapping information for this particular fiscal year comes from a pamphlet the City Council published.[4] It covers the period 1 July 1849–30

June 1850, instead of the 1 September 1849–31 August 1850 span reported in the paper. (It may be that the continuing controversy between the city and the Neck prompted officials to make expenses known.) This printed record is invaluable in documenting all aspects of City Council's work. It gives details on a variety of city tasks and improvements; it also helps explain the continuing support of the city fathers for the hiring-out practice and how that issue could become one of the hotly debated points in the battle between the city and the Neck. The pages detail numerous instances of the city itself hiring slaves to work; indeed that occurs on nearly every page of council expenditures. In July 1849, for instance, Robert Elfe was paid $12 for one month's hire of a Negro; J. D. Yates was paid $24 for a month's hire of two Negroes in October. John Ryan, for one month's hire of a Negro, got $12, while John King for this month's hire of three Negroes was paid $36. There are also entries for horses and carts and drivers (probably slaves) who were hired. They cost significantly less than labor of whites or free persons of color. The record shows that white laborers were paid $1 a day. One could hire a slave for a whole month for $12, which would only pay for a free laborer for 12 days. The city obviously saw the economic sense of this and so participated in the hiring-out practices it promulgated and policed.

There are also numerous entries regarding badges in this year's worth of financial records. Badges brought in $199 in July and $79 in August. In the same month, a report was made that W. M. Rouse was paid $2.06 for "75 extra copper badges (making)." This means that apparently not enough badges had been made earlier in the year to last out the fiscal term. P. Cantwell was paid $10.62 for "1 mo[nth], less 3 days hire of a negro." In September, badges brought the city income of $45; $81 came in October and $52 in November. In the same month, $16 was returned to "M.A. Waring for badges improperly taken out in 1848." Then D. H. Deveaux was paid "for making Badges for Carts, drays, omnibuses, & c." in December 1849: 145 carts, 415 Drays, 35 Omnibuses, 595 at 5 cents, $29.75. (This shows that Deveaux was indeed the tin badge maker for this year, and not the copper badge maker, as reported in the press.) Only $4 came in this month for badges.

In January 1850, when the new badges for the year went on sale, the city received $7,542 in income; this month it "Paid William Rouse, for making 2,400 Servants; 1,400 Porters; 400 Mechanics; 180 Fruiterers; 100 Fishers." The copper badges, "4,480 at 2 1/2 cents each [cost] [$]112. 20 Sweeps, tin at 13 cents each, 2.60; 30 extra porters in Oct. (copper), .82. 15 Dray licenses, tin, at 6 cents, .90, [totaling $]116.32."

For the first time, there is a number given for how many badges the city made in each category for a particular year. (This is the information used to derive the formula for estimating the number of badges sold each year; see appendix.) Servants, including washers, constituted, by far, the highest category with 2,400 made. It was followed by 1,430 porters, which was the word used to also cover carters, drayers and day laborers. (There were 1,400 porters made, following 30 made earlier in October.) The next highest category was the mechanic class, or "handicraft tradesman," numbering 400. The next category was 180 fruiterers or hucksters, followed by 100 fishers.

Were this many badges, 4,510 (4,480 plus 30) actually sold in this period covered in the pamphlet? Probably not. (The number 4,510 does not include the 75 extra badges made in August; if they were sold in August, these would have been counted in the previous fiscal year; but if they were sold after 1 September, they *could* be included in this fiscal year. The 30 extra porter badges made in October probably had "1849" stamped on them.) If all were sold, the amount brought into the city would have amounted to something like $14,520. (Servant badges cost $2, porters, $4, mechanics, $7, fruiterers, $5, fisherwomen, $2 and fishermen, $4. For the sake of parity, it is assumed one half of the fisher badges were men, and one half women.) Instead of $14,520, the amount mentioned in the newspaper for the end of the fiscal year was $13,290 and the total of all monthly sales listed in the pamphlet comes to $13,223. From these totals, it does appear, however, that a high percentage of the 4,510 were sold. *(4,135 is the formula's estimate.)* Failing any other data turning up, archeological evidence may help show how many badges in each category were really made and used, for if a badge number approximating the figure given for any category is found, it can show that the number made and circulated match the number estimated.

The published record continues to offer interesting glimpses of the process. February 1850 reveals a $6.75 expense of the Police Office to E. R. Stokes for purchasing "three Badge Books," obviously to keep the records. $3,577 for badges came in that month, with six chimney sweep licenses sold ($35 worth were sold the month before, the first time such went on sale), and City Council paid D. H. Deveaux $7.55 for making "151 extra dray and cart badges." In this month, A. C. Welton was paid $45 for the hire of three Negroes, these costing more, perhaps for the special skills they needed in helping on the artesian well. John Ryan was paid another $10.37 for the hire of a Negro in January, and many more were listed as well. $616 for badges came in during March; and $4 for a porter's badge was "returned to Mrs. M. May, by resolution of Council, 20th March 1850." Of interest this month is the fact that H. M. Bruns was paid $30 for "negro hire" in the high school. For badges $354 came in during April. The next month saw $42 coming into City Council coffers from Edward Sebring "for badges that should have been taken out in 1849, but which were not." Sebring had earlier petitioned City Council back in July of 1840 for relief from double payment of badges and surtaxes.

In the same month as this, E. Martin purchased a fruit license, something that happens other months, too, but no badge was mentioned. Licenses were needed (but not badges) if the person selling fruit, etc., was not a slave.[5] For $5 this month, one sweep license (again not a badge, but a license for a non-slave) was sold, too. An extra $375 in "servant's" (slave) badges came in then, too. This month also saw $262 in income from dog badges, the first amounts coming in from the new statute.

Charlestonians were informed of the need for dog badges in articles in the local press in 1850; on 1 May of that year, the *Mercury* noted that City Council had had a second reading of that bill and it would be read the third time at the next meeting. "The City Treasurer shall provide a sufficient number of metal badges suitable for dogs, marked CC and numbered from 1 upwards, and dispose of the same for the sum of two dollars each to such persons as may apply for the same." William Rouse made 250 brass badges for dogs at 12 cents each for $30, paid out by City Council. June shows $308 coming in for slave badges and $252 for badges for dogs; William Rouse was paid another $12 for making 100 additional brass badges for dogs in this month.

This superb record for 1850 is important. For the first time there is not just the gross number of badges expected to be sold in a specific period, but a breakdown by category is also given. From the badge book reference, it is seen that the badge books were kept by the Police. And it also shows how expensive badges were to make.

Since the census reports that in 1850, there were 19,532 slaves in Charleston, if 4,510 were hired out, that would make 23 percent in that category. What perhaps is most telling of all is the reliance of the city of Charleston on the system. Slaves were hired out for just about every type of work, from the high school to the Sheriff's office of Robert Elfe.

Most badges in this era were diamond-shaped and varied slightly from year to year.

## *1841*

The 1841 badge, made by John Mood, is different from the ones made by W. M. Rouse in this and the previous decade. Mood's badges are larger than Rouse's (with the exception of Rouse's 1836 badge). Mood also used different dies in his lettering. The order of information on this diamond-shaped badge is: "Charleston," badge number, occupation, and date. All information is stamped, except for the badge number, which is punched.

### *1842*

These badges, made by W. M. Rouse, followed the same pattern of those made by John Mood the year before: "Charleston," badge number, occupation, "1842."

### *1843*

Rouse made these badges just as he had the year before, but he switched the order of information somewhat. "Charleston" on the first line was followed by "1843," then the occupation, and the badge number.

### *1844*

This badge made by John Mood is similar to the one he made in 1841, aligning in size, shape and text information.

### *1845*

Rouse made these badges smaller than Mood had the previous year and placed "Charleston" on the first line, the date on the next, followed by occupation, and then the badge number on the last line.

### *1846*

This is nearly an exact duplicate of the year before except that the position of the badge number and the year is reversed. The badge number is on the second line, the year on the fourth.

### *1847*

Rouse changed the pattern this year. Instead of punching a hole in a corner, which would make the suspended badge hang in a diamond shape, he made his holes in the center of the top side, making it now a square. This is the only time Rouse designed a square badge. The order of text follows the 1845 badge: "Charleston," "1847," occupation, and badge number.

## *1848*

This is a very distinctive year for slave badges, for there are two different types bearing the year 1848. This was the year that hostile action was taken by the leaders of Charleston Neck (the area of the peninsula above Boundary Street to Line Street) and leaders of the city (see Chapter 2). The Neck was not incorporated in the city of Charleston and was governed by a board of commissioners, who demanded that the city of Charleston give up some of its money that came from slave-hire badges. When City Council refused, the "government" on the Neck then began making its own badges. This is the only year in the whole era of slave badge usage that slaves working north and south of Calhoun or Boundary Street had to have badges for both geographic areas.

The 1848 badge for the city of Charleston followed the example of those Rouse made in 1846. Diamond-shaped, they had information in this order: "Charleston," badge number, occupation, and date.

The badges made for the Charleston Neck are completely different from Rouse's 1848 badges in both size and manner of fabrication. (Badges for the Neck went on sale in February 1848.) They are labeled C. N. There are not many badges from the Neck in this year known: a few servant and a few porter badges. The two different occupations have different sizes, similar to the round ones Charles Prince made between 1801 and 1803. It is possible that other occupations have different sizes as well. Another telling difference is that although the lettering on the badges is parallel to the bottom and top sides of the badge, as if a square, the hole punched for suspending the badge is in the upper corner, the left corner in a servant badge, and in the right upper corner in the porter badge. This would make the suspended badge assume the shape of the diamond and the lettering would be at an angle, not parallel to the ground. This would be able to be seen immediately and the difference in size and hole placement would fulfill two functions. At a glance, one would be able to tell if a slave carrying on a particular task was wearing the proper badge, and, secondly, police on the Neck would be able to see if the slaves hired out on the Neck were wearing C. N badges, visually different from Charleston city badges.

There is yet another obvious difference to these C. N badges: all the letters and numbers are hand-punched; i.e., each letter and number was individually hammered or forced onto the metal, instead of there being a pre-set die; it could have been the speed with which the program was set up on the Neck that disallowed the time needed to make the form.

It may be that the maker of these badges was D. H. Deveaux, a graphic artist, and brother to the city coroner. Deveaux would be selected by City Council in 1850 for the contract to make the tin cart and dray badges for the city; perhaps this artistic bent of his made him a candidate for badges made on the Neck. Or perhaps not. The badge maker's name will, hopefully, one day come to light.

### *1849*

This year continued the trend of having two different badges, one for the city and one for the Neck. But with the change of the law, however, a slave who worked both south and north of Boundary Street did not need to wear badges from each district. Now a slave had only to wear one badge no matter where he or she worked; if his or her owner lived on the Neck, the badge was purchased there; city dwellers purchased a city badge.

The 1849 badges for the city of Charleston are diamond-shaped. Made by Rouse, they carry information in this order: "Charleston," date, occupation, and badge number.

The 1849 badges for the Neck are very similar, for they were also made by Rouse. They are the same size, and also diamond-shaped. They state their location as "Charleston Neck," not "C.N" as the year before; then there follows the badge number, occupation and date. Unlike the previous year Neck badges, the information (all but for the badge number) is stamped. The year before, all data was punched. Only the badge number is punched on the 1849 Charleston Neck badge.

### *1850*

This is the last year that two different badges, one for the Neck and one for the city, were made. Again, both were made by Rouse. They follow the same pattern as the 1849 badges; both city and Neck badges are diamond shaped and of the same size; both also reverse the order of information in the second and fourth lines. City badges present data ordered "Charleston," badge number, occupation, then date; and the Neck badges are slightly different: "Charleston Neck" is on the first line; then comes the date, the occupation, and finally the badge number. After this year, with the incorporation of the Neck into the city, only "Charleston" badges were made.

Although the 1850 badges, either Neck or city, were good both above and below Boundary Street, Council went the extra length to assure everyone of that. On 1 October 1850, it noted "that all badges, cart and dray licenses for 1850, heretofore taken out, either from City or Neck, be considered as authorizing the holders to pass and repass without interruption through all the present city Wards" (*Courier,* 1 October 1850).

As mentioned above, this is the first year dog badges were issued for the city of Charleston, and apparently the Neck. They were marked "CC" and numbered sequentially.

In 1850, the city designated a second badge maker, just as it had in 1849. David H. Deveaux was now chosen to make the tin badges for carts and drays. He was born in Charleston ca. 1816, and he attracted attention early for his painting skills. The *Courier* (3 September 1846) noted that "A fine miniature painting of the 'Fire on Magwood's wharf,' Jan. 28th, 1845, executed by Mr. DAVID H. DEVEAUX, a young artist of our city, may be seen at the Exchange Reading Room, where it has been placed for exhibition for a few days. We understand that it is the property of the Hope Fire Co." He married Julia E. Harper in 1849, about the time he was being awarded contracts for tin badges for the city; he obviously used it as a way to make money, for he advertised himself as a painter in the 1852 Charleston City Directory. His end was not a happy one, as this article (*Charleston Daily Courier*, 21 June 1855), attests:

> DAVID H. DEVEAUX, aged 35 or 38 years, an ornamental painter, of this city, was found yesterday afternoon, about half-past 12 o'clock, in the northeast corner of the Hall of the Hope Fire Engine Company, quite dead. In his pockets were found a paper of arsenic and a razor. The Acting Secretary of the Company, having occasion to visit the Hall, discovered his body suspended. An inquest was held in the afternoon by JOHN A. GYLES, Esq., Magistrate, when the following verdict was returned: 'That the said David H. DeVeaux deprived himself of life on the 19th day of June, 1855, by hanging himself in the saloon of the Hope Fire Engine Company, under mental aberration.' He left a wife and a child.

In the next generation, in 1880, another DeVeaux, possibly David's nephew, would be coroner of the county, following in the shoes of another J.P. Deveaux who was coroner in 1849. This later DeVeaux, ironically, would become involved in a duel in which the other person was a Mr. Rouse, apparently W. M. Rouse, the long-time slave badge maker, who also made badges in this same era.[6]

Tabulated the statistics for these years are thus (with estimates in *italics*):

| *Fiscal Year* | *Badge year* | *# of Badges* | *Income* | *Expenses* | *Maker* |
|---|---|---|---|---|---|
| 1840-1841 | 1841 | (3,800*) *3,908* | 12,555.00 | 169.80 | Mood |
| 1841-1842 | 1842 | *3,842* | 12,345.00 | 132.90 | Rouse |
| 1842-1843 | 1843 | *4,101* | 13,178.00 | 143.85 | Rouse |
| 1843-1844 | 1844 | *4,275* | 13,737.00 | 151.20 | Mood |
| 1844-1845 | 1845 | *3,843* | 12,347.00 | 143.44 | Rouse |

| *Fiscal Year* | *Badge year* | *# of Badges* | *Income* | *Expenses* | *Maker* |
|---|---|---|---|---|---|
| 1845-1846 | 1846 | *3,776* | 12,133.00 | 131.85 | Rouse |
| 1846-1847 | 1847 | (3,775*) *4,171* | 13,401.00 | 157.90 | Rouse |
| 1847-1848 | 1848 | (3,775*) *4,277* | 13,741.00 | 189.20 | Rouse |
| 1848-1849 | 1849 | *4,279* | 13,750.00 | 164.60 | Rouse |
| 1849-1850 | 1850 | (4510*) *4,135* | 13,290.00 | 173.62 | Rouse |

(For the years 1847-1848, 1848-1849, and 1849-50, only the statistics for the city of Charleston are given, as for all the earlier years. The totals for Charleston Neck are unknown.) Since male fishers cost $4 and females cost $2, the figure of $3 was used in the above estimations.

*Derived from press reports, and in the case of 1849-50, from the pamphlet *Statement of Receipts and Expenditures.*

"Badge year" denotes the predominant badge sold in the fiscal year.

## CHAPTER 8

# 1851–1860

### *1850-1851 (1851 badges)*

In November 1850, the city council advertised for "Proposals for making, lettering and numbering at least 6,150 Copper Badges, and finding Copper, for finding Tin, making, painting and numbering about 1,050 Badges for Carts, Drays and Omnibuses, and 50 sweeps; also 500 Brass Badges for Dogs" (*Courier*, 9 November 1850). W. M. Rouse, it was soon announced (*Courier*, 20 November 1850), got the contract for making badges. (Based on this figure—the growth from 4,510 to 6,150 in the number of badges ordered—one might speculate that this increase of 1,640 badges might mean that about 1,640 were made the year before for the Neck.[1] Knowing now that all on the Neck and the city would buy the same badge, the Treasurer could have estimated and advertised a total reflected a combination of Neck and city amounts.)

1851 Porter, No. 892. (W. M. Rouse). This year was the first time that Rouse did not clip the corners on all of his "Servant" badges.

In February, City Council rejected John Wilson's request "to be refunded a tax, the price of a Porter's Badge" (*Courier*, 12 February 1851). But in March, Ann M. Cambridge was successful in seeking exchange of a cart license for a badge (*Courier*, 5 March 1851). Henry S. Tew asked for permission to return a badge and be refunded the money he had paid for it; it was granted (*Courier* 19 March 1851). The next month, Henry S. Griggs had a badge of B. Ellis transferred to him; the badge was taken out for a servant in February, and this slave was purchased by Griggs on the 5th of March (*Courier*, 25 April 1851).

Many of these just mentioned transactions show up again in another publication; for this year, the city also published a pamphlet on its income and disbursements, *Statement of Receipts and Expenditures by the City Council of Charleston, from the 1st September 1850, to 1st September 1851*, aligning the report with its fiscal year. Again the data supplied is invaluable; it shows the city's heavy reliance upon hired slaves. Sheriff Robert Elfe continued to pay out for their hire, as did a variety of others. Slaves were hired for help with the artesian well, in the lazaretto, and were used by the street inspector in the upper wards of the city, once the Neck. (Slaves were also hired out for the fire department in these years.) And revenue came in, too: $92 for badges and $16 for dog badges in September, $52 for badges in October, and $6 for dog badges; November saw $40 coming in for badges. December just saw $8. Those taking out fruit licenses were listed in January 1851: F. White, S. Lacombe, S. Shem, A. Anthony, M. Hutchinson, and S. Generet paid $5 each; six sweep licenses were sold, too. (These were non-slaves doing this type of work.) Ninety-two dog badges at $2 each brought in $184 in this same month, while the January amount for badges, when most people would buy for the whole year, came to $6,556. The city had taken out advertisements in January 1851 announcing that the badges were available and what the prices were: Handicraft Tradesman, $7; Carter, Drayman, Porter or Day Laborer $4; Fisherman, $4; House Servants or Washerwoman, $2; Fruiterer, $5; Chimney Sweep Badges, $5. Contrary to the 1840 law, there was no category listed for fisher woman; that law said those badges would go for $2. (In December 1859 the press would go back to advertising fisher badges for women at $2, so this lack in 1851 was probably just an oversight.) Dog licenses were also advertised at $2, all available from the city treasurer. "Negroes found working out on hire, without a Badge, after the 1st prox. will subject their owners to the penalty affixed by Law" (*Mercury*, 8 January 1851).

The pamphlet on finances, in February 1851 noted that W. M. Rouse was paid for "making the following Badges: Servants, 3,500; Porters, 1,600; Mechanics, 600; Fruiterers, 500; Fishers, 150; Drays, 700; Carts, 400." These amounts exceed the 6,150 slave badges advertised for by the city a few months previously.[2] The numbers shown actually add up to 6,350 slave badges; and although the city in its proposal only asked for 1,050 badges for drays, carts, and omnibuses, Rouse actually made 1,200. (The number of badges made is a great step up from the 4,510 made the year before. As stated, this could be due to the fact that now the city proper extended north of Boundary or Calhoun Street, and encompassed more territory and more slaves needing badges. Based on this demographic and geographic enlargement, one would expect the dollar amounts and gross numbers of badges sold to be larger than ever, and this certainly is the case in the next few years, as the numbers and table below show.)

In that same month of February, badges brought in $3,237; dog badges amounted to $74. Also, T. A. Hindman was refunded $4 for the amount of a porter's badge "as twice taken out."

It is known that cart and dray badges were numbered like the slave badges because in March 1851, "Cart License No. 147, [was] returned by Miss Ann M. Cambridge, and money refunded her by order of City Council, March 4, 1851." Furthermore, police records of the 1850s often refer to cart numbers in issuing fines for their being used improperly. According to the *Statement of Receipts and Expenditures*, badges brought in $519 that month; the amount for dog badges was $116. In April, the amounts were $275 and $152 respectively. May brought in $308 and $68 in those categories. June ("see badge book," citation notes) brought in $235, and dog badges earned the city $28. H. S. Tew was refunded $2, as shown earlier, for a badge by order of Council 18 March 1851, but wasn't paid until June. Dog badges earned the city $10 in July and slave badges brought in $189. That month, $1.50 was paid out to make extra dog badges; apparently the 500 proposed by the city and made by Rouse were not enough. In the final month of the fiscal year, badges brought in $104.

The upper wards of the city, once the Neck, had their records kept separately. (The reason for this was due to the nature of the joining of the two: income from the Neck was to go to better the neck, it was decided, so separate bookkeeping was necessary; some of these records for the upper wards from the 1850s have survived.)[3] In September 1850, badges for dogs on the Neck brought in $14. In October, the amount was $26, and $18 for Negro badges, with a fruit license listed separately. No income is shown in these categories in November and December. January 1851 witnessed income from badges for dogs amounting to $152; badges for slaves, with the new 1851 badges going on sale this month, brought in $2,031, with $25 for sweeps. In February 1851, slave badges sales amounted to $866, and badges for dogs came to $44. March 1851 saw $192 from slave badges, $22 for dogs, and $5 for sweeps. In April, $82 came from slave-hire badges, and $122 from dogs; May brought in $104 for badges, and $12 for dogs. June brought in $62 and $10 respectively. Slave badges brought in $34 in July, with dog badges listed twice at $2. August sales mentioned only slave badges at $14. The total for slave badges in the upper ($3,403) and lower wards ($11,615) comes to $15,108, a rise over the year before, as would befit a greater number of badges called for this year versus the year before (6,150 called for in the press, 6,350 made, compared to 4,480 the year before). The newspapers, reporting on finances for the year, noted $11,615 in income from the lower wards and $3,403 from the upper wards, matching the totals from the pamphlet exactly (Charleston *Mercury,* 30 August 1851 and 1 September 1851). Also, the newspaper and pamphlet figures nearly tally for expenses in making the badges; the newspaper puts down the figure as $243; while using the figures in the pamphlet, one comes up with $237.

For the first time, a month-by-month tally of badge income matches the gross amount of income listed in the press at the end of the fiscal year. *By the formula for estimating slave badge sales based on income, the number of badges sold comes to 4,668, quite a bit less than the number actually made.* The census of 1850 tabulated 19,532 slaves in Charleston; using the *estimated* figure of slave badges, one can guess that 23 percent of the slaves in Charleston were hired out. (If all badges were actually sold, that would have meant 32 percent of slaves were hired out.)

For that and other reasons, it is likely that all the badges made this year were not sold in the fiscal year of 1850-1851 or calendar year of 1850; if one multiples the number of badges in each category by the fees for each badge category, and adds them together, the total comes to $20,700, a far cry from the $15,018 actually made. It seems likely that some badges made this year would be carried over to the next. (The possibility also exists that badges were sold illegally, with the income not showing up on the city's financial books.)

### *1851-1852 (1852 badges)*

To prepare for this next year, the city, as usual, advertised for proposals for "making, lettering and numbering at least 5,600 Copper Badges, and finding Copper; for finding Tin, making, painting and numbering about 1,010 Badges for Carts, Drays and Omnibuses, and 50 Sweeps; also, 600 Brass Badges, for Dogs" (*Courier,* 6 November 1851). With no pamphlet published of financial records, there is only the newspaper's annual report. Badges brought in $11,442 in the lower wards. Chimney sweep licenses, according to newspaper figures, only brought in $40, and $528 came into the city coffers for dog badges. The cost of making the badges was given as $290.26 (*Mercury*, 30 August 1852). Separate figures were given for income for the upper wards: there slave badges brought in $3,401; dog badges brought in $248, and sweeps, $60. It appears, from the badges themselves that Rouse again got the contract. City Council minutes confirm that (*Courier,* 5 December 1851).

The combined total from lower and upper wards for slave badges is $14,843. *(The formula used for estimating the number of badges sold pegs the figure at 4,588, about 1,000 less than the number of badges the city ordered.)* Since the paper also gives the number of slaves below (12,450) and above (3,823) Boundary Street, the total slaves in the city that year is known to be 16,273. If the city sold 5,600 badges, the percentage of hired-out slaves that year would have been 34 percent, but only 28 percent of slaves were hired out, if the *estimated* number of badges sold is used.

### *1852-1853 (1853 badges)*

Proposals for making at least 5,600 Copper badges and finding copper; finding tin and making about 1,010 badges for carts, drays and omnibuses, 50 for sweeps and 600 Brass badges for dogs (the exact number in each category of the previous year) began to appear in the papers in the fall of 1852 (*Courier* 27 October 1852). W. M. Rouse got the contract by 1 December. The report for the fiscal year was not published until October, and many of the following years showed this same trend. The 31 October edition of the *Mercury* reported that $10,486 came in from badges in the lower wards, where $128 came in from dog badges, and carts and drays brought in $6,155. "Badges, cost of making" was $243.30. In the upper wards, badges for slaves brought in $3,572, carts and drays, $2,730, and dog badges, $76. The totals come to: badges, $14,058; carts and drays, $8,885, and dog badges, $204. *According to the formula, 4,346 badges sold.*

### *1853-1854 (1854 badges)*

Again, the same numbers were advertised in all categories for proposals for badge making: 5,600 copper; 1,010 tin for carts, drays and omnibuses; 50 sweeps; and 600 brass dog badges (Charleston *Mercury*, 9 December 1853). A. M. Rouse, a mistake for W. M. Rouse, was announced as recipient of the contract (Charleston *Mercury*, 22 December 1853).

In May of 1854, Charles Jugnot petitioned the Committee on Relief to be "relieved for paying a tax on a negro, for whom he had taken out a Porter's Badge, who died the day after" (*Courier*, 27 May 1854). His petition was granted at the next meeting (*Courier*, 6 June 1854). Death records for the city of Charleston show that this unfortunate slave was named Sam, he had been born in Charleston, was 60 years old and he died of small pox on 14 February. He was buried in the City Burial Ground.[4]

It was not until October that reports for the fiscal year ending in August appeared (*Mercury*, 26 October). Income in the lower wards was shown as $10,108, with $220 for dog badges and $5,580 for carts, drays and carriages, with $349.40 being paid out for their making. In the upper wards, $3,357 was collected for badges, $22 for dog badges, and $2,755 for carts and drays, bringing the grand totals in the respective categories to $13,465, $242, and $8,335. *Estimates put the number of badges sold at 4,162.*

## *1854-1855 (1855 badges)*

Almost all the same numbers in each category were part of the proposals sought in December 1854 *(Mercury* 9 December 1854). Again, at least 5,600 copper badges were sought, but now about 1,200 tin badges for carts, drays and omnibuses were to be made, with 50 for sweeps, and 600 brass badges for dogs. A new man, B. O'Connor, the papers announced (*Courier*, 21 December 1854), won the contract for furnishing tin and copper badges.

O'Connor appeared in the 1852 city directory listed as a watchmaker on Beaufain Street; in 1855, his name (misspelled as O'Commer) was in the directory, listing him as a watchmaker on Savage Street, where he turned up again the following year, in the era in which he made badges. He is not listed in the 1859 or 1860 lists of taxpayers compiled by the city, so it is not known if he owned slaves or not. After the Civil War, W.G. O'Connor, Jeweler and Silversmith, was at 217 King Street, with a residence on Wentworth Street.

In March, a petition from Samuel C. Black to be refunded the amount paid for a servant's badge, requested in February (*Courier,* 20 February 1855), was denied (*Courier*, 20 March 1855).

It was not until October that the city's annual financial report was published (*Mercury*, 19 October 1855). In the lower wards, badge income was $9,215.96, and badge expenses were $266. Badges for dogs brought in $106, and sweeps brought in $35 in licenses. In the upper wards, badge income amounted to $3,188. Badges expenses were not listed, and so perhaps they were subsumed in the above figure. In the upper wards, the amounts for dogs ($24) and sweeps ($30) were given, too, and there is a helpful notation: "(most of the dogs are paid for in Tax Returns.)" This paying for dog badges or paying taxes on dogs also showed up in the newspaper reports where the amount of taxes collected was noted; and at a special meeting of the City Council reported in the Charleston *Mercury* on 10 May 1856, Council decreed that citizens would be taxed, "two dollars on every Dog kept within the city, for which a badge has not been taken out." In the lower wards, in this year, it stated that $106 came in for dog badges, but a further 383 licenses brought in $766, at $2 each for 1854 taxes. (It appears that instead of just buying a badge, people could pay a tax.) In the year 1855, taxes brought in a further $810 (405 dogs). In the upper wards, an extra 190 dogs brought in $380 in tax dollars in 1854, and taxes for 179 dogs brought in $388 in revenue in 1855. This fiscal report shows there were 11,950 slaves taxed in the lower wards in 1854 and 11,687 in 1855; there were 4,512 slaves taxed in the upper wards in 1854 and 4,337 in

1855. (The demographics of free people of color are given as well.) Totaling the highest numbers for both areas of town, it can be inferred that Charleston had as many as 16,462 taxed slaves. If 5,600 badges were sold, as suggested by the newspaper report, that means that at least 29 percent of the slaves in town were hired out this fiscal year, a very significant percentage. The total income for this year from badges came to $12,403.96. *Estimates derived from this total put the number of badges at 3,834; however, this total is well shy of the 5,600 called to be made.* And if this is the right number, this would bring down the percentage of slaves hired out to the more usually seen 23 percent.

### *1855-1856 (1856 badges)*

This year repeated the same proposed numbers of the year before; at least 5,600 copper badges, "about 1,200" tin badges for carts and drays, 50 sweeps, and 600 brass badges for dogs (*Mercury*, 13 December 1855). W.D. Veronee was awarded the contract (*Courier*, 21 December 1855). At this time, too, the police office in Charleston reminded the public in advertisements of the 1843 statute regarding drays and carts, that anyone losing the badge from the vehicle had to inform the city treasurer, who would issue the person a certificate saying that it replaced the tin badge. One reason for this advertisement was to remind people of the new ordinance ratified 25 January 1854 amending cart, dray and wagon licenses. This amendment now demanded that "the number of the license of each Cart, Dray and Wagon shall be painted or fastened on each blind of the bridle of the animal drawing the same, under the penalty of not less than twenty dollars for each and every violation of this provision. The above will be strictly enforced on and after Monday 26, inst. By order of the Mayor." Dated 22 November, it ran in the 22 December 1855 issue of the *Charleston Daily Courier*.

On 30 October 1856, the *Courier* printed a number of financial statistics of the city, breaking each category on either side of December 11. In Receipts and Expenditures of the lower wards in the city from 1 September to 11 December 1855, the city brought in $9 for slave badges and $12 for dog badges. For the same lower wards, from 12 December 1855 to the end of the fiscal year (31 August 1856), the city's balance sheet for badges showed income at $10,311 and expenses reaching $457.50. Dog badges brought in $170 and sweeps, $35.

"Consolidated Transactions for the Lower Wards" for the whole period were totaled: badge income was $10,401, with expenses totaling $457.50. The total amount for dog badges was $182, and sweeps, $35.

For "Upper Wards: Receipts and Expenditures 1 Sept–11 December 1855," badges brought in $10; from 12 December 1855 through 31 August 1856, the income in that category was $3,458, with dog badges bringing in $54 and sweeps, $60. "Consolidated Totals for the Upper wards" were badges, $3,468; dog badges, $54; and sweeps, $60.

Again, tax totals that were printed showed that many dogs were accounted for under taxes and not under the badges column. Explaining the odd break on December 11 is the fact that it was the date that City Treasurer W. H. Inglesby left office, replaced by N. R. Middleton. In total for the year, income from slave-hire badges was $13,869, and expenses, $457.50. The total for dogs was $236 and that for sweeps, $95. *It is estimated that 4,287 slave badges were sold in this period.*

As usual in these years, the numbers and sex and age breakdown of free people of color are given; there are gross numbers for slaves, taxed at $3 each, too: in the lower wards, 11,758, and in the upper wards, 4,575, for a grand total of 16,333. If 4,287 slaves had badges, that would mean 26 percent of the slaves were hired out.

According to the paper, W. D. Veronee was awarded the contract. There is a W. B. Veronee, tinsmith, in the 1852 City Directory at the Corner of State and Linguard Streets, with another W. Veronee living there, too. G [eorge] H. Veronee, Tinner and William Veronee, Tinner, are listed at 63 State Street in 1855, as is "Veronee and Brother, Stoves and Tinware." W.B. Veronee reappears in the 1856 Directory as a tinplate worker at State and Guingard Streets, with a residence on King Street. (He had done some work for the city earlier; in October of 1851, the city had paid him $38.70 for "129 ft. gutter pipe for Picket Guard House."[5]) William, another tinsmith, was listed as living elsewhere on King Street, along with Cornelius Veronee, also a tinsmith; while George, a tinner, lived at 22 Line Street, as did another William Veronee, with a Samuel Veronee living nearby, all in 1856. It seems there were two brothers and possibly their various sons, in the tinning business.

One unusual thing known of Veronee, due to some city financial records that have survived, is what he was paid. In winning the contract, he apparently was to be paid per badge he made for the city. Under the title "Rates of Contracts," this appears: "W.B. Verronee, Badges of Copper & Brass, 3 c[ents] ea; for Bread Carts, 23 [cents]; carts & drays, 2½ [cents]; sweeps, 15 [cents each].[6]

In August of 1856, a series of debates began in City Council on an issue related to slavery. Reacting to a new ordinance that abolished the sale of slaves on the street north of the Customs House (then at the Exchange Building on East Bay Street at the foot of Broad Street), more than 60 citizens petitioned the Council to reverse that decree:

> With no law to appeal to, the great protection of the slave is an enlightened and humane public, and the effort of our lawmakers should be to remove him from conditions and situations in which the violations

> of humanity escape detection. It is not wise nor consistent with the sentiment of our people that the sale of our negroes should be done in a corner. Instances have been known when the indignation of bystanders have prevented the separation of families and the anxiety of your memorialists that the arrangements which have permitted and encouraged this feeling should not be interfered with, is increased by the consideration that an alteration may be regarded as an acquiescence in opinions unsound and erroneous [*Courier*, 7 August 1856].

On 27 November, the same paper reported that the committee appointed to confer with the committee of slave brokers, in response to several similar petitions, had not been able to make "any satisfactory arrangements for the establishment of a mart," and that since many people did not want one, the committee recommended that "brokers be allowed to sell on the grounds north of the customs house, negroes and all other property, except animals, vehicles, merchandise and other chattels, as will interfere with the use of the street; Provided always, that each of them using said grounds ... shall pay to the city $100 per annum...."

A group of more than 50 gentlemen then counterpetitioned City Council, stating that the ordinance not be overthrown. They took offense at the "insinuations of hostility and mawkish sentimentality towards the public sales of slaves." In their counterattack, they blamed slaves themselves:

> Our complaint is against the evils attendant upon these sales. The crowd who collect, and particularly the number of idle negroes attracted, are most frequently so great that this, one of, if not the greatest of, our business thoroughfares, become completely obstructed. ... To those whose business confine them to the immediate neighborhood, the annoyances are innumerable.... The space North of the Custom House is too small for the purpose for which it is attempted to apply it ... and not infrequently the negros to be sold are sufficiently numerous to crowd the space assigned to property and purchases [*Courier*, 8 January 1857].

These latter petitioners prevailed; the ordinance forbidding sales at the Customs House was kept, and a mart for slave sales was built and used. (City Council had been debating this since the mid–1830s.) This was the site that Northern journalists and abolitionists visited after the war and where they found their horrific trophies to take away and display in the North.

## *1856-1857 (1857 badges)*

The new year 1857 would not start off auspiciously for the city. Citizens were greeted with the following on 17 December 1856 in the *Mercury*:

> The Committee on Contracts, who was authorized to advertise for offers to supply the different public institutions, and for other purposes, announced that they were not fully prepared to report. And, on motion of Alderman Evans, it was resolved that the election of Contractors be referred to a Special Committee, whose duty it will be to act with the Committee on Contracts, and report at the next meeting. And it shall also be the duty of those Joint Committees to inquire into the expediency and propriety of re-organizing the whole system of city contracts.

On 24 December, the paper reported that "The Special Committee, to whom was referred the re-organizing of the system of City Contracts, report that they recommend all boards and persons in the service of the city, heretofore supplied by these contracts, be allowed to supply themselves with the same articles in the best manner they can, and of whom they please." So, after thinking it would restructure the process, the city just went on with the old ways.

The year-end annual report appeared in the *Charleston Mercury* on 21 October 1857, breaking the income from badges (with no report on expenses) into lower and upper wards, with the former being $8,534, and the latter amounting to $3,370, for a grand total of $11,904. Sweep licenses brought in $30 in the lower wards, and $60 in the upper, for a total of $90. In 1856, in the lower wards 482 dog badges were sold, with 549 sold in the upper. In 1857, those figures were 219 and 245 respectively. It was decreed that all dogs kept within the city, for which badges had not been taken out, be taxed (*Mercury,* 17 January 1857). *It is estimated that 3,680 badges were sold.* Most of this information was repeated exactly in a pamphlet published by Mayor William Porcher Miles, reporting on the activities of the past year (*Mayor's Report on City Affairs. Submitted to Council, at a Meeting Held Tuesday, September 20th, 1857*). The tax records in the Mayor's report show that 482 dogs were taxed in the lower wards and 549 in the upper wards, agreeing with the figures given under badges in the newspaper accounts.[7]

These tax records also tell us that there were 11,758 slaves taxed in the lower wards in 1856 and 11,572 in 1857. In the upper wards, there were, respectively, 4,525 and 4,533 slaves. This would make for, at most, 16,291 slaves this year; and if the estimate for the number of badges sold is correct, then 22 percent of Charleston slaves were hired out.

The numbers for free people of color taxed are also given, in demographic breakdowns:

| *Lower Wards* | *1856* | *1857* |
|---|---|---|
| Females from 14 to 18 years | 36 | 32 |
| Females from 18 to 50 years | 347 | 344 |
| Males from 16 to 21 years | 51 | 47 |
| Males from 21 to 60 years | 166 | 159 |

| *Upper Wards* | *1856* | *1857* |
|---|---|---|
| Females from 14 to 18 years | 54 | 51 |
| Females from 18 to 50 years | 389 | 388 |
| Males from 16 to 21 years | 44 | 58 |
| Males from 21 to 60 years | 264 | 272 |

These free people of color, their numbers noted again and again in the coming years, would soon become involved with the slave badge issue.

## *1857-1858 (1858 badges)*

The ads appeared in December:

> Office of the City Treasury, December 8, 1857. – Proposals will be received at this office, until Tuesday, 15 instant at 2 o'clock, P.M., for finding copper, making, lettering and numbering at least (4,500) four thousand five hundred COPPER BADGES; for finding tin and making, painting, numbering and lettering at least (2,800) twenty-eight hundred TIN BADGES and SIGNS for Licensed Taverns. The whole of the above to be approved by and executed under the direction of the City Treasurer, and will be delivered at this office in such quantities and at such times as he shall direct. Persons whose offers shall be accepted, will call at the office of the City Attorney with their sureties, and execute bonds within ten days after their acceptance. A. Campbell, City Treasurer.

**1858 Mechanic, No. 450. (W. M. Rouse). The highest mechanic badge number of any year found to date. Note the double stamp of "Charleston." Imperfections often occur.**

The most important term in this ad is the word "at least." It suggests that, at a very minimum, this will be the amount of badges made. As noted earlier, in the fiscal year 1850-1851, a certain amount was listed in the paper to be made, but the city had made and paid for more.

The report for that year did not appear in the papers until November (*Courier,* 2 November 1858). Income was $10,457, and expenses came to $135 for the lower wards. Dog badges brought in $80 with no expenses listed, suggesting that all badge expenses were subsumed in the first expense category. Upper wards brought in $5,017 in income, and again, $135 was listed as the expense. The total for slave-hire badges brought in was $15,474, with $135 for expenses. *As many as 4,783 badges, close to the 4,500 called for, were made, according to estimates.* Dogs brought in $22 more, for a grand total of $102.

The tax receipts are shown again, allowing more vital information. They also compare the previous year. The year 1857 saw 11,572 slaves in lower wards, and 11,348 slaves there in 1858. For upper wards the year amounts for slaves were 4,533 and 4,502. (As for dogs, in 1857, there were taxes paid on 549 in the lower wards, and 556 in the next year; in the upper wards, the totals showed 245 and 230.) From these figures, with as many as 16,105 slaves in the city of Charleston, it can be estimated that 29 percent of the slaves were hired out, an increase over the 22 percent of the year before, with the number of slaves hired out jumping from 3,680 to 4,783.

Something else seems to have been on the rise this year; either the subject had not been discussed in the full board meetings, or no infractions were happening, but for a good while, there were no reports in the press of slaves caught laboring without badges. (Extant police records for 1855-56, showing arrest records, also show no infractions.) Suddenly, they are in the news again: Mrs. M. H. Laurens petitioned council "that a fine imposed for a slave working out without a badge be remitted." It was referred to the Committee on Retrenchment and Relief (*Courier,* 18 February 1858). Then on 18 March, J.V. Harrell petitioned for the same relief, and a free woman of color, Catherine Clark, asked that her capitation tax also be relieved. That is the tax each free person of color had to pay to the city annually. The amounts varied, depending on the age and sex of the free person. It was a way the city had of generating income; the annual recapitulations in the press in these years reported on the numbers and the fees brought into the city.

From this point onward, both free people of color and slaves were caught for their particular infractions in growing numbers and frequency. At the meeting of 20 April 1858, (reported in the *Courier*, 22 April), statistics showed that 21 slaves (20 males and one female) were caught for "working out without badge." Four free men of color and seven free women were also found not to have paid their capitation tax. In May, four males were apprehended for working without badges, and one male and two free females of color did not pay their capitation taxes (*Courier,* 27 May 1858). The numbers increased in the next month according to the paper (*Courier,* 24 June 1858). Twenty-two men and one woman were found working without badges, and four free men of color and two free women did not pay their capitation tax. In July, three male slaves were discovered to be working without badges (*Courier* 22 July 1858). In the next few weeks, there were three more male slaves and one female found committing the same infraction (*Courier*, 19 August 1858).

## *1858-1859 (1859 badges)*

The ad calling for proposals picked up the same language and numbers as the year before, calling for "finding copper, making, lettering, and numbering, according to patterns in this office, at least (4,500) four thousand five hundred COPPER BADGES" and at least 2,800 tin badges and signs for licensed taverns. "Persons whose offers shall be accepted, will call at the office of the City Attorney, with their sureties, and execute hands for faithful performance of contract, within ten days after their acceptance" (*Mercury*, 4 December 1858).

Results of the fiscal year were published in October (*Courier*, 4 October 1859). From the lower wards $9,241 came in for badges, with $4,458 coming in from the upper wards, totaling $13,699, a step down from the year before. The expense amount was only $122.08, the lowest figure in years. Dog badges brought in $88 in lower wards, $20 in the upper. (In the lower wards, 556 dogs were taxed in 1858, and 588 in 1859. The figures were 230 and 234 for the upper wards.)

The accounts also gave the number of slaves, 11,348 and 11,090 in the years 1858 and 1859 in the lower wards (taxed at $3 each), and 4,502 and approximately 4,413 or so in the upper wards in the two calendar years.[8] At most, there would have been 15,850 slaves in Charleston this year; *with estimates giving the number of slave badges sold at 4,235*, the percentage of slaves hired out in Charleston would have been nearly 27 this fiscal year.

One other item that must be noted is the new phrase appearing in the advertisement to make slave badges, "according to patterns in this office." It did not appear in earlier ads. Now it seems the city had an idea of what it wanted slave and other badges to look like. It implied it would not be up to the wishes of the selected contractor, but the badges this year did not differ markedly from other years. The pattern, different from the year before, was similar to that of 1820 and 1826.

Again this year, Council reported statistics for those working out without badges and not paying their capitation tax, among other things. Apparently it was so common for free people of color not to pay their tax that the city had fill-in-the-blank forms printed up for this purpose.[9] Three male slaves had no badge, and one free man was caught for not paying his tax in September

(*Courier*, 18 September 1858). The next month, one slave of each gender was caught with no badge, and three free men and one free woman of color had been found not to have paid their tax (28 October). In November, just one male slave was caught, but 27 free men and 26 free women became statistics for their infractions of no tax (11 November). Three free men and one free woman were caught without receipts for their capitation taxes by the next meeting, and three male slaves were found with no badge (23 December). In the new year, the infractions continued, with two male slaves and one free man and one free woman of color caught (19 March). Sixteen slaves (13 men and three women) working without badges were then discovered, as were two men and one woman with no proof that they had paid their capitation tax (14 April). Then 15 more slaves (seven male, eight female) were caught without badges, and four free people of color (one male and three females) were shown to have paid no annual tax (12 May). The authorities continued in their round-ups; three free men without tax receipts and five male and two female slaves without badges were caught in June (23 June), and five male slaves and one female slave, as well as four free men and seven free women, were apprehended in July (21 July). Something was happening.

### *1859–1860 (1860 badges)*

The advertisement for the coming year repeated the same numbers as the year before: at least 4,500 copper badges would be needed, along with 2,800 tin badges and signs for tavern licenses. The treasurer soon listed the prices for the badges:

> Handicraft Tradesman, 7.00; Carter, drayman, porter or day laborer, 4.00; Fisherman, 4.00; Fisherwoman, 2.00; House servant or washer-woman, 2.00; Seller of fruits, cakes and objects not prohibited 5.00.

Every person applying to the City Treasurer, the notice said, quoting the statute,

> for a Badge or Badges, shall take and subscribe before him the following oath to wit: "I. A.B. do solemnly swear (or affirm) that the negro or negroes (stating the name and number) is or are my property, and is or are of the ages respectively stated, or the property of C.D. (as the case may be), and that the employment of every such slave when working on hire, is to be no other than such as is now mentioned by me: so help me God." And the City Treasurer shall grant no Badge unless such oath or affirmation be previously taken and subscribed before him by the person applying [*Mercury,* 23 December 1859].

One has to wonder if this unusual appearance of this extra information in the paper was accidental or not. It may very well have been planned, for this year, the badge laws were much in debate, as the secession crisis and the break over slavery loomed. Many levels of government had been asked to crack down on slave hiring, and perhaps the city, in a show of virtue, was declaring its intent to do just that.

As had happened in the early 1700s as competition with slaves began, white mechanics competing with the hired-out slaves were again trying to halt the practice. In October 1858, white mechanics met in the Masonic Hall to denounce the practice of slaves who hired their own time and to chastise the local government for not following its own laws prohibiting this practice. Such laws, as quoted earlier, they declared, were "dead letters upon the Statute Books."[10] One hundred and sixty-three men signed a petition to the state legislature requesting "more rigid enforcement" of the laws. Resolutions in favor of it were passed by the Charleston Mechanics' Society, the South Carolina Mechanics' Association, and the Charleston Grand Jury.

A few months earlier, in February of 1858, these mechanics had petitioned Charleston City Council on the same issue, but the city, too tied to the process and profiting too much from the slave-hiring practices, had refused to act, postponing it indefinitely.[11] Then a yellow fever epidemic broke out, affecting white mechanics more than the blacks. Once that waned, there came that October meeting when the mechanics made their demands on the state legislature. They asked that the owners of slaves who were caught hiring their own time be penalized and fined $100. (At this time, due to a statute passed by the state in 1849, the penalty was only $50.) They also asked that all slaves in the state be prohibited from following "any mechanical pursuit" at all, be it on their own or being hired out legally.

The legislature agreed with the mechanics that it was terrible for slaves to act as if they were free; but nevertheless, it ruled that the relationship between the master and slave was sacrosanct, and that it was not the legislature's role to meddle in something so basic to a slave holding society. "We are a slave holding people," legislators replied, begging the question. They angered the petitioners even more by acknowledging how difficult it truly was to enforce all the laws on slave hire; technically, every time a hired-out porter went from one task to another, his owner should do the negotiating. That was impossible to do, the legislators agreed; so they, in effect, suggested that all existing laws be winked at, the exact opposite of what the petitioners were requesting. Specifically, the Committee on Colored Population recommended that most hired-out slaves, domestics, porters, etc. (but not mechanics), be allowed to hire their own time.

The white mechanics, predictably, were upset. They went back to Charleston City Council with a petition asking the city to ban all slaves hiring their own time, with a $50 fine to be levied against the person employing the slave and the slave's owners. Again, the city refused to act, saying that such would be a great inconvenience, and labor would be forced out of the hired slave's hands into that of others, which is exactly what the mechanics wanted.[12]

All of these actions were aimed specifically at hired-out slaves, but linked to slaves working and making money were free people of color who also sometimes worked as day laborers and skilled artisans. Charlestonian James Eason, owner of a foundry, in 1860, for instance, had introduced a bill in the South Carolina legislature to ban free *and* hired-out blacks from competing with the white laborers in town. A petition of his garnered nearly 500 signatures of those wishing "to prevent Free Negroes or persons of color from carrying on any Mechanical trade or calling, in their own name, or name of others."[13] The city profited too much, however, from the practice of hiring slaves for its own use and of generating income from their licensing to abolish the practice. But Mayor Charles MacBeth did give in on some points, tightening enforcement of some badge laws. Arrests for those working without badges, for instance, rose dramatically the previous fiscal year, as just shown in the various monthly tabulations. And on 10 December 1859, the *Mercury* editorialized on the subject, noting under the title, "BADGES FOR SERVANTS":

> An attendance at the Mayor's court for a few days will convince any person that the procuring of badges for slaves is a matter very much neglected by parties having servants to hire. Scarcely a day passes that some owner has not to pay the penalty incurred for this neglect, and as the police have positive instructions to rigidly enforce the ordinance relative to this matter, we deem it our duty to call the attention of those who are innocently, or willfully amenable. The fine imposed for one omission would pay for a badge for five to ten years.

The warning in the press did not work. The increase of infractions rose from none in January, February and March 1860, to 27 in April, 45 in May, 32 in June, 40 in July and 93 in August 1860. (Arrests for people of color not paying their capitation taxes also rose—from under five in January, February, March and April, to 25 in May, 25 in June and 20 in July.)[14] This could have been a gesture to the white mechanics. This stepped-up enforcement of the badge and other laws wreaked havoc on the lives of a class of Charlestonians not normally linked to the slave-hiring out system. The city and state governments, reluctant to restrict the slave-hiring laws, perhaps, as a token to the white mechanics, did concede on one point and allowed restrictions to come into play on the free people of color.

Theirs had been a crisis in the making since 1820, when the lawmakers of South Carolina made it impossible for owners to manumit or free their slaves without petitioning both houses of the legislature. Two years later, after the Denmark Vesey insurrection, the legislature further emended the law stating,

> That from and after the first day of June next, every free male negro, mulatto or mestizo in this State, above the age of fifteen years, shall be compelled to have a guardian, who shall be a respectable freeholder of the district in which the said free negro, mulatto or mestizo shall reside. And it shall be the duty of the said guardian to go before the clerk of the court of the said district, and before him signify his acceptance of the trust, in writing; and, at the same time, he shall give to the clerk aforesaid, his certificate, that the said negro, mulatto or mestizo for whom he is guardian, is of good character and correct habits; which acceptance and certificate shall be recorded in said office, by the clerk, who shall receive for the same fifty cents; and if any free male negro, mulatto or mestizo shall be unable to conform to the requisitions of this Act, then, and in that case, such person or persons shall be dealt with as this Act directs for persons of color coming into this State contrary to law.[15]

The penalties for this were spelled out in the 1820 law restricting emancipation: free people entering South Carolina could be apprehended by any white person and taken to a magistrate. The free person of color would then be ordered to leave within 15 days. Failing that, he or she would be fined $20; if that were not paid, the free person of color could then be sold into service for up to five years "and the amount of sale shall be divided, one half to the informer, and the other half for the use of the State."[16]

These laws were enforced in the era of the Vesey rebellion. Once the crisis passed, however, vigilance slacked and attention grew lax; many free blacks did have guardians, but did not bother to record the relationship with the clerk of court.

This still left the law of 1820 forbidding manumissions to complicate the lives of the free people of color community. To get around the law, those slave owners wanting to free their slaves deeded their slaves to a trustee in a deed of trust; the terms of the trust declared that the slave was to be allowed to act as if free, a deft maneuver to make the law work for the benefit of the slave. Often these slaves married and had children, and the trust declared their children to be free. Those living in the free people of color community, obeying the laws, paid a special tax each year, based on age and gender. This receipt for their free people of color tax was used as proof that the payer was free.

For two generations now this system had worked; but it all started unraveling with the stricter vigilance the police began to give to the badge laws around 1860. The problem had really escalated some 20 years earlier, when in

**1860 Mechanic, No. 176. (W. M. Rouse). Many badges taken out this year were worn by free people of color who were caught in rigid enforcements of slave codes.**

1841, the state legislature had passed "An Act to Prevent the Emancipation of Slaves, and for Other Purposes." In that act, it was declared

> That any bequest, gift, or conveyance, of any slave or slaves, accompanied with a trust or confidence, either secret or expressed, that such slave or slaves shall be held in nominal servitude only, shall be void and of no effect; and every donee or trustee, holding under such bequest, gift, or conveyance, shall be liable to deliver up such slave or slaves.[17]

Again, only the lax enforcement of the law prevented the "freed" slaves from being taken up. For years now, "free" men and women of color working without badges showed their annual tax receipts to prove they were free. But now in this era of closer attention being paid to the letter of the law (prompted, it seems, by the anger white mechanics felt towards hired-out slaves), the free persons of color were caught. According to the legal definition of freedom in South Carolina, one had to have been free in South Carolina before 1820 *or* be the child of a woman freed before then. *And,* since 1820, males also had to have a white trustee. Many of those "freed" by a deed of trust did not fit the letter of the law, and many males in this category (as well as those legally freed) had neglected to record a white guardian. So any person of color rousing a white person's attention in Charleston around 1860 could be questioned and found wanting.

Panic set into the free community; "there are cases" of people, one free person of color lamented in a letter on 20 August 1860, "who for 30 yrs have been paying Capitation Tax & one of 35 years that have to go back to bondage."[18] They were sold back into slavery (for a term of five years), as the law directed, or at the very least, the person in question had to find someone to deed him or her away in a new deed of trust. If that happened, one could no longer continue the charade of being free, since it really took an act of the legislature to become free, if one were not born of a free person of color. So, a person of color working in Charleston in this era could be caught for breaking a number of laws. This drove many in the free community to despair and to leave the city for good. (The law gave people 15 days to leave the state once warned to do so.)

Those who stayed stampeded the treasurer's office. On 9 August 1860, just a few weeks before the end of the fiscal year, the following article appeared in the *Courier*:

> Sale of Badges—It is estimated that in the last two or three days as many as three or four hundred badges have been sold by the City Treasurer. Some sixty or seventy negroes have been brought up by the Police before the Mayor for working out without a badge. Most of them were under a mistaken notion that they were free and did not require it. The law of 1822 [*sic*—really 1820], however, forbids the emancipation in this State of any slave after that year. Many owners have liberated their slaves since 1822, without, perhaps, taking this law into consideration. Their slaves must have at least an owner in trust. The announcement by the Mayor that such negroes were not free, created considerable commotion among those outside who were similarly situated as the parties arrested—The rush to the Treasurer's office for badges, has, in consequence, been unusually large.[19]

If they weren't arrested for not being literally free, they could be arrested for being non-free Negroes working without a badge. Those who could afford badges for the category they were already working in rushed out to buy an appropriate badge to try to hedge their bets and buy some sense of security. (The laws, however, said no badges could be sold to Negroes themselves, but had to be delivered to a white person; perhaps they had sympathetic whites go get the badges for them.) Money poured in too, from people trying to make up for non-payment in past years. "The Derreefs have had to pay some $80 in fines," wrote free person of color James Johnson.[20]

Others who took out badges did not feel safe, but fled. A journalist wrote of the plight of those he saw arriving in Philadelphia. "Some," he wrote, " have brought with them their copper badges, which read thus: Charleston, 1860, Servant, 1,243." The journalist was right about this badge, for this is exactly the order of information on badges that were worn in 1860; but he got the larger picture a bit garbled, writing that free people of color had to "wear a copper badge, bearing his number."

The Southern press seized upon this mistake and wrote in reply, "It is not true that there is any law in South Carolina, or in Charleston, requiring the free people of color to wear a distinctive badge."[21] This, indeed, was true, and had not been in effect since 1789; the newspaper, however, used this error to also say that the Philadelphia paper was wrong in saying there was a crisis for free people of color in Charleston. For, indeed, there was.

The tragedy for the free people of color was appalling, a trap sprung just as secession loomed to cut them off further from free states. But in cold print, their plight showed up as more income for the city. The fiscal year report did not appear in the *Courier* until 29 November 1860. It showed $11,450 in income for badges in the lower wards, the price for badge-making being $172. Most of the free people of color lived in the upper wards, and there the income was greater than it had ever been, $5,358, bringing badge income to the highest total ever, $16,808. *Estimates put the number of badges sold this year, also the highest ever, at 5,196.* The tone in the article in August of 1860 was amusing. The whites in town apparently thought the mad scrambling of the free people of color to save their freedom something comical, perhaps like bugs scrambling away from the light. The city made money on their tragedy.

The year-end report showed business as usual. In the lower wards, carts and drays brought in $7,742 against $219.73 for expenses, perhaps making badges; the upper wards brought in $5,600 for a total of $13,342. (Dog badges brought in $816 and $602 in the lower and upper wards.) There were 11,090 slaves in 1859 and 11,212 in 1860 in the lower wards; and 4,413 slaves in 1859 and 4,730 in 1860 in the upper wards. The number of slaves grew in each area as the number of free people of color decreased; 675 free people of color taxed in the lower wards in 1859 went down to 581 in 1860, and 959 taxed in the upper wards in 1859 lowered to 934 in 1860 in the upper wards. This is not surprising, for many free blacks were both being enslaved and leaving. According to estimates, all things being equal, with there being as many as 15,942 slaves in Charleston, a full 32 percent might have worn slave badges this year. But the number must be lower, for a large number of badge wearers were those who considered themselves free.

This then was the financial situation for the city, before it witnessed the Secession Convention in December 1860, and the starting of war in April 1861.

In appearance, the badges for these years were very similar to the ones created the decade before.

## *1851*

William Rouse did not clip the corners of some of his badges this year, so for the first time, there were sharp points on the "diamond" of some of his badges. Many servant badges with sharp corners have been found; but porter badges have been discovered with clipped corners. Clipped or not, the order of information was: "Charleston," date, occupation, and badge number. Rouse stamped all the information on these badges in this era, except for the badge numerals, which he punched.

## *1852*

These badges made by Rouse, diamond-shaped and corners clipped, bore their data in the order of "Charleston," badge number, occupation and date.

## *1853*

Starting with badges made this year, Rouse stopped clipping the corners of all badges, this perhaps being a time and cost saving gesture. Many of these unclipped badges have been excavated with corners bent, either from wear, or from the wearer deliberately bending them to make them more comfortable and to keep the sharp edges from snagging and unraveling fabric of clothes. Diamond-shaped as usual, they bear data in the same order of the 1851 badges: "Charleston," "1853," occupation, and number.

**1853 Mechanic, No. 171. (W. M. Rouse). This year none of the badges had their corners clipped. The same holds true for the next year, 1854.**

## *1854*

Rouse continued the pattern of diamond-shaped badges with unclipped corners. He put information on the badge in the same order of the 1852 badges.

## *1855*

This year the contract was awarded to William O'Connor. Like Rouse, O'Connor did not clip the corners of his badges; he used different lettering and numbering dies. The order of information he used was "Charleston," number, occupation, and then date. Like all the work of Rouse before him, O'Connor stamped all the data except for the badge number, which he punched.

### *1856*

W.B. Veronee, a tinman, or tinsmith, made badges this year. Veronee did not clip his corners on his badges this year, and his diamond-shaped badges followed the order of information of the year before, "Charleston," number, occupation, and date. Here again as with his predecessors before, all data, except for punched badge numbers, were stamped.

### *1857*

Rouse again got the contract in this and the following year, and returning to the contract, he returned to his earlier practice of clipping most corners of his badges. He followed the order of information of the preceding two years, stamping all the data, but for the punched badge number.

**1857 Servant, No. 2010. (W. M. Rouse). By this time, Rouse was clipping the corners of all the badges and occupations.**

### *1858*

Examples have been found with both clipped and unclipped corners of this year's diamond-shaped badges made by Rouse. "Charleston" is on the top line; next comes the date, the occupation, and the hand-punched badge number.

### *1859*

As noted earlier, the advertisements for proposals for slave and other badges placed in the papers at the end of 1858 for the 1859 badges noted that they would now be made "according to patterns in this [the treasurer's] office." Obviously, the pattern in the office allowed unclipped corners, for all those that follow have this feature. For the first time since 1826, the occupation is on the second line of text, after "Charleston" and before the badge number on the third line and the date on the bottom. Perhaps this had to do with the pattern decided upon by the treasurer's office. No announcement of who was awarded the contract has been found, but archeological evidence, showing how the dies match those used in 1856, suggest that the maker was Veronee.

### *1860*

The badges Rouse made this year were diamond-shaped with clipped corners; the information given followed the 1858 model, "Charleston, "1860," occupation, and badge number. Thus it appears that the "pattern" desired by the City Treasurer did not specify order of text after all.

This is a tabulation for the final full decade of slave badges (*italics* for estimated numbers):

| *Year* | *Badge year* | *# of badges* | *Income* | *Expenses* | *Maker* |
|---|---|---|---|---|---|
| 1850-1851 | 1851 | (6,350*) *4,668* | $15,108.00 | $243.00 or $237.00 | Rouse |
| 1851-1852 | 1852 | *4,588* | $14,843.00 | $290.26 | Rouse |
| 1852-1853 | 1853 | *4,346* | $14,058.00 | $243.30 | Rouse |
| 1853-1854 | 1854 | *4,162* | $13,465.00 | $349.40 | Rouse |
| 1854-1855 | 1855 | *3,834* | $12,403.96 | $266.00 | O'Connor |
| 1855-1856 | 1856 | *4,287* | $13,869.00 | $457.50 | Veronee |
| 1856-1857 | 1857 | *3,680* | $11,904.00 | ? | Rouse |
| 1857-1858 | 1858 | *4,783* | $15,474.00 | $135.00 | Rouse |
| 1858-1859 | 1859 | *4,235* | $13,699.00 | $122.08 | Veronee |
| 1859-1860 | 1860 | *5,196* | $16,808.00 | $172.00 | Rouse |

From 1851-1852 through 1855-1856, the press called for "at least" 5,600 badges.

From 1857-1858 through 1859-1860, the press called for "at least" 4,500 badges.

*6,350 made according to *Statement of Receipts and Expenditures*; 6,150 called for in the press.

Since the badge laws called for fisher badges to sell for $4 for men, and $2 for women, the price of $3 was used in estimating badge sales this decade.

"Badge year" denotes predominate badge sold in the fiscal year.

# CHAPTER 9

# 1861–1865

## *1860-1861 (1861 badges)*

In December 1860, the city began its annual process of advertising for proposals for badges (*Mercury*, 4 December 1860):

> Proposals in writing will be received at this office until 2 o'clock, P.M., of the 4th of December next, for finding Copper, Making, Lettering and Numbering, according to patterns in this office, at least 6,400 COPPER BADGES; for finding Tin, Making, Painting, Numbering and Lettering at least 2,800 TIN BADGES and SIGNS FOR TAVERN LICENSES; the whole to be approved by and executed under the direction of the City Treasurer, and delivered at his office at such periods and in such quantities as he shall direct.

Suddenly the number of badges was up from the "at least 4,500" for the past three to four years. Maybe this shows that indeed the 4,500 figure was low and surpassed every year, or maybe it shows that with the new enforcement of laws on free people of color, more were now needed. Obviously, the white mechanics were defeated, and reading this, they could see it; most whites were now joining together in defense of slavery.

Although this advertisement makes it seem that things were on a normal course in the city, they were not. Just a few days after the period for badge proposals was closed, Charleston was the scene of fateful events. On 20 December 1860, delegates signed a document that took South Carolina out of the Union. The Federal Troops on Sullivan's Island outside Charleston evacuated Fort Moultrie a few days later for the more key and strategic Fort Sumter in the middle of the harbor. War loomed.

These were extraordinary times. On 15 January 1861, City Council found it expedient to publicly put forth its budget. "About seven hundred and fifty-five thousand ($755,000.00) dollars will be required to meet the current expenses, and pay the maturing bonds and interest on city debts," George W. Williams, William Ravenel, E. W. Edgerton, and Charles Macbeth, Mayor, reported. The city listed only ten categories for income, one being "From Badges, Carts, Drays, etc." $25,000 would be needed; $47,000 in taxes on slaves was expected, too (Charleston *Mercury*). When the city published its fiscal report for the year ending August 1861, it showed "Badges for Negros" amounting to $13,381, with $422.05 in expenses, making the net receipt $12,958.95.[1] This figure can be checked in some of the few surviving financial records known from the city. A ledger book contains gross dollar amounts in a running total.[2] In the beginning of the new fiscal year, starting 1 September 1860, badges went on sale; the records tell us that $226 in badges had been sold by October, $291 worth by November, and $298 by the end of the year. Once 1861 badges went on sale in January, the gross totals jumped to $6,461 by the end of January and $11,095.95 by the end of February; the cents suggested that the amount paid the badge maker was deducted. March saw the total reach $11,768.95; April, $12,343.95; by the 31st of July, the amount reached $12,839.95 and the final amount at the end of August was $12,958.95, matching the amount listed in the paper. The total for carts and drays was $10,734.75, and dogs brought in a mere $224. The total amount from all badge sources equaled $23,917.70, very close to the $25,000 budgeted. *The estimated number, based on income, is 4,136 badges sold.*

## *1861-1862 (1862 badges)*

With the firing on Fort Sumter in April 1861, the city and the rest of the country went to war. It was raging mostly elsewhere, however, when the city advertised for the coming year. "Proposals in writing, will be received in this office until 2 o'clock P.M., of the 4th of December next," the treasurer noted (*Courier*, 26 November 1861). The proposal would be

> for Finding Copper, Making, Lettering and Numbering, according to the patterns in this Office, at least 4,500 COPPER BADGES; for finding Tin, Making, Painting, Numbering and Lettering at least 1,400 TIN BADGES and Signs for Tavern Licenses. The whole to be approved by and executed under the direction of the City Treasurer, and delivered at his Office at such periods, and in such quantities, as he shall direct. Persons whose offers shall be accepted will have to call on the City Attorney and execute sufficient Bonds for the fulfillment of their contracts. A. Campbell, City Treasurer.

**1862 Porter, No. 1128. (William Veronee). Much definition was lost when this badge was turned over and re-stamped.**

The change is obvious; there is not only a drop in the number of slave badges from the estimated 6,500 of the previous year to "at least 4,500"; there is also a reduction by half of the number of tin badges for carts and drays. This reduction may be attributable to the wartime economy; with the harbor blockaded, there was no need for moving materials around town, and horses and equipment could have been pressed into service elsewhere. Besides, many people were being told to prepare to leave. Planters as far south as the South Edisto Inlet were warned in a notice just below the treasurer's advertisement to be ready to evacuate. Metal was soon to be in short supply, what with the creation of ironclad ships, as noted in an advertisement on this same page. More ominously still, there was a call on this page for "DONATIONS or SUBSCRIPTIONS IN AID OF THE DEFENSES OF THE CITY."

On 1 January of 1862, the city treasurer posted a notice in the *Courier* that badges would be on sale for the prices as shown in earlier years; the oath necessary to swear out was listed as well. But things were not the same; the following article appeared in the *Courier* a week later (8 January 1862): "Iron and copper—in fact all the important and valuable metals, except tin—are found abundantly within the Confederate States, and yet in some places, from delay or insufficiency in transportation, there is a short supply." This lack of tin could help explain why only half the number of tin badges was called for. The city kept on using copper, however. The fact that it did and went on licensing slaves and creating badges for them out of scarce materials shows how wedded it was to the system of hiring out. (As a result of the metal shortages, badges were soon recycled; many of those found show evidence of having their backs used for the subsequent year.)

On 1 February 1862, the city listed the receipts and expenditures for calendar year 1861, and estimated receipts for 1862 (*Courier*). It noted that $12,000 was expected from badges, with $8,000 expected from carts and drays, totaling $20,000; the projected income is not too far down from the $25,000 projected the year before.

On 25 February 1862, police records show the arrest of Isaac Morrison, a free person of color for nonpayment of his 1861 capitation tax, but the charges were dismissed. A. M. Jones was arrested on a similar charge on 3 April 1862, as was Ralph Coffin on 8 August 1862, who was fined $40 for nonpayment of his 1861 and 1862 capitation taxes.[3]

When the fiscal year ended in August, the report, not published until 31 December 1862, was not good (*Courier*). The city had brought in only $9,624.50 in badges, and it had cost significantly more ($588.30) to make them, perhaps due to the scarcity of materials. (According to financial records dated 13 January 1862, however, the city actually had expected to pay out as much as $1,200 for these badges.)[4] *The estimated number of badges sold is 2,975.* The ledger surviving from the time contains figures that match exactly those published in the press. $108 worth of badges had come in by 31 October 1861; $131.50 by the end of December. By 28 February 1862, the amount had grown to $7,980.20; the amount was $8,883.20 by the end of May and $9,046.20 by the end of August. That matches to the penny the amount of income reported in the press ($9,624.50) minus expenses ($588.30).

According to the financial report, there were 15,637 slaves in Charleston in 1861 and 12,903 the next year. So the percentage of slaves hired out fell between 18 and 22 percent for this last year in which there are population statistics. Carts and drays brought in $7,366; dogs brought in only $52. Sweeps (after the fire of December 1861 which laid waste to a large part of town) brought in $70, more than usual. Obviously, people were now scared of fire and checking their chimneys; the disaster also had a great effect on the local economy, reducing income from slave-hiring and carts and drays. Life in Charleston, if just read from the balance sheet, could be seen to be changing.

## *1862-1863 (1863 badges)*

"CITY BADGES," the headline ran in the ad in the 22 December 1862 edition of the *Charleston Daily Courier*.

> Proposals for materials, making, painting & C. COPPER or TIN BADGES, for the year 1863, according to patterns, as shall be shown in the Treasurer's Office, and of such quantities as he shall direct, will be received under seal addressed to the City Treasurer. These Badges to be delivered by the 1st of January next.

This did not leave much time (less than ten days or so) to stamp them out; tellingly, no number here was stated, just quantities, as the treasurer would direct.

War was certainly takings its toll, but the newspaper ran an article about the high price for Negroes, nine being sold recently, "three of them of an inferior description" nevertheless selling for high rates (*Charleston Daily Courier*, 8 January 1863). Other similar notices appeared on 21 January, 26 February, and 4 March, but there were also articles on the difficulty of buying salt and the abridgement of some lessons in the high school (14 January). More telling perhaps was an advertisement of John Mood's, once the provider of slave badges for the city. "ZINC! ZINC! ZINC!" went the top line of his ad (26 March 1863). "OLD COPPER! OLD COPPER! BRASS! BRASS! BRASS! BRASS! BRASS! THE HIGHEST PRICE WILL BE PAID FOR THE above at JOHN MOOD'S 336 KING-STREET." One wonders if people turned in old brass dog badges and old copper slave badges to this former slave badge maker.

On 24 January 1863, the city published its upcoming budget for the year in the *Courier*, noting that it expected to get just $5,000 for badges, so certainly there were less made. Fiscal reports now ceased to appear in the papers. (Eight thousand slaves were slated to bring in $24,000 in taxes; and free people of color were slated to bring in $6,000, down from $7,000 the year before.)

A city ledger provides information that the papers no longer provide. As of 1 January 1863, only $63 had come in for badges; by the end of April, the amount was $6,446.50; by 1 July it grew to $7,282.50, and the total at the end of the fiscal year was $7,385.50, showing more income than actually budgeted.[5] In fact, the total income was actually $7,704; another city record spanning the time period 1860 to 1884 notes that the expenses this year were $318.50 and that the figure $7,385.50 was arrived at by subtracting expenses from total income.[6] (Carts and drays brought $5,560; and dogs, $54.) *According to the formula, as many as 2,381 slave badges may have been sold.*

Fewer badges were being sold, and there seemed to be more lawbreaking going on, or perhaps a more vigilant police force looking for spies and firestarters in the streets of Charleston. Police records show that many slaves were being caught for working without badges. (The records also show men deserting from gunboats and forts around the city.)

Mr. Gibson, a free man of color, was fined $20 for nonpayment of his capitation taxes on 17 November 1862, according to police arrest records. Lizza Wadsworth was fined $40 on 2 January 1863 for not paying her taxes for two years. The slave "Amos to Mr. Johnson" was taken up on 5 February 1863 for "working out without a badge," as was Gail to Tom Small, Charles to Dr. Mitchell, Gabriel to Mr. Williams, and Sam, James and Stephen to Mr. Therin. Most were fined $20, half to the arresting officer, half to the city. Amos to Mr. Johnson was discharged. "Grad to Mrs. Rogers" was taken up for the same offense on 7 February; of the $20 paid, half went to the policeman, half to the city; as it did for Dinah to J.T. Elsworth, "working without a badge." John to Charles Hankel and Patty to H. Nelson (listed as free, perhaps meaning a free person of color) were also taken up for this charge but had their cases dismissed. Vinney to Mr. McElmoy was assessed a fine of $10, paid to the officer only. The crackdown continued. Joe to Mr. Bailey was taken up for working without a badge on 10 February, and on 1 March, Huldah to T. N. Gadsden was also arrested for working out without a badge. The fine was $20; but the city's half was rescinded; the other half went to the arresting officers. Police records end on 18 March; no other arrests are known.[7]

## *1863-1864 (1864 badges)*

City Council records (published in the 26 November 1863 *Charleston Mercury)* show that the clerk of council was instructed to advertise for proposals for two city printers; no ads for proposals for making slave badges have been found. The few slave badges found for 1864 show that the badges for 1863 were often reused. Many 1864 badges (but not all) have been stamped on the back of 1863 badges. This was due to the fact that metal was scarce. On Tuesday morning, 5 January 1864, the following notice from "Headquarters, Dept. SC. GA and FLA," dated Charleston, S.C., 3 January 1864, appeared in the *Courier*: "Citizens are particularly requested to refrain from purchasing from soldiers in this Department, any copper, brass, or zinc of any description, all of which are wanted by the Ordnance Officers of Charleston."

The need for metal was so great that bells were taken from steeples. As early as 1862, the governor and executive committee of the state had paid Frederick Paturzo for removing 11 bells from St. Philips Church, seven from St. Michael's, one from the Scotch Church (First Scots, at the corner of Tradd and Meeting Streets), and one bell from St. Paul's. The next week, bells were removed from the Lutheran Church, from Magnolia Cemetery, the Palmetto Engine House, Flynn's Church (Second Presbyterian Church), Arsenal tower, the workhouse tower, and railroad shops. But slave badges were still being made and used.[8]

On 14 January 1864 (*Courier*), all slave owners in Charleston were

> hereby summoned to deliver ONE FOURTH of their male slaves, between the ages of sixteen and fifty, at the Depot of the South Carolina Rail Road in Mary Street, on Monday, the twenty fifth day of January instant, at 10 O'clock A.M. for thirty days labor on the Fortifications.

No doubt badges were not required for this mandatory service, and maybe the free persons of color were exempted from badges, if not from work:

**1863 Servant, No. 44. (William Veronee). Due to scarcity of copper, an 1862 Porter badge, No. 1128, was reused to stamp this on the back. Many badges from 1862 onward were double-stamped.**

Free Persons of Color, males, between the same ages, are hereby ordered to report on the same day, time and place above mentioned. Those failing to do so will be impressed and sent down to work on the fortifications along the coast.

As the city fell into chaos, still nevertheless, the papers noted "High Price of Negroes" on 29 January 1864. Their bondage would not last long.

But while it did, slaves were being hired out. The city ledger shows that $3,500 in income came in from slave badges by 1 April 1864; by 1 July, it inched up to $3,660, and the end of the fiscal year showed a total of $4,042. A parallel city record, however, notes that this latter figure is really the total less expenses of $540, meaning that the true gross income for badges was $4,582. (Carts and drays amounted to $5,960 and $35 came in from sweeps. No dog badge income is given.)[9] Indeed, as these figures attest, life was now different in the city for slave and free, and the hired-out. *Only 1,416 badges may have been sold this year.*

### *1864-1865 (1865 badges)*

The papers were no longer printing such ordinary things as advertisements for proposals for slave badges as 1865 dawned, but archeological evidence shows that while it teetered on chaos and collapse, the city nevertheless carried on with slave hiring, diverting scarce metals from defense of the city to their defense of the slave-hiring system. At least two 1865 badges are known. The surviving city ledger, so reliable on all foregoing entries, states that $5,504 had accrued in the badge category; it also states that carts and drays totaled $10,862. (Furthermore, it states that only $64 had come in the new fiscal 1864-65 year by 31 December 1864.) Perhaps the only way to make sense of these figures is to construe the amounts as running totals continued from 31 August

1864. At that point, as shown above, slave badge totals amounted to $4,042, and carts and drays totaled $10,211.80. It is conceivable that $1,462 came in from badges from 1 September 1864 through 31 January 1865, with only $64 coming in by the end of 1864, making the total for January 1865, $1,398. (The amount for carts and drays would have been $650.20.) But one can make sense of that by adjusting for inflation. The cost of everything was going up dramatically, including prices for all the badges in all categories. On 23 January 1865, less than a month before the fall of the city, the following appeared in the *Courier:*

> THE FOLLOWING rates have been established by City Council:
>
> | | |
> |---|---|
> | Servant's Badge | $10 |
> | Porter's Badge | 20 |
> | Fruiterer's Badge | 25 |
> | Mechanic's Badge | 35 |
> | Private Cart License | 10 |
> | Public Cart License | 60 |
> | Bread Cart License | 60 |
> | Hack License | 150 |
> | Omnibus License | 200 |
>
> and must be taken out during the month of January.

So those who did buy their badges in January bought them at excessively high prices; by 1840, the prices had stabilized: $2 for a servant; $4 for a porter; $5 for fruiterer, a mechanic going for $7. In January 1865, badge prices were now going for five times the amount they had gone for the past 20 years. (That no fisher badges were listed might be an oversight, or telling. With so much warfare going on in the harbor, marshes and rivers around the city, fishing was not only dangerous, but the possibility existed of slaves going over to the enemy, as Robert Smalls had done in the *The Planter.*) *Estimates based on the premises above point to only 88 badges being sold in 1865.*

However many in 1865 sold, they were the last. On 18 February 1865, Federal troops entered Charleston, the city that had brought more slaves into the country than any other. The institution which had supported and shaped the city and which the city had fashioned into a type of bondage peculiarly its own was now overthrown. Scattered about in the dust of its destruction were countless slave badges, which surfaced over the years, and which are still surfacing, to tell their story.

As for the badges themselves, they, as noted above, are quite scarce, with fewer found for each year of the reign of the Confederacy. Books printed in the Confederate States of America from the point of secession in December

1860 through early 1865 are collectible for being Confederate Imprints. The same can be said of the badges made these final years. The badges from these years started with the look from the decade before.

### *1861*

The badges made this year are attributed to Rouse due to their resemblance to the ones he made and the dies he used. They are diamond-shaped, with clipped corners, and are the smallest badges found. The information was stamped, but for the badge number, which was punched, in the following order: "Charleston," badge number, occupation and date.

### *1862*

It appears that Veronee was the maker of badges for this year, and it also appears that he would see out the procedure to its final days. The badges he made this year were diamond-shaped, with clipped corners and with information ordered "Charleston," date, occupation, and badge number. Veronee also, it seems, started the practice of double-stamping the badges, i.e., stamping 1862 on the back of 1861 badges, to save the copper. The 1862 badges that are not double-stamped are just marginally larger than the smallest badges of the year before.

### *1863, 1864 and 1865*

Many, if not nearly all of the badges from these years found show strikings on both sides, a practice carried out by Veronee, who also appears to be the maker of these badges. But since at least one from this era shows no strikeovers, it must be argued that new badges were made in these waning years of the Confederacy. The order of information on these last badges was "Charleston," badge number, occupation, and finally the year.

One 1865 slave badge discovered is a number 13, a servant, double-stamped on the back of an 1864 servant badge, number 541, possibly carried by the same slave/servant two years in a row.

The slave who carried it (and the badge itself) saw the end of slavery. Today, this particular item is damaged. Part of this damage is due to it having been stamped on the reverse of the 1864 badge, but the other destruction seems deliberate. There is a hole in its center as if someone drove a nail through the surface. Did a freed slave take a badge from his or her pocket, and nail it to a post to prove the end of slavery? If so, it would have hung in plain view, testifying to a past misery, while still encouraging those around to reflect and never forgot the horror of its wearing. (See color image on page H of insert.) It, along with all others that have been discovered, and those yet to emerge from the earth, continue to compel and tantalize. They carry a weight of unanswered questions and unguessed significance. The deciphering of their story, sketched in this volume, remains unfinished. New information can turn up with any random turn of the earth, or with the discovery and/or return of records to the city of Charleston.

This is a tabulation of the final years (with estimates in *italics*):

| *Fiscal Year* | *Badge Year* | *# of badges* | *Income* | *Expenses* | *Maker* |
|---|---|---|---|---|---|
| 1860-1861 | 1861 | (6,400*) *4,136* | $13,381.00 | $422.05 | Rouse |
| 1861-1862 | 1862 | (4,500*) *2,975* | $9,624.50 | $588.30 | Veronee |
| 1862-1863 | 1863 | *2,381* | $7,70400 | $318.50 | Veronee |
| 1863-1864 | 1864 | *1,416* | $4,582.00 | $540.00 | Veronee |
| 1864-1865 | 1865 | *88* | $1,398.00 | | Veronee |

*Called for in the press.

"Badge year" denotes the predominant badge sold in the fiscal year.

## AFTERWORD

# A Note on Counterfeits

There is no way any participant in the slave-hire practice (slave, legislator, badge maker or purchaser) could have foreseen the frenzy and interest these bits of copper have triggered in the scholarly and collecting community in the last decades of the twentieth century and the beginning of the twenty-first. These tangible pieces of history are now desperately sought after, bought and sold in auctions for higher and higher amounts, selling for more than what a slave would have brought in the nineteenth century. So desirable are they, that they, unfortunately, are now being created in counterfeit.

Many fakes are quite easy to spot. They look brand new and name impossible places, like plantations and conditions, claiming to be passes excusing the bearer for being found on the road at night. On the Internet, many of these are being sold under the category of "fantasy badges," a title that is particularly apt. Other badges, however, are quite good forgeries. The authors of this book have foreseen the fact that the information offered here can help possible purchasers avoid the pitfalls of counterfeits, but we realize, as well, that counterfeiters may also use the information presented here to produce better fakes. To help consumers combat this, we recommend that all badges purchased be checked against the data presented herein for individual years. We have neither discovered nor presented all that is possible to know about badges and their appearance. We have not seen badges from three years, 1804, 1808 and 1809; nor have we seen all the possible names for some early categories. Nor have any badges before the year 1800 ever turned up. We suggest that careful attention be paid to the patina of the badges, the history offered, and all the lettering, position, and order of text, including whether the letters and numbers are punched, engraved or stamped. One thing not often taken into consideration, and something overlooked (until now) by counterfeiters, is the subject of numbering. As shown earlier, the numbering system of the very early years is not known. It has not been shown if badges were numbered in categories, or just in a total sequence. It is obvious, however, that badges were numbered within categories at least by 1807, when two badges in different categories are known to share the same number. (This could have been the practice as early as 1803.) This fact has not been published until now, so forgers have often inadvertently slipped up. There was, for instance, a badge from the late 1850s advertised for sale in the year 2000; it came with a very intriguing and plausible history and a patina that suggested it had rested in the earth. What made it suspect were some of the letters (appearing too smooth and modern and regular); but what made its falsehood glaring was its occupation and number. It was a "Carpenter," making it questionable, since such badges from that time period were most often called "Mechanics," there being no "Carpenter" known to the authors later than 1813. While this would not totally disqualify it, what did, without a doubt, was its number. No more than 600 mechanic badges were made in the 1850-1851 fiscal year, the period when the number of badges made in each category was reported. This particular "Carpenter" badge bore a number in the 800s range, making it quite implausible.

Counterfeits such as these tend to be very recent in origin. The contemporary laws against counterfeits were fairly severe, and while it seems that some enforcement of the statutes was quite lax, still there is not much evidence that counterfeiters flourished. Slaves were to be whipped, put in the stocks and confined in the workhouse, according to the laws; whites would be fined. Although most antebellum police records for the city of Charleston have not survived, there is no mention of counterfeiting badges in those records that are known. Moreover, while newspapers and pamphlets on city finances occasionally mention other infractions regarding badges, such as working without a badge, or a citizen being refunded for a badge, there is no mention of counterfeiting. The minutes of the City Council that were printed in the newspaper press (and thus saved), took up all sorts of issues regarding badges, transferring them, refunding their costs, etc. Never was the issue of counterfeiting raised. Nor was it listed as an offense in any of the tables compiling crime statistics. Furthermore, none of the mechanic petitions of the late 1850s and early 1860s, and no other document complaining of the lax enforcement of the laws, ever mentioned counterfeiting either. What is suggestive, too, is that the penalty for counterfeiting did not change over the years in the ordinances, while other elements, the cost of badges, the penalties and punishments for working out without badges, etc., did. Certainly, if counterfeiting were rampant, the city authorities would have clamped down on it.

Nevertheless, there do seem to be some fairly old counterfeits on the market and in museums. Theresa Singleton, in her landmark article on badges, included an image of irregular-shaped badges, from 1834 and 1844. Their shapes alone should warn that they are counterfeits; none in those peculiar formats have ever surfaced. The lettering of "Charleston" in the 1834 badge is suspect, not matching any sort of letters from any other year. And even more telling is the lack of the letters "No." preceding the slave badge numeral; no badges lacking that have appeared in this era.

Suspect in the 1844 badge is the splitting of the year into two sets of numerals, 18 and 44, but odder still (odder even than the very irregular shape) is the inclusion of "S.C." the letters that split the year. No other badge from any other year includes the abbreviation of South Carolina. There would be no reason for badge makers to have included it. So why would a counterfeiter?

Certainly, through ignorance. But images of these badges were published in the first modern article on the items long before they became so hotly collected. These two badges had been in the Charleston Museum's collection for numerous years. The 1834 badge was given to the museum in 1933, and the 1844 badge was donated in 1966.[1] There were no connections necessarily with Charleston and South Carolina with the donors; the items had been in their families for a while, and it was the notation of "Charleston" that prompted heirs to donate them to the museum.

Recently, another similar badge with "Charleston, SC" stamped on it was found in the city of Charleston. For all intents and purposes it did appear to have rested in the earth for a number of years; certainly clever forgers could have aged it, or made it and buried it, biding their time. But the person who found it did actually unearth it. Could this mean that it is a forgery from the times of slavery?

Not likely; for counterfeiters at the time could not have hoped to have this type of work pass muster, even on a casual inspection. Counterfeiters would have obviously known what the badges for the particular year looked like and would have made their false copies accordingly. So, who could have possibly made such an egregious error long enough ago to have the badge be in the earth for a number of years?

A clue comes, fittingly enough, from the first person known to have tried to unravel the history of slave badges. That was John Bennett, originally from Ohio, who, when he first visited Charleston in 1898, was immediately intrigued with the place and all its customs. Especially intriguing to him were the local African Americans. He studied their language of Gullah and published a scholarly treatise on it; he collected and transcribed spirituals and wrote down much of the African American oral folklore rapidly passing out of existence. In 1903, as noted in the beginning of this book, he wrote the first truly objective piece on slave badges. In it, he ridiculed those who believed that all slaves had worn such badges, and he also criticized those who were trying to pass off fake items, such as railroad claim badges. For the first time since the end of the Civil War, Charleston was experiencing a flood of tourists from the rest of the country. Even President Theodore Roosevelt and author Samuel Clemens had come to attend the South Carolina Interstate and West-Indian Exposition on the outskirts of town, now the site of the urban Hampton Park.

As mentioned in Bennett's article, tourists were coming to town, anxious to find what they could buy and take away regarding the city and its slave-tainted history. The Exposition itself had many trinkets for sale, such as seashells, booklets, pillows and scarves, all noting the name and Charleston, SC.[2] One cannot help but wonder if someone in this era (or earlier, perhaps catering to the abolitionists' horror of the practice so identified with the city) had, with imperfect knowledge, manufactured a piece of history for tourists. Such a trinket, if it just stated "Charleston" would not necessarily have satisfied a tourist specifically wanting to carry away of piece of history from this South Carolina city; it could be confused with Charleston, West Virginia, or other Charlestons elsewhere in the country. So, to appeal to these customers, forgers at the time, with just vague recollections of the badges, but with more of an eye on possible buyers, could have created items to sell. (And as noted in the introduction, slave owners, those who saw such badges all the time, and even the owners of a slave museum were all muddled on the appearance and uses of the badges.) Counterfeiters, in fact, could have even stumbled across some of the original dies and stamps of the makers, some of them, like William O'Connor and William Rouse, living into the late nineteenth century. Stamping odd pieces of metal, and catering to a hunger for history, they could have created many of the old counterfeits. These may have been purchased and passed on in families for a generation or two. Descendants, inheriting them, having no reason to doubt their authenticity, could have in all sincerity turned them over to museums as gifts or sold them on the collector's market. Some could have even been lost and thrown out over the years, where they are still being unearthed today.

This is only a suggestion, but one that can answer all the questions arising from such blatant forgeries. Only further discoveries over time may reveal the truth of this and other issues related to these pieces of slave history. Hopefully readers of this book will continue the search, and much information, looted from Charleston during or after the Civil War, lost in walls, underground, and in archives and libraries, will come to the surface, as badges themselves often do, to add their testimony to the story.

# Appendix 1: A Note on the Mathematical Formula

In order to estimate the number of badges created and/or sold in any given year, a formula was needed. It was developed based on the year for which the most complete set of data was known. In 1850, the City of Charleston published the pamphlet *Statement of Receipts and Expenditures by the City Council of Charleston from the 1st July 1849, to 1st July 1850.* Although there are some questions regarding the total number of badges created that year (see Chapter 7 for details), the pamphlet states that in January 1850, the city had a specific number of badges made in each category. Using the number of badges in each category, a model was created for estimating the number of badges sold or created in other years. These categories and their corresponding percentages in 1850 are as follows:

| *Badge Category* | *Number of Badges Made in 1850* | *Percentage of total* |
|---|---|---|
| Servant | 2,400 | 53.6% |
| Porter | 1,400 | 31.3% |
| Mechanic | 400 | 8.9% |
| Fruiterer | 180 | 4.0% |
| Fisher | 100 | 2.2% |
| Total: | 4,480 | 100.0% |

Using the total revenues recorded in other years, the formula was applied as such:

Total badges = Total revenues/(Price of Servant badge × 53.6 percent) + (Price of Porter badge × 31.3 percent) + (Price of mechanic badge × 8.9 percent) + (Price of fruiterer badge × 4.0 percent) + (Price of fisher badge × 2.2 percent)

Basically, this formula matches the percentages calculated above with total badge revenues and individual badge prices to derive the total number of badges made/sold in any given year. The figure for total revenue for any given year may give one a sense of increase and decrease; i.e., if the number of badges sold rose or fell from year to year, but is not totally reliable. If badge prices increased, the gross revenue would increase, but the number of badges made and sold could have decreased. So knowing the price of badges for each year and the percentages sold is key. Using this one year of data available is fraught with dangers, however, for there is no way of knowing if this year and the categories made in it were in any way typical. But it is the only way to make any workable estimates as to the number of badges sold, and thus the number of slaves hired out in any given year.

It is necessary to note that the city published a similar pamphlet the next year, and the categories and gross numbers are all different. This was to be expected, for in this year (1851), the city now encompassed the Neck, so a much larger number of badges would be sold. For 1851 and after, a formula similar to the one above was used to estimate the badges sold from then until 1865.

Key to the derivation of the estimate is the dollar amount of income. For some years, expenses and income is given, and for some years, income minus expenses is known. Instead of second guessing what the figure means, the authors have just used the most reliable figure, assuming it to be income. There are some problems with prices of badges for some years, too, but these are noted in the particular chapters.

# Appendix 2: A Note on Sources

Many city records, key to interpreting the badge laws and the system, are unknown. But many do exist in a variety of formats.

For the most part, statutes have been published and are available in various compilations, digests and/or microfilm. The researcher must be aware, however, that some compilations were not published until years after laws were originally passed, so if they were emended or overturned, the full text of the original laws may not be included; turning to the newspapers is often the only way to find the original law. And not all slave badge laws were codified under those headings; in the 1830s, the City of Charleston made some changes to the slave badge laws in the bills passed to raise income for the city.

City Council records are vital in reconstructing the badge system and all aspects of city government. Except for two volumes, no original City Council minutes are known. One volume covers the period of 1822, it being the scratch copy of minutes that would have been copied over in fair hand. The other volume covers parts of the years 1834–36 and was for years in fragments and unusable. Extensive work by Liz Newcombe and Harlan Greene of the South Carolina Room, Charleston County Public Library, has returned this source to usability. Much of the manuscript could not be recovered, and there are large gaps in the pages and the text.

At some point, the City of Charleston began to publish its City Council minutes in the newspapers of the day; fragments appeared in the early years of the nineteenth century; full transcripts of the meetings were printed in the local press in the 1830s. A century later, the Works Progress Administration put people to work transcribing these minutes from the nineteenth century newspapers. The workers transcribed what they could find from the 1830s until the late 1850s; they are now housed in the South Carolina Room of the Charleston County Public

Library. Realizing that scholars would have to go back and check the holograph copies against the printed minutes for accuracy, the staff went back to the microfilm and printed out those City Council minutes from the newspapers for researcher use. More research is needed to determine what other records are in the papers.

Financial records, for the most part, do not exist for the City of Charleston until the 1850s; those scattered records that are known are in the South Carolina Room of the Charleston County Library. The authors of this book have made extensive use of the fiscal year-end reports published by the city in the newspapers from roughly 1783 to 1865. The city was incorporated in August of 1783, and its fiscal year always ended on the last day of that month. For nearly every year between 1783 to 1865, the authors have located published accounts of the city's expenses and income, usually printed in early September. These records contain much information of use to economic historians and those interested in the day-to-day operation of the city. The city also published a few pamphlets that laid out expenses and income for the city for year-long periods. They exist for the 1849-1850 and 1850-1851 periods; with some similar information available for the 1836-1837 era.

The badge books, crucial to any true understanding of the system, are not known. Not one scrap from scores of years of such records is among city records, while similar records noting the taxes paid by free persons of color (called the Capitation books) do exist. One can only wonder if they were destroyed each year or were destroyed after the Civil War. They could have been taken by souvenir hunters, could still lay undiscovered in someone's attic or basement, or could possibly even have been sold on the streets of Charleston in the late 1940s.

This possibility is related to what is known of the antebellum City of Charleston records. About 90 percent of the records known from this period came out of the Charleston Orphan House before the building was torn down in the late 1940s. The Orphan House, a monumental structure at the corner of Calhoun and St. Philip's streets, was a city-run institution. When Charleston came under siege in 1863, the Mayor moved his office to the Orphan House, beyond Union shells. It appears that City Records were moved here, as well.

All Orphan House records survived the Civil War; and it may be that city records did as well. Mr. J. V. Nielsen of the City's Historical Commission toured the orphan house before it was torn down. According to its minutes (in Special Collections of the Charleston County Public Library), "he reported on the careless removal of the contents of the Orphan House Library, and his having purchased for a very small amount a number of books including 4 bound volumes of official manuscript records, viz. Reports to the Commissioners from one of the departments. These reports he had already promised to give to the South Carolina Historical Society." In fact, nearly all the known antebellum records of the City of Charleston were thus turned over to the Historical Society, which later turned them over to the City of Charleston once a records management department was established.

Continuing on, the minutes note that Mr. Nielsen "stated the books were thrown on the floor in great confusion, and apparently no effort was being made to dispose of them, any that were not sold, it was presumed would be left for destruction when the building is razed."

Apparently, some books were sold from the Orphan House; some of the "books" could very easily have been the manuscript badge books. And apparently, there were records in the building when it was torn down. A local family purchased some of the bricks from the Orphan House; when they were delivered, a destroyed volume was in the load. It was turned over to the South Carolina Historical Society and later to City Archives; with much work, staff of the Charleston Public Library put the destroyed and shredded pages back together, reconstituting the City Council minutes from 1834 through 1836. The only other known volume of minutes, 1822, was earlier taken out of the building and obtained by Nielsen.

Over the years, other stray volumes of city records have turned up, often having been saved by city employees, or having turned up in estates. When the police station on St. Philip Street was razed in the 1970s a bystander saved some antebellum and Civil War police records for the City of Charleston and turned them over to the Charleston Library Society.

By this time, the city had a very professional Archives and Records Management Division, which amassed all early city records and worked heroically to catalogue and find them, overcoming centuries of oversight. (Most American cities did not start such programs until this time; Charleston's program is both an early and admirable one.) To better make these valuable records accessible to the public, the City of Charleston and the County of Charleston worked out a transfer of the records from the former to the latter. Early records are now in Special Collections of the Charleston County Library and are being catalogued and microfilmed for researcher use. It is hoped that, over time, more records, such as the city's badge books, will surface and be added to the archives where they can be used for the public's benefit.

# Chapter Notes

## *Introduction*

1. Walter J. Fraser, Jr., *Charleston! Charleston! The History of a Southern City* (Columbia: University of South Carolina Press, 1989), 6.
2. Quoted in Edmund L. Drago, *Broke by the War: Letters of a Slave Trader* (Columbia: University of South Carolina Press, 1991), 3.
3. Drago, *Broke by the War*, 3.
4. John Bennett, "'Slave Tags' for Tourists: Railroad Local Trunk Checks at Two Dollars Each," *Sunday News (and Courier)*, 3 May 1903.
5. Daniel Elliot Huger Smith, *A Charlestonian's Recollections, 1846–1913* (Charleston, SC: The Carolina Art Association, 1950), 64.
6. John Andrew Johnson, *The Experience of A Slave in South Carolina* (London: Passmore & Alabaster, 1862), 25.
7. I. Jenkins Mikell, *The Rumbling of the Chariot Wheels* (Columbia, SC: The State Company, 1923), 41–42.
8. Miriam Bellangee Wilson, *Slave Days* (Charleston, SC: Old Slave Mart Foundation, 1946), 9–10.
9. Daria Macomber, *A Clearing in the Fog* (New York: The World Publishing Co., 1970), 119.
10. Pam Durban, *So Far Back* (New York: Picador USA, 2000), 208.
11. Richard C. Wade, *Slavery in the Cities: The South 1820–1860* (New York: Oxford University Press, 1964), 49–50.
12. Theresa Singleton, "The Slave Tag: An Artifact of Urban Slavery," *South Carolina Antiquities*, 1984, vol. 16, pp. 41–65.
13. Personal communication between Singleton and the author, January 2000.
14. Bennett, "'Slave Tags' for Tourists."
15. This was slave William Garner. Edward A. Pearson, *Designs Against Charleston: The Trial Record of the Denmark Vesey Slave Conspiracy of 1822* (Chapel Hill: University of North Carolina Press, 1999), 74. Although this source has been recalled by the press for its faulty transcription of the Vesey trial manuscripts, its narratives and lists are still useful.
16. Quoted in Michael P. Johnson and James L. Roark, *Black Masters: A Free Family of Color in the Old South* (New York: W. W. Norton Co., 1984), 181.
17. Quoted in Pearson, *Designs Against Charleston*, 73.
18. Edward Ball, *Slaves in the Family* (New York: Ballantine Books, 1999), 89.
19. Bennett, "'Slave Tags' for Tourists."

## *Chapter 1. 1670–1822: Laws of the Colony and the Early Republic*

1. David J. McCord and Thomas Cooper, eds. *The Statutes at Large of South Carolina* (Columbia, SC, 1840) Vol. 7, 343.
2. McCord and Cooper, *Statutes*, vol. 7, 363.
3. McCord and Cooper, *Statutes*, vol. 7, 380.
4. Quoted in Singleton, "The Slave Tag," 45.
5. Quoted in Mary Allison Carll, *The Role of the Black Artisan in the Building Trades and the Decorative Arts in South Carolina's Charleston District, 1760–1800* (PhD dissertation, University of Tennessee, Knoxville, 1982), 71.
6. *South Carolina Gazette*, 8 November 1742, quoted in Singleton, "The Slave Tag," 46.
7. *South Carolina Gazette*, 6–13 May 1751, cited in Singleton, "The Slave Tag," 46.
8. David J. McCord, *Statutes at Large of South Carolina* (Columbia, SC, 1841), vol. 9, 704.
9. *South Carolina Gazette*, 31 March–25 August 1764.
10. McCord, *Statutes*, vol. 9, 704.
11. *South Carolina Gazette*, 24 September 1772.
12. McCord, *Statutes*, vol. 9, 704.
13. Quoted in Leila Sellers, *Charleston Business on the Eve of the American Revolution* (Chapel Hill: University of North Carolina Press, 1934), 100.
14. *South Carolina Gazette and General Advertiser*, 28 November 1783.
15. *South Carolina Gazette and General Advertiser*, 28 November 1783.
16. *South Carolina Gazette and General Advertiser*, 28 November 1783.
17. Alexander Edwards, *Ordinances of the City Council of Charleston* (Charleston: W. P. Young, 1802), 68.
18. Singleton, "The Slave Tag," 47.
19. Edwards, *Ordinances of the City Council of Charleston*, 193.
20. Edwards, *Ordinances of the City Council of Charleston*, 224.
21. Edwards, *Ordinances of the City Council of Charleston*, 397–98.
22. Minutes of the proceedings of City Council of Charleston, 13 April 1837 (printed in the *Courier*, 1 May 1837).
23. Charleston City Council, *Digest of the Ordinances of the City Council of Charleston: From the Year 1783 to July 1818* (Charleston: Archibald E. Miller, 1818), 191.
24. Pearson, *Designs Against Charleston*, 74.
25. Quoted in Pearson, *Designs Against Charleston*, 71.
26. Quoted in Douglas R. Egerton, *He Shall Go Out Free: The Lives of Denmark Vesey* (Madison, WI: Madison House Publishers, 1999), 53.
27. Quoted in Pearson, *Designs Against Charleston*, 70.
28. McCord, *Statues at Large of South Carolina*, vol. 7, 462.
29. Quoted in Pearson, *Designs Against Charleston*, 155.
30. Quoted in Pearson, *Designs Against Charleston*, 73.
31. Quoted in Loren Schweninger, "Slave Independence and Enterprise in South Carolina, 1780–1865," *South Carolina Historical Magazine* Vol. 93, no. 2 (April 1992), 101–125, 115.
32. David C. R. Heisser, " Bishop Lynch's Civil War Pamphlet on Slavery," *The Catholic Historical Review*, Vol. LXXXIV, No. 4 (October 1998), 689.

## *Chapter 2. 1823–1866: Laws of the Antebellum and Civil War Periods*

1. It appears nothing was done about this complaint regarding the street criers. In May 1846, "Ralph Rhyme" sent a poem to the *Courier*, rhapsodizing on the street crier's calls. Quoted

in Charles R. Rowe, *Pages of History: 200 Years of the Post and Courier* (Charleston: Evening Post Publishing Co., 2003), 105. Years later the City of Charleston would pass out awards for the best street cries in its annual Azalea Festivals.

2. City Council of Charleston, *Collection of Ordinances: 1826–1832*, 8.

3. City Council of Charleston, *Collection of Ordinances: 1826–1832*, 41.

4. City Council of Charleston, *Collection of Ordinances: 1826–1832*, 41–2.

5. City Council of Charleston, *Collection of Ordinances: 1826–1832*, 59.

6. City Council of Charleston, *Ordinances of the City of Charleston From the 5th Feb., 1833, to the 9th May, 1837* (Charleston: A. E. Miller, 1837), ordinance no. 2, commencing page 2, and ordinance no. 7, commencing page 18.

7. City Council of Charleston, *Ordinances of the City of Charleston: 1833–1837*, ordinance no. 11, commencing page 36, and ordinance no. 19, commencing page 60.

8. City Council of Charleston, *Ordinances of the City of Charleston: 1833–1837*, ordinance no. 42, p. 116.

9. Fragments of manuscript copy of City Council minutes, South Carolina Room, Charleston County Public Library.

10. Proceedings of City Council, 13 April 1837, printed in the Charleston *Courier*, 1 May 1837.

11. City Council of Charleston, *Ordinances of the City of Charleston: 1833–1837*, ordinance no. 52, commencing page 141.

12. City Council of Charleston, *Ordinances of the City of Charleston: 1833–1837*, 149.

13. Proceedings of City Council, 22 November 1837, printed in the Charleston *Courier*, 29 November 1837.

14. City Council of Charleston, *Ordinances of the City of Charleston: From the 24th May 1837, to the 18th March, 1840* (Charleston: B. R. Getsinger, 1840), 43.

15. City Council of Charleston, *Ordinances of the City of Charleston: 1837–1840*, 67.

16. Horlbeck Brothers Account book, p. 17 (South Carolina Historical Society item number 33-100-05.)

17. City Council of Charleston, *Ordinances of the City of Charleston, 1837–1840*, 244, 237.

18. George B. Eckhard, *A Digest of the Ordinances of the City Council of Charleston: From the Year 1783 to Oct. 1844* (Charleston: Walker & Burke, 1844), 21–23.

19. Proceedings of City Council, 22 April 1851, printed in the Charleston *Courier*, 25 April 1851.

20. Proceedings of City Council, 31 May 1841, printed in the *Southern Patriot*, 2 June 1841.

21. H. Pinckney Walker, *Ordinances of the City of Charleston From the 19th of August 1844, to the 14th of September 1854* (Charleston, A. E. Miller, 1854), 52.

22. South Carolina Legislature, *The Statutes at Large of South Carolina: Containing the Acts from 1838, Exclusive*, Vol. XI (Columbia, SC: Republican Printing Company, 1873), 563–64.

23. Quoted in Schweninger, "Slave Independence and Enterprise," 115.

24. Robert Young Hayne, *Report of the Proceedings of the City Authorities of Charleston During the Past Year Ending September 1, 1837; with Suggestions for Improvement of the City* (Charleston: A. E. Miller, 1837), 12.

25. Quoted in Claudia Dale Goldin, *Urban Slavery in the American South, 1820–1860: A Quantitative History* (Chicago: University of Chicago Press, 1976), 48.

26. *The Southern Patriot*, 2 November 1840.

27. John H. Honour, Jr., ed., *A Directory of the City of Charleston and Neck for 1849* (Charleston: A. J. Burke, 1849), iii–iv.

28. Charleston *Courier*, 28 January 1848.

29. Charleston *Courier*, 28 January 1848.

30. Charleston *Courier*, 29 January 1848.

31. Charleston *Mercury*, 5 February 1848.

32. Commissioners of the Crossroads, *The Rules and Regulations for Charleston Neck to which are annexed The Acts of the Legislature which Relate Exclusively to Charleston Neck* (Charleston: Burges, James & Paxton, 1848), 4–7.

33. Charleston *Mercury*, 26 February 1848.

34. Charleston *Mercury*, 1 January 1849.

35. Charleston *Mercury*, 11 January 1849.

36. Rebecca Moses account book from the estate of Henry Aaron Alexander, courtesy of Judith Shanks.

37. Charleston *Mercury*, 24 November 1849.

38. South Carolina Legislature, *The Statutes at Large of South Carolina*, Vol. XI, 564–65.

39. Proceedings of Charleston City Council meeting of 22 January 1850, printed in the Charleston *Courier*, 24 January 1850.

40. Charleston *Courier*, 24 January 1850.

41. City Council of Charleston, *Statement of Receipts and Expenditures by the City Council of Charleston, From the 1st July 1849, to 1st July 1850* (Charleston: A. E. Miller, 1850), 135.

42. Proceedings of Charleston City Council meeting of 1 October 1850, printed in the Charleston *Courier*, 4 October 1850.

43. Walker, *Ordinances of the City of Charleston: 1844–1854*, 48–49.

44. Bernard E. Powers, Jr., *Black Charlestonians: A Social History, 1822–1885* (Fayetteville: University of Arkansas Press, 1994), 15. Minutes, Charleston Board of Fire Masters, 18 June 1849, originals in South Carolina Room, Charleston County Public Library.

45. John R. Horsey, *Ordinances of the City of Charleston: From the 14th September, 1854, to the 1st December, 1859* (Charleston: Walker, Evans & Co., 1859), 19–20.

46. Walker, *Ordinances of the City of Charleston: 1844–1854*, 157.

47. Edwards, *Ordinances of the City Council of Charleston*, 178–179.

48. Eckhard, *A Digest of the Ordinances of the City Council of Charleston*, 57–58.

49. Walker, *Ordinances of the City of Charleston: 1844–1854*, 87–88.

50. D. T. Corbin, *Ordinances of the City of Charleston: From December 1st, 1859 to September 6th, 1870* (Charleston: Charleston Courier Book and Job Presses, 1871), 13.

## *Chapter 3. 1800–1810*

1. Diary of Timothy Ford, published in *The South Carolina Historical Magazine*, volume XII, no. 3 (July 1912), p. 142

2. The only way available to check this theory is to use it for the years just discussed above. For these years, it's known what the newspapers reported, with some problems in the numbers being noted. It is encouraging to note, however, that the formula, when used for the least problematic years, results in totals close to the historic numbers. The 1801 data given in the paper is 2,116 badges sold; the formula gives the number as 2,480; while the difference is significant, one must also remember that research suggests that this year may have a heavily inflated revenue (and it is upon revenue that the formula is based), with revenue for next year's badges reported in this fiscal year. The problematic number given in the press for 1802 is 2,373 badges sold, which, as noted, seems to include some badges from the year before, while revenue—which is an essential part of the formula—seems to be lower than badge numbers would suggest. Instead of 2,373, statistical projections give the number as 1,451 badges sold. But for the next year, 449 is the number given in the press for 1803 badges sold; the formula used by these authors supplies the number 388. The formula number is 86 percent of the historical number. The next two years are closer still. 1,574 is the number given in the press for 1,804; the formula produces the end number 1,638; the derived number is 104 percent of the historical one. 1,354 is the number of badges sold supplied by the 1805 press, while the formula suggests 1,203. The statistically derived number is 88 percent of the given number. Given the fact that the formula rests on the percentages of categories (and what they cost) for the year 1850, and knowing that the same percentage of each category probably varied year by year, this may be as close

as we can get to any reliable numbers. If more information is found, the formula and resulting numbers may very well change.

3. Cited in Pearson, *Designs Against Charleston*, 316.
4. Jacob Milligan, *The Charleston Directory* (Charleston: W. P. Young, 1794),
5. Milby Burton, *South Carolina Silversmiths: 1690–1800* (Charleston: Charleston Museum, 1942), 15–17. Charleston *Times*, 23 October 1800.
6. Hartzog Auction Catalogue referenced in "Charleston, South Carolina Slave Hire Badges: The John J. Ford, Jr. Collection," Auction Catalogue in possession of authors.
7. Although not identified as such, an image of the badge appears in Martha A. Zierden, *Excavations at 14 Legare Street, Charleston, South Carolina* (Charleston: The Charleston Museum, October 2001), p. 4–39
8. Burton, *South Carolina Silversmiths*, 102–103.

## *Chapter 4. 1811–1820*

1. Cited in Pearson, *Designs Against Charleston*, 316.
2. Will of Richard Holmes Cheevers, WPA typescript, Volume 28, 379–380.
3. Will of Peggy Cheever, CWA Will typescripts, Volume 49, 760–61.
4. [Charleston City Council], *List of Taxpayers of the City of Charleston for 1860* (Charleston: Evans and Cogswell, 1861), 317.
5. Abraham Motte, *Charleston Directory and Stranger's Guide* (Charleston: Printed for the Publisher, 1816), 54.
6. Burton, *South Carolina Silversmiths*, 115.
7. Charleston City Death Records record his place of birth as Ireland, and he was buried in St. Mary's Catholic Church cemetery. See also, Susan S. King, *Roman Catholic Deaths in Charleston*, (Columbia, SC: SCMAR, 2000), 200.
8. Federal Census, City of Charleston, 1810, 1820, 1830.
9. See Pearson, *Designs Against Charleston*, 297–310. Adam Bellamy was owned by James H. Merritt; Pierre Chapeau, owned by Monsier Chappeau, was also known as Pierre Lewis; Panza Mitchell was owned by James Michel; Louis Remoussin was owned by Mr. Cromwell; Jacob Stagg was owned by Jacob Lankester; Sandy Vesey was owned by R. W. Vanderhorst; and John Vincent was owned by D. Cruckshanks.
10. See bill of sale by Cheevers *et al.*, 29 December 1800, Bills of Sale, 3N, 501, SC Department Archives and History.
11. Bills of Sale, volume 3x, p. 75, SC Department Archives and History.
12. Addendum to document cited in note 11 above.
13. Bills of Sale, volume 3x, p. 72, SC Department of Archives and History.
14. Bills of Sale, volume 3x, p. 76, SC Department of Archives and History.
15. Bills of Sale, volume 4 F, p. 82, SC Department of Archives and History.
16. Bills of Sale, volume 4 I, p. 168, SC Department of Archives and History.
17. Will of Barsheba Cattle, CWA will book volume 34 (1818–26), 97.
18. "Inventory of the Estate and Effects of Barsheba Cattle, deceased, taken ... this second day of July 1819," Charleston County Inventories, book F, 1819–1824, 81–82.

## *Chapter 5. 1821–1830*

1. Wade, *Slavery in the Cities*, 235.
2. Egerton, *He Shall Go Out Free*, 124.
3. There is a drawing of an 1824 badge with "Lafar" stamped on the front in Burton, *South Carolina Silversmiths*, 103. The image contradicts the text which says the stamping of Lafar is on the reverse of the Charleston Museum's 1824 and 1825 badges.

## *Chapter 6. 1831–1840*

1. Fragments, Charleston City Council Minutes, 1835, SC Room, Charleston County Public Library.

2. Fragments, Charleston City Council Minutes, 1835, SC Room, Charleston County Public Library.

3. Fragments, Charleston City Council Minutes, 1835, SC Room, Charleston County Public Library.

4. Since most of the badges for this calendar year might have been sold by the time this rate increase went into effect, the lower price, $5, was used in estimating the number of badges sold this year.

5. Despite the increase in income, this had been a bad year for the city, for the fire of April 1838 had burned down a large portion of the center of town. Histories state that 560 buildings and 600 outbuildings were destroyed with a loss of three million dollars. This catastrophe and the chaos and losses and necessary resulting loans prompted the city to publish a pamphlet on its finances (*Report, Containing a Review of the City Authorities, from the 4th September, 1837, to the 1st August 1838; With Suggestions for the Improvements of the Various Departments of the Public Service, Presented to the City Council, August 6, 1838* by Henry L. Pinckney, Mayor). Oddly only 11 months are accounted for, "from the 4th of September, 1837, to the 1st August, 1838."

In that pamphlet, the city expenses were recapitulated, as well, with some more information given about badges, but much of it is puzzling. On page 31, the line of type reads as follows, "Cart and Dray Licenses, 4,764, and Badges, 2,032 $16,707." This gives then the number of licenses and the number of slave badges, with the amount of income made from the two. For every other known year, more income came from slave badges than from licenses for carts and drays, so the numbers may be reversed. Perhaps 4,764 slaves were really hired out. That would be a big increase over the last few years, and over the following ones, too. (The next year, it would be stated that about 3,700 badges would be needed, and the income would very nearly match income for this year under discussion.) But perhaps more slaves were hired out with all the rebuilding and restructuring of lives necessary. (One could argue as well that maybe the numbers *aren't* reversed, and there were more carts hired out, as needed for rebuilding, etc.) Although some categories in the pamphlet and the annual report in the newspaper are close, there seems to be no way to align the figure $16,707 in the pamphlet with figures published in the press at the end of the fiscal year.

6. Burton, *South Carolina Silversmiths*, 131–32.

7. Thomas McAlpin Stubbs, *Family Album: An Account of the Moods of Charleston, South Carolina, and Connected Families* (Atlanta: Curtis, 1943), 25–27, 56; Susan Millar Williams, *A Devil and A Good Woman, Too: The Lives of Julia Peterkin* (Athens: University of Georgia Press, 1997), 4.

8. Burton, *South Carolina Silversmiths*, 160–62.

## *Chapter 7. 1841–1850*

1. Lydia Jane Waring Account Book, 24. South Carolina Historical Society.

2. Anne W. Chapman, "Inadequacies of the 1848 Charleston Census," *South Carolina Historical Magazine*, Vol. 81, no. 1 (January 1980), 24–34.

3. Honour, *Directory of the City of Charleston and Neck for 1849*, 148.

4. *Statement of Receipts and Expenditures by the City Council of Charleston From 1st July 1849, to 1st July 1850;* published by order of Council (Charleston, A. E. Miller, 1850). The companion volume, for the next year, is *Statement of Receipts and Expenditures by the City Council of Charleston, From 1st Sept. 1850, to 1st Sept., 1851, With a List of the Tax Paying Citizens in the Upper and Lower Wards—Separated*, Published by Order of Council (Charleston, A. E. Miller, 1851).

5. Free people of color had to obtain a license to sell fruits, but not wear a badge. City Council of Charleston, *Collection of Ordinances, 1826–1832*, 11. An Elizabeth Martin, free person

of color, does appear in the 1850 census—and in the 1850 book on capitation taxes for free people of color of the city of Charleston.

6. *An Historical and Descriptive Review of the City of Charleston* (New York: Empire Publishing Company, 1884), 167.

## *Chapter 8. 1851–1860*

1. If one accepts the estimate 4,135 badges sold, instead of the 4,510 made, however, that would mean an extra 400 or so were expected, boosting the estimate of the neck to about 2,000. For the 1850-51 fiscal year, it is known that $3,403 came in for badges on the neck. Using the mathematical formula for estimation, it appears that only 1,052 badges were sold on the neck in 1850-51. This might be closer to the number sold on the neck for 1849-50 and previous years.

2. From this year onward, these are the figures used in the formula to estimate the number of badges sold. Servant badges are 55.1 percent of the total; porter badges, 25.2 percent; mechanic badges, 9.4 percent; fruiterer badges, 7.9 percent, and fisher badges, 2.2 percent for a total of 100 percent. These values were used in the formula explained in the appendix.

3. Originals in Special Collections, Charleston County Public Library.

4. Return of Deaths/Lists of Interments City of Charleston, 12 February 1854–18 February 1854.

5. *Statement of Receipts and Expenditures by the City Council of Charleston, From 1st Sept. 1850, to 1st Sept., 1851, With a List of the Tax Pay Citizens in the Upper and Lower Wards—Separated*, Published by Order of Council (Charleston, A. E. Miller, 1851), 19.

6. Treasurer's Account Book, 1855–1865, p. 18. Special Collections. Charleston County Public Library.

7. William Porcher Miles, *Mayor's Report on City Affairs Submitted to Council at a Meeting, Held Tuesday, September 29th 1857* (Charleston: Walker, Evans & Co., 1857), 37.

8. The number given in the paper (44,113) is obviously a misprint; but if the dollar amount slaves brought in, at $3 each, $13,239, is correct, that comes to 4,413 slaves.

9. There is such a form filled in against Maria Louisa Silvanneau, dated 28 June 1849, in Special Collections, Robert Scott Small Library, College of Charleston, Charleston, SC.

10. Quoted in Johnson and Roark, *Black Masters*, 173.

11. Johnson and Roark, *Black Masters*, 179.

12. Johnson and Roark, *Black Masters*, 183.

13. Barbara Bellows, *Benevolence Among Slaveholders: Assisting the Poor in Charleston, 1670–1860* (Baton Rouge: Louisiana State University Press, 1993), 186.

14. Cited in Michael P. Johnson and James L. Roark, *No Chariot Let Down: Charleston's Free People of Color on the Eve of the Civil War* (Chapel Hill: University of North Carolina Press, 1984), 94.

15. McCord, *Statutes at Large*, vol. 7, 462.

16. McCord, *Statutes at Large*, vol. 7, 459.

17. McCord, *Statutes at Large*, vol. 7, 154–55.

18. Johnson and Roark, *No Chariot Let Down*, 85.

19. Cited in Johnson and Roark, *No Chariot Let Down*, 95–96.

20. Johnson and Roark, *No Chariot Let Down*, 85.

21. Johnson and Roark, *No Chariot Let Down*, 144–146.

## *Chapter 9. 1861–1865*

1. Undated clipping in financial record book, City of Charleston, Special Collections, Charleston County Public Library; clipped from a newspaper, the annual report bears the date of 21 September 1861.

2. Treasurer's Ledger, Balances, 1860–1873, Special Collections, Charleston County Public Library.
3. City of Charleston Police Day Book 1861–1863, Charleston Library Society.
4. Journal, 1855–1887, City of Charleston, Special Collections, Charleston County Public Library.
5. Treasurer's Ledger, Balances, 1860–1873, Special Collections, Charleston County Public Library.
6. Financial Statements Record Book 1860–1884, City of Charleston, Special Collections, Charleston County Public Library.
7. City of Charleston Police Day Book 1861–1863, Charleston Library Society.
8. John Bennett, "Story of Forgotten Bells, Sacrificed to Confederate Guns, Is Told," *News and Courier*, 12 December 1937.
9. Treasurer's Ledger, Balances, 1860–1873, and Financial Statements Record Book, 1860–1884, Special Collections, Charleston County Public Library.

## *Afterword*

1. Information provided by staff of the Charleston Museum.
2. Anthony Chibbaro, *The Charleston Exposition* (Charleston, SC: Arcadia Publishing Company, 2001), 103–117.

# Bibliography

## Manuscript Sources


### *Charleston County Public Library*

Charleston County Estate Inventories (microfilm)
City Council of Charleston Minutes
City of Charleston Records of Deaths and Interments
City of Charleston Treasurer's Records
CWA Charleston County Will Transcriptions
Federal Census Schedules, South Carolina (microfilm)
Free Negro Capitation Tax Books (microfilm)

### *Charleston Library Society*

City of Charleston Police. Day Book, 1861–1863.

### *Robert Scott Small Library, College of Charleston. Special Collections.*

Miscellaneous Manuscript Series

### *South Carolina Division of Archives and History. Columbia, South Carolina.*

Bills of Sale
Charleston District Court of Common Pleas. Judgment Rolls.

### *South Carolina Historical Society. Charleston.*

John Bennett Collection
Horlbeck Brothers Account Book
Lydia Jane Waring Account Book

### *Privately Held Materials*

Rebecca Moses Account Book. Henry Aaron Alexander Estate. Courtesy of Judith Shanks

## Contemporary Newspapers
## (All Charleston)

*City Gazette* (printed under various titles)
*Columbian Herald*
*Courier*
*Mercury*
*Morning Post*
*The Southern Patriot*
*South Carolina Gazette* (printed under various titles)
*Times*

## Printed Primary Sources

Barnwell, Joseph W., ed. "Diary of Timothy Ford: 1785–1786." *South Carolina Historical and Genealogical Magazine.* Vol. XIII, No. 3 (July 1912), 132–147.

City Council of Charleston. *A Collection of the Ordinances of the City Council of Charleston: From the 10th Day of October, 1826, to the 13th Day of March, 1832.* Charleston, SC: Archibald E. Miller, 1832.

City Council of Charleston. *Digest of the Ordinances of the City Council of Charleston: From the Year 1783 to July 1818.* Charleston, SC: Archibald E. Miller, 1818.

City Council of Charleston. *List of Taxpayers of the City of Charleston for 1860.* Charleston, SC: Evans & Cogswell, 1861.

City Council of Charleston. *Ordinances of the City of Charleston From the 5th Feb., 1833, to the 9th May, 1837.* Charleston, SC: A. E. Miller, 1837.

City Council of Charleston. *Ordinances of the City of Charleston From the 24th May 1837, to the 18th March, 1840.* Charleston, SC: B. R. Getsinger, 1840.

City Council of Charleston. *Statement of Receipts and Expenditures by the City Council of Charleston, From the 1st July 1849, to 1st July 1850.* Charleston, SC: A. E. Miller, 1850.

City Council of Charleston. *Statement of Receipts and Expenditures by the City Council of Charleston, From the 1st Sept. 1850, to 1st Sept, 1851, With a List of the Tax Paying Citizens in the Upper and Lower Wards—Separated.* Charleston, SC: A. E. Miller, 1851.

Commissioners of the Crossroads. *The Rules and Regulations for Charleston Neck to which are annexed The Acts of the Legislature which Relate Exclusively to Charleston Neck.* Charleston, SC: Burges, James & Paxton, 1848.

Corbin, T. C. *Ordinances of the City of Charleston: From December 1st, 1859 to September 6th, 1870.* Charleston, SC: Charleston Courier Book and Job Presses, 1871.

Dawson, J. L., and H. W. DeSaussure. *Census of the City of Charleston, South Carolina for the Year 1848 Exhibiting the Condition and Prospects of the City, Illustrated by Many Statistical Details.* Charleston, SC: J. B. Nixon, 1849.

Eckhard, George B. *A Digest of Ordinances of the City Council of Charleston From the Year 1783 to Oct. 1844.* Charleston, SC: Walker and Burke, 1844.

Edwards, Alexander. *Ordinances of the City Council of Charleston.* Charleston, SC: W.P. Young, 1802.

Hayne, Robert Young. *Report of the Proceedings of the City Authorities of Charleston During the Past Year Ending September 1, 1837. With Suggestions for Improvement of the City.* Charleston, SC: A. E. Miller, 1837.

Horsey, John R. *Ordinances of the City of Charleston: From the 14th September, 1854, to the 1st December, 1859.* Charleston, SC: Walker, Evans & Co., 1859.

Honour, John H., Jr., ed. *A Directory of the City of Charleston and Neck for 1849.* Charleston, SC: A. J. Burke, 1849.

McCord, David J., and Thomas Cooper, eds. *The Statutes at Large of South Carolina; edited, Under the Authority of the Legislature*, 10 vols. Columbia, SC. 1836–1840.

Miles, William Porcher. *Mayor's Report on City Affairs Submitted to Council at a Meeting Held Tuesday, September 29th 1857.* Charleston, SC: Walker, Evans & Co., 1857.

Milligan, Jacob. *The Charleston Directory.* Charleston, SC: W.P. Young, 1794.

Motte, Abraham. *Charleston Directory and Stranger's Guide.* Charleston, SC: Printed for the Publisher, 1816.

Pinckney, Henry L. *Report, Containing a Review of the City Authorities, from the 4th September 1837, to the 1st August 1838; With Suggestions for the Improvements of the Various Departments of Public Service, Presented to the City Council, August 6, 1838.* Charleston, SC: Thomas J. Eccles, 1838.

South Carolina Legislature. *The Statutes at Large of South Carolina: Containing the Acts from 1838, Exclusive*, Vol. XI. Columbia, SC: Republican Printing Co., 1873.

Walker, H. Pinckney. *Ordinances of the City of Charleston From the 19th of August 1844, to the 14th of September 1854.* Charleston, SC: A. E. Miller, 1854.

## Secondary Works

Ball, Edward. *Slaves in the Family.* New York. Ballantine Books, 1999.

Bellows, Barbara. *Benevolence Among Slaveholders: Assisting the Poor in Charleston, 1670–1860.* Baton Rouge: Louisiana State University Press, 1993.

Bennett, John. "'Slave Tags' for Tourists: Railroad Local Trunk Checks at Two Dollars Each." *Sunday News (and Courier)*, 3 May 1903.

Bennett, John. "Story of Forgotten Bells, Sacrificed to Confederate Guns, is Told." *News and Courier*, 12 December 1937.

Burton, Milby. *South Carolina Silversmiths: 1690–1800.* Charleston, SC: Charleston Museum, 1942.

Carll, Mary Allison. *The Role of the Black Artisan in the Building Trades and the Decorative Arts in South Carolina's Charleston District, 1760–1800.* PhD dissertation, University of Tennessee, Knoxville, 1982.

Chapman, Anne W. "Inadequacies of the 1848 Charleston Census." *South Carolina Historical Magazine.* Vol. 81, No. 1 (January 1980), 24–34.

Chibarro, Anthony. *The Charleston Exposition.* Charleston, SC: Arcadia Publishing Co., 2001.

Dawson, Victoria. "Cast in Bondage" *Smithsonian*, Vol. 33, No. 11 (February 2003), 20, 22.

Drago, Edmund L. *Broke by the War: Letters of a Slave Trader.* Columbia, SC: University of South Carolina Press, 1991.

Durban, Pam. *So Far Back.* New York: Picador USA, 2000.

Egerton, Douglas R. *He Shall Go Out Free: The Lives of Denmark Vesey.* Madison, WI: Madison House Publishers, 1999.

Fraser, Walter J. *Charleston! Charleston! The History of a Southern City.* Columbia, SC: University of South Carolina Press, 1989.

Goldin, Claudia Dale. *Urban Slavery in the American South, 1820–1860: A Quantitative History.* Chicago: University of Chicago Press, 1976.

Heisser, David C. R. "Bishop Lynch's Civil War Pamphlet on Slavery," *The Catholic Historical Review*, Vol. LXXXIV, No. 4 (October 1998). 681–696.

Hewatt, Alexander. *An Historical Account of the Rise and Progress of the Colonies of South Carolina and Georgia.* London: A. Donaldson, 1779. [Spartanburg, SC: The Reprint Co., 1962].

*An Historical and Descriptive Review of the City of Charleston.* New York: Empire Publishing Co., 1884.

Hodder, Michael. "Charleston, South Carolina Slave Hire Badges: The John J. Ford Jr. Collection: Earlier, from the Collections of F.C.C. Boyd, Virgil M. Brand, and David Proskey." *United States Gold, Silver and Copper Coins.* New York: Stacks Auction House, 8 September 1993.

Johnson, John Andrew. *The Experience of a Slave in South Carolina.* London: Passmore & Alabaster, 1862.

Johnson, Michael, and James L. Roark, *Black Masters: A Free Family of Color in the Old South.* New York: W. W. Norton Co., 1984.

Johnson, Michael, and James L. Roark. *No Chariot Let Down: Charleston's Free People of Color on the Eve of the Civil War.* Chapel Hill: University of North Carolina Press, 1984.

King, Susan S. *Roman Catholic Deaths in Charleston.* Columbia, SC: SCMAR, 2000.

Macomber, Daria (Pat Robinson and Nancy Stevenson). *A Clearing in the Fog.* New York: The World Publishing Company, 1970.

Mikell, I. Jenkins. *The Rumbling of the Chariot Wheels.* Columbia, SC: The State Company, 1923.

Pearson, Edward A. *Designs Against Charleston: The Trial Record of the Denmark Vesey Slave Conspiracy of 1822.* Chapel Hill: University of North Carolina Press, 1999.

Powers, Bernard, Jr. *Black Charlestonians: A Social History, 1822–1885.* Fayetteville: University of Arkansas Press, 1994.

Rowe, Charles. *Pages of History: 200 Years of the Post and Courier.* Charleston, SC: Evening Post Publishing Company, 2003.

Rulau, Russell. *Standard Catalog of Hard Times Tokens:* 1832–1844. Iola, WI: Kraus Publications, 2001.

Schweninger, Loren. "Slave Independence and Enterprise in South Carolina, 1780–1865." *South Carolina Historical Magazine*, Vol. 93, no. 2 (April 1992), 101–125.

Sellers, Leila. *Charleston Business on the Eve of the American Revolution.* Chapel Hill: University of North Carolina Press, 1934.

Singleton, Theresa. "The Slave Tag: An Artifact of Urban Slavery," *South Carolina Antiquities*, 1984, Vol. 16, Nos. 1 & 2, 41–65.

Smith, Daniel Elliot Huger. *A Charlestonian's Recollections, 1846–1913.* Charleston, SC: The Carolina Art Association, 1950.

Stubbs, Thomas McAlpin. *Family Album: An Account of the Moods of Charleston, South Carolina, and Connected Families.* Atlanta: Curtis, 1943.

Wade, Richard C. *Slavery in the Cities: The South* 1820–1860. New York: Oxford University Press, 1964.

Williams, Susan Millar. *A Devil and A Good Woman, Too: The Lives of Julia Peterkin.* Athens: University of Georgia Press, 1997.

Wilson, Miriam Bellangee. *Slave Days.* Charleston, SC: Old Slave Mart Foundation, 1946.

Zierden, Martha A. *Excavations at 14 Legare Street, Charleston, South Carolina.* Charleston, SC: The Charleston Museum, 2001.

# Index